ENGLISH WRITERS OF THE EIGHTEENTH CENTURY

English Writers

of the Eighteenth Century

EDITED BY

JOHN H. MIDDENDORF

COLUMBIA UNIVERSITY PRESS · NEW YORK AND LONDON

Copyright © 1971 Columbia University Press
Library of Congress Catalog Card Number: 70-175643
ISBN: 0-231-03516-0
Printed in the United States of America
10 9 8 7 6 5 4 3

95509

PREFACE

TRADITIONAL VIEWS of eighteenth-century England and its literature emphasizing their uniformity are recognized today largely as legacies of either unsympathetic—or, in some cases, nostalgic—nineteenth-century critics. Social historians have brought sceptical eyes to the older, superficially attractive, but never very convincing picture of brawling London mobs held in check by an almost too-civilized minority, with a bypassed and outmoded landed gentry looking on scornfully from the sidelines. Political historians have begun to reveal the intricate relationships of family and interest implicating what were once comfortably thought to be rather easily separable Whig and Tory ideologies. And economic historians examining the origin and development of industry and the new agriculture have thrown out of joint the neat patterns of progress favored by an age more certain of its destiny than are we.

In literary studies, poems earlier dismissed as immediately and completely comprehensible have been found to be as structurally complex and texturally dense as the best of any other age; and examinations of the variety of rhetorical resources used and effects created by eighteenth-century poets have assigned older criti-

cal formulations and catchwords to the dustbin. Eighteenth-
century novels are no longer interesting mainly as increasingly
mature ancestors of "superior" modern novels but as sophisticated, finished examples of a genre sensitively responding to
and reflecting the most vital social and intellectual forces of the
time. Biographical studies have emphasized the sharply individualistic nature of a once gray crowd, and new scholarly editions of
letters, memoirs, and literature have emphasized the diversity,
vigor, and endurance of their ideas.

From this kind of reinvestigation and re-evaluation what has
emerged? Certainly no new labels, no overarching explanations.
Complexity has taken the place of simplicity, and subsequent attempts to find unifying elements, through studies of the essentials
of what used to be called neoclassicism or studies of what appear
to be recurrent controlling ideas, archetypes, or metaphors, have
been at least as successful in emphasizing what still must be done
as what has been done. Yet understandably the desire for uniformity still lingers. Concepts such as "neoclassicism," with its accompanying associations of tradition and form, and "reason," with its
accompanying associations of order, objectivity, and control, continue to attract, and this despite writers like Swift and Johnson (to
name only two) whom modern studies have made it forever impossible to classify. The rage for order besets most naturally the
editors of volumes of the kind here represented: unifying themes
are sought, and if not easily discovered, occasionally devised.

The compilers of this volume wished to bring together a
collection of essays concerned with the literature of the eighteenth
century and written by students of one of the most active and influential modern scholars of that period, James Lowry Clifford,
for whom this book was made and to whom it is gratefully dedicated. They frankly recognized the state of knowledge about the
eighteenth century as one of unresolved complexities, and frankly
invited contributors to submit their best efforts on aspects of the
period about which they are best qualified to speak. The task of
finding order in diversity—if it may ever be found—lies in the fu-

ture. The essays here presented may therefore be said to be uniform in one sense only—their concern with the literature of eighteenth-century England and with its clarification. The subjects considered, the approaches taken, the style of presentation and documentation, and the conclusions reached are as diverse and individualistic as that age itself. Therein, we believe, will be found one of the principal interests of this volume.

The Editorial Committee

CONTENTS

ENGLISH WRITERS OF THE EIGHTEENTH CENTURY

Problems of Biography

CHESTER F. CHAPIN

Johnson and Pascal

ON GOOD FRIDAY, 1779, Johnson and Boswell attended church together. On their return home, Johnson continued his religious devotions, and that he might not be interrupted, handed Boswell a copy of Pascal's *Pensées*. The loan turned out to be a gift. Boswell asked Johnson to inscribe the book, and kept it "with reverence." [1] Johnson had made the acquaintance of the *Pensées* much earlier: he cites a passage from one of them in *Rambler* 92 (1751).[2] Some seventeen years later, on September 18, 1768, Johnson noted in his diary that he had "this day read a great part of Pascal's Life." [3] What he read was probably the life

[1] Samuel Johnson, *Diaries, Prayers, and Annals,* ed. E. L. McAdam with Donald and Mary Hyde (Vol. 1, Yale Edition, New Haven, 1958), pp. 293–94.

[2] Cf. the first paragraph of *Rambler* 92 with Pensée No. 932 on "poetic beauty." References in my text to the *Pensées* are to Martin Turnell's translation (New York, 1962). The Turnell numbering follows that of the French edition of Louis Lafuma (2nd ed., Paris, 1952). Where the pensée is quite lengthy, I have followed the number with page references to Turnell.

[3] *Diaries,* p. 119.

by Pascal's sister, Gilberte Périer, which could be easily read in one sitting. Probably in 1769 Johnson and Mrs. Thrale discussed whether number is infinite, Johnson siding with Pascal that it *is* proper to speak of "infinite number" as against Soame Jenyns, who thought this phrase a contradiction in terms.[4] In 1781 Johnson reproved Hannah More "with pretended sharpness for reading 'Les Pensées de Pascal,' or any of the Port Royal authors," alleging that as a good Protestant, she "ought to abstain from books written by Catholics." But when Miss More began to defend herself, Johnson said, with tears in his eyes, and with the most affecting earnestness, "I am heartily glad that you read pious books, by whomsoever they may be written." [5]

It is clear that Johnson, making the acquaintance of the *Pensées* in the 1750s or earlier, retained a lifelong esteem for this "pious" book. The evidence hardly entitles us to claim that Johnson was influenced in his own religious attitudes by his knowledge of Pascal. But parallels can be illuminating, especially since it has not been usual to associate Pascalian religious emphases with those of eighteenth-century Anglicans. There is only one reference to Pascal in Leslie Stephen's massive *History of English Thought in the Eighteenth Century,* nor does the more recent work of C. J. Stranks, G. R. Cragg, Norman Sykes, and Horton Davies support the view that Pascal had any perceptible influence on eighteenth-century Anglican thought.[6]

Nevertheless, the many admiring references to Pascal, from that of John Locke in 1694 to that of John Wesley in 1790, demonstrate the high esteem in which Pascal was held by Anglicans of

[4] *Thraliana,* ed. Katharine C. Balderston, 2nd ed. (Oxford, 1951), I, 191, n. 1; and compare Pensée No. 343, pp. 200–01.

[5] *Johnsonian Miscellanies,* ed. G. B. Hill (Oxford, 1897), II, 194.

[6] I have in mind Stranks's *Anglican Devotion* (London, 1961); Cragg's *Reason and Authority in the Eighteenth Century* and his *From Puritanism to the Age of Reason* (Cambridge, 1964 and 1966); Sykes's *Church and State in England in the Eighteenth Century* and his *From Sheldon to Secker* (Cambridge, 1934 and 1959); and Davies's *Worship and Theology in England from Watts and Wesley to Maurice* (Princeton, 1961).

all sorts. Locke speaks of "that prodigy of parts, Monsieur Pascal," and for Wesley Pascal exemplifies what is best in religion: "I do not mean external religion, but the religion of the heart; the religion which Kempis, Pascal, Fénelon enjoyed: that life of God in the soul of man, the walking with God and having fellowship with the Father and the Son." Other admirers of Pascal included John Dennis, Joseph Addison, John Arbuthnot, Joseph Spence, Joseph Warton, and Bishop Berkeley. And we learn that one Brian Fairfax (1676–1749), commissioner of customs, kept "Mons. Paschal's Thoughts" on his study table alongside that sober Anglican treatise, the enormously popular *Whole Duty of Man*.[7]

It would appear that esteem for Pascal was widespread during the early and middle years of the century—during just that period when Anglicanism is popularly thought to have declined into a kind of easy going Pelagian version of Christianity. But the *Pensées* are thoroughly Augustinian, not at all Pelagian. In sharp contrast to Pelagian views, they strongly affirm the reality of the Fall and original sin, and assert the necessity of supernatural grace as indispensable for salvation.[8]

It may well be that the work of Pascal—more especially the

[7] See Locke, *Essay Concerning Human Understanding*, ed. A. C. Fraser (Oxford, 1894), I, 199–200—the comment on Pascal was added to the 2nd (1694) edition—and Wesley, *Selected Letters*, ed. F. C. Gill (New York, 1956), p. 231. For references indicating the esteem in which Pascal was held by John Dennis, Joseph Addison, and Bishop Berkeley, see the indices to the E. N. Hooker edition of Dennis's works (Baltimore, 1939), the Donald F. Bond edition of *The Spectator* (Oxford, 1965), and the A. A. Luce and T. E. Jessup edition of Berkeley's works (London, 1964). For the esteem in which Pascal was held by John Arbuthnot, Joseph Spence, and Joseph Warton, see respectively, Kathleen Williams, *Jonathan Swift and the Age of Compromise* (Lawrence, Kansas, 1965), p. 153; Austin Wright, *Joseph Spence* (Chicago, 1950), p. 26; and *Eighteenth-Century Critical Essays*, ed. Scott Elledge (Ithaca, N.Y., 1961), II, 755. For Fairfax, see John Nichols, *Literary Anecdotes of the Eighteenth Century* (London, 1812), V, 433.

[8] For the argument that Augustinianism was much more widespread in eighteenth-century England than has been supposed, see Donald Greene, "Augustinianism and Empiricism: A Note on Eighteenth-Century Intellec-

Pensées—was of such an intimate, fragmentary, and "non-public" nature that it did not lend itself well to the kind of published work upon which our conception of "Anglican thought" is largely based. In any case, the possibility arises that eighteenth-century Anglicans really understood Pascal's argument in the *Pensées,* and that they understood it because it was not new but a part of their religious heritage. Their admiration for Pascal, then, would be that of men who found in Pascal a more eloquent and penetrating expression of sentiments and modes of reasoning by no means unfamiliar to them.

According to Joseph Wood Krutch, Johnson

accepted the Bible as revelation, but only because he had, or thought he had, good rational reasons for believing that it *was* revelation. In other words, his arguments in favor of the Christian religion were founded almost exclusively upon an acceptance of those "Christian evidences" which seemed so much more solid than they have seemed, even to most churchmen, in any century since his own.[9]

Krutch has in mind the traditional historical arguments from miracles, prophecies, and testimony. Johnson *does* use these arguments; in fact he insists upon them. The fullest and clearest instance of Johnson's appeal to the facts of history is doubly significant because he made it at a time when he knew he was dying. William Windham asked Johnson's opinion of "natural and revealed religion." Bypassing the traditional theistic proofs in support of "natural" religion, Johnson chose to discuss revealed religion only:

For revealed religion, [Johnson said] there was such historical evidence, as, upon any subject not religious, would have left no doubt. Had the facts recorded in the New Testament been mere civil occur-

---

tual History," *Eighteenth-Century Studies* (Fall, 1967), I, 33–68. It is worth noting that D. G. James long ago advanced the opinion that John Locke was nearer to Pascal than to the deists in his religious beliefs. See James, *The Life of Reason* (London, 1949), pp. 111–14.

[9] *Samuel Johnson* (New York, 1944), pp. 250–51.

rences, no one would have called in question the testimony by which they are established; but the importance annexed to them . . . created doubts unknown upon any other subject. Of proofs to be derived from history, one of the most cogent, [Johnson] seemed to think, was the opinion so well authenticated, and so long entertained, of a Deliverer that was to appear about that time. . . . For the immediate life and miracles of Christ, such attestation as that of the apostles, who all, except St. John, confirmed their testimony with their blood; such belief as their witness procured from a people best furnished with the means of judging, and least disposed to judge favourably; such an extension afterwards of that belief over all the nations of the earth, though originating from a nation of all others most despised, would leave no doubt that the things witnessed were true, and were of a nature more than human.[10]

I call attention to Johnson's emphasis on "the opinion so well authenticated, and so long entertained, of a Deliverer that was to appear about that time." On another occasion, Johnson told Boswell that "the Christian revelation is not proved by miracles alone, but as connected with prophecies, and with the doctrines in confirmation of which the miracles were wrought." [11] These statements reflect Johnson's belief in the cogency of that proof known to history as the argument from prophecy. The remark to Boswell has been thought "astonishing" from the mouth of the orthodox Johnson since it expresses an opinion "very close" to one condemned by the Sorbonne in the 1750s—that is, that the New Testament miracles "were efficacious as proofs of Christianity only if considered in conjunction with the prophecies." [12] However, Pascal also stressed the argument from prophecy.

Modern readers are impressed with the so-called existentialist aspect of the *Pensées,* with their "depiction of the human condi-

[10] *Johnsonian Miscellanies,* II, 384.
[11] Boswell's *Life of Johnson,* ed. Hill-Powell (Oxford, 1934–1950), III, 188; and compare *Life,* I, 445, where Johnson, after a defense of miracles against Hume's criticism, adds: "Then, Sir, when we take the proofs derived from prophecies which have been so exactly fulfilled, we have most satisfactory evidence."
[12] Robert Shackleton, "Johnson and the Enlightenment," *Johnson, Boswell, and Their Circle* (Oxford, 1965), p. 91.

tion as absurd." As E. B. O. Borgerhoff points out, the *Pensées* "are admired either as a kind of drama or poem of the human paradox or as a record of personal anguish, an *examen de conscience* of the sort we have taken for granted since Rousseau and recently witnessed in Gide. Indeed Gide himself spoke of Pascal's 'splendid outcries' much as T. S. Eliot spoke of his 'broodings.' " Certainly, there is this element of personal anguish in the *Pensées* but, as Borgerhoff convincingly shows, the *Pensées* are notes for an argument. Readers impressed by particular passages expressing Pascal's sense of man's alienation from himself, his world, or his God may tend to overlook the fact that this depiction of the human condition as "absurd" constitutes, for Pascal, a thoroughly "rational" argument in favor of the proposition that "faith is not terminally absurd and that, in the face of our conclusions about the human situation, Christianity makes sense." [13] Such readers may also forget how much of the book is devoted to discussion of the traditional Christian evidences. H. F. Stewart, however, speaks rightly of the argument from prophecy as "dear to the heart of Pascal and his friends." [14]

It seems reasonable to assume, then, that a part of Johnson's esteem for the *Pensées* is based upon the fact that Pascal drives home the importance of the concrete, historical proofs of revelation. But Pascal combines the historical argument with another. "As against adversaries who did not admit historical certainty," Pascal produced "a wholly psychological argument and, by starting from the study of the human soul," arrived at God—and not

[13] E. B. O. Borgerhoff, "The Reality of Pascal: The *Pensées* as Rhetoric," *Sewanee Review* (Winter 1957), 2, 19.

[14] *Pascal's Pensées,* trans. Stewart (London, 1950), p. xv; and compare this from the preface to the Port-Royal edition (1670) of the *Pensées* (Turnell, p. 83): "M. Pascal next embarked upon the task of proving the truth of religion from the prophecies, and he devoted far more time to this subject than to the others, As he had done a lot of work on it and held views which were peculiarly his own, he explained them in a manner which was very easy to grasp; he showed their meaning and the way in which they were linked with a marvellous ease: and he stated them in all their clarity and all their force."

at some vague theistic God but at the Christian God specifically.[15]

Johnson also argues from the nature of man to the existence of God, and his argument at major points of emphasis is essentially that of Pascal. Basically this argument—or, I should say, that part of it isolated for discussion here—points to the unhappiness of human life as evidence of man's transcendent destiny. Here it must be remembered that Pascal and Johnson were Augustinians: they believed in the reality of the Fall and original sin. They believed that at one time the founders of the human race had lived a life of consistent happiness, at harmony with themselves, with God, and with all creation. What this meant in practice they could hardly tell, but they had as part of their tradition the idea of an earthly utopia, whereas the modern secularist, bereft of this idea, may be willing to "settle for less" with regard to the possibilities of earthly happiness.

But Pascal and Johnson are also hard-headed pragmatists. If they believe that life is full of frustrations and miseries, they justify this belief on empirical grounds. Pascal asks his unbelievers, in effect, to look into their own hearts, to match his description of "la misère de l'homme" with their own experience, and then to say, if they dare, that the life of man is "happy." For Johnson human history amply demonstrates the truth of the proposition that "human life is everywhere a state in which much is to be endured, and little to be enjoyed" (*Rasselas,* ch. 11).

There are, of course, the obvious calamities afflicting man— disease, war, poverty, natural catastrophes, and the like. But these are in the nature of accidents. Some men may never suffer them. But there is one affliction which those who escape greater misfortune can hardly expect to avoid. Man is the only creature afflicted with boredom, ennui, *tedium vitae.* In his sections "Ennui," "Le Divertissement," and elsewhere, Pascal insists upon the universality of this affliction. I need hardly document Johnson's emphasis upon what he calls the "vacancies" or "vacuities" of life. Life

[15] Joseph Lataste, article, "Pascal," in *The Catholic Encyclopedia* (New York, 1913), XI, 512.

must be filled up, a man must do *something,* there is no instance
"of any man who is left to lay out his own time contriving not to
have tedious hours." [16] From this apparently minor affliction, Pascal and Johnson draw an important conclusion. Man is subject to
boredom and restlessness because of "the insufficiency of human
enjoyments." [17] Man is possessed of a constitutional inability to
find lasting enjoyment—or even what might seem reasonable
content—in any activity or state of being. Pascal and Johnson
find proof of this in man's inability to live fully in the present.
"Let each of us examine his thoughts," says Pascal,

and he will find that they are all occupied with the past or the future.
We can scarcely think of the present; and if we do think of it, it is
only in order to find our bearings for mapping out the future. The
present is never our goal; the past and present are our means; the future alone is our goal. Thus we never live, but we hope to live; and as
we are always preparing ourselves to be happy it is inevitable that we
never are happy (No. 84).

Or, as Johnson says in *Rambler* 207, "such is the emptiness of
human enjoyment, that we are always impatient of the present.
Attainment is followed by neglect, and possession by disgust; and
the malicious remark of the Greek epigrammatist on marriage
may be applied to every other course of life, that its two days of
happiness are the first and the last." Both men agree that "the
mind of man is never satisfied with the objects immediately before
it, but is always breaking away from the present moment, and losing itself in schemes of future felicity." And so it follows that "the

[16] On this, see W. J. Bate, *The Achievement of Samuel Johnson* (New
York, 1955), p. 64; for the quotation, see *Boswell for the Defence,* eds. W.
K. Wimsatt and F. A. Pottle (New York, 1959), p. 128.

[17] Cf. Imlac on the great Pyramid (*Rasselas,* ch. 32): "I consider this
mighty structure as a monument of the insufficiency of human enjoyments.
A king whose power is unlimited and whose treasures surmount all real
and imaginary wants, is compelled to solace, by the erection of a pyramid,
the satiety of dominion and tastelessness of pleasures, and to amuse the te-
diousness of declining life, by seeing thousands labouring without end, and
one stone, for no purpose, laid upon another." For Pascal, "a king without
pastimes is a man bowed down by misery" (No. 270).

natural flights of the human mind are not from pleasure to pleasure, but from hope to hope" (*Rambler* 2).

But if men find no lasting satisfaction in action, they cannot
endure inaction. In a famous phrase Pascal remarks that he once
thought men would be happy if they were capable of "sitting down
quietly in a room and relaxing." But he knows how impossible
this is: "Movement is the essence of our nature; complete repose
is death to us" (No. 162). "Nothing is more intolerable to man
than a state of complete repose, without desires, without work,
without amusements, without occupation" (No. 160). Thus activity, desire, and hope, however frustrating or self-defeating, are indispensable to life. As Johnson says, "such are the vicissitudes of
the world, through all its parts, that day and night, labour and
rest, hurry and retirement, endear each other; such are the changes
that keep the mind in action; we desire, we pursue, we obtain, we
are satiated; we desire something else, and begin a new persuit"
(*Rambler* 6).

It is not, then, the intention of Pascal or Johnson to condemn
man for his restlessness. Indeed, they recognize that man is not
satisfied with mere variety, with mere succession of "day and
night, labour and rest." Over and above this, man wants what
Johnson calls "novelty" and Pascal "excitement." Man's mind
seeks the stimulation of the new and the strange, his senses the
stimulus of "violent headstrong action" (No. 269, p. 177). Thus,
for Pascal, those who pretend to play the philosopher and think it
"very unreasonable of people to spend the whole day chasing a
hare that they would not have bothered to buy, have a poor
knowledge of human nature" (No. 269, p. 176). There is nothing
wrong in seeking excitement "provided that it is only regarded as
a distraction; what is wrong is that men seek it as though possession of the things they seek would make them truly happy." And
men make this mistake of everything they seek, of the pursuit of
"high office" as well as hares (No. 269, pp. 176–77).

This point is crucial. Here is where men go wrong, where
they misunderstand their own true nature. They think possession

of the things they seek will make them truly happy. I know of no better commentary on Pascal's remark than Johnson's *Rasselas*. At the very end of the tale, although by this time he should certainly know better, Rasselas still dreams of happiness through possession of "a little kingdom, in which he might administer justice in his own person, and see all the parts of government with his own eyes" (ch. 49).

Here we come to the point where Pascal and Johnson turn this analysis of the human condition into an argument for religion. A secularist might accept the human need for change, vicissitude, novelty, excitement—but presumably would have to define happiness in terms of some sort of optimum adjustment to this need. But Pascal and Johnson think of true happiness as a condition where this need itself is transcended, done away with. No doubt this concept—Pascal speaks of a *"vision* of happiness" (No. 246, p. 170: italics mine)—reflects the Christian association of change with imperfection when considered in contrast to the unchanging perfections of God. But the persistent human illusion that attainment of the immediate goal will be followed by happiness rather than discontent is for Pascal and Johnson ample proof that men inevitably tend to conceive of happiness as perpetual and unalloyed felicity. They do not think, or refuse to think, of satiation and discontent as in a sense necessary to happiness as we know it in this life. And so, as Pascal says, man "wants to be happy, and cannot wish not to be happy, but how is he to set about it? In order to make a good job of it, he would have to make himself immortal" (No. 266).

Men do have intimations of immortality. They can imagine a kind of felicity which, in duration and intensity, partakes of that eternal joy which—their reason should tell them—can never be theirs under the limitations of finite existence. Where could such a concept of happiness come from, unless from God? And why should God have implanted this concept within man, unless as a sign of man's transcendent destiny? As Johnson points out in *Rambler* 41, the beasts, unlike man, do appear to live fully in the present moment: "they seem always to be fully employed, or to be completely at ease without employment," and to have no "higher faculties, or more extensive capacities than the preservation of themselves or their species requires." The beasts are self-suffi-cient, well adapted to their environment. But man is not. He is de-pendent, "incomplete," in a sense unfitted for the world in which he finds himself. "If man were happy," says Pascal, "he would be all the happier if he amused himself less, like the saints and God. —Yes, but is not the pleasure we derive from amusements a way of being happy?—No, because they come from somewhere else and from outside us; which means that man is dependent and nev-ertheless exposed to a thousand accidents that inevitably lead to affliction" (No. 265). If men were truly happy their happiness would be like that traditionally ascribed to God, an everlasting fe-licity unaffected by dependence on anything outside itself.

Although aware of what he calls man's "greatness," that spiritual part of man which marks him as "raised above the whole of nature and made like God" (No. 246, p. 170), Pascal prefers to dwell on a core of emptiness within man, a certain ineradicable dissatisfaction with self. Why is a state of complete repose so in-tolerable? Because in such a state man "becomes aware of his nothingness, his abandonment, his inadequacy, his dependence, his emptiness, his futility. There at once wells up from the depths of his soul weariness, gloom, misery, exasperation, frustration, de-spair" (No. 160). Thus for Pascal the need for diversion derives from man's need to escape from himself: "Men's sole good there-fore lies in the discovery of some form of distraction which will stop them from thinking about their condition" (No. 269, p. 176). For Pascal this unhappy situation can be adequately explained only in terms of Christian teaching. It is a consequence of man's "fallen" nature: "It lies in the *natural* misfortune of our feeble and mortal state which is so wretched that when we give it serious thought, nothing can console us for it" (No. 269, p. 175: italics mine).

Johnson is also much aware of our "desire of abstraction

from ourselves," of the fact that "almost every man has some art, by which he steals his thoughts away from his present state." Whether alone or in company men are ever prone to seek "forgetfulness" of themselves (*Idler* 32). But Johnson prefers to emphasize man's overreaching spirit as a sign of his transcendent destiny. That "so few of the hours of life are filled up with objects adequate to the mind of man" is for Johnson "strong proof of the superior and celestial nature of the soul of man" (*Rambler* 41). Even that curiosity which leads men to the study of polite arts and abstruse sciences points to the same conclusion, for this curiosity, "which always succeeds ease and plenty, was undoubtedly given us as a proof of capacity which our present state is not able to fill, as a preparative for some better mode of existence, which shall furnish employment for the whole soul, and where pleasure shall be adequate to our powers of fruition" (*Idler* 37). And so for Johnson it is scarcely to be imagined "that Infinite Benevolence would create a being capable of enjoying so much more than is here to be enjoyed" unless there will "come a time, when every capacity of happiness shall be filled, and none shall be wretched but by his own fault" (*Adventurer* 120).

Thus, while Pascal sees in the insufficiency of human enjoyments a sure sign of man's "wretchedness," of his fallen nature, Johnson points to this insufficiency as evidence of man's "greatness," a sign of his immortal destiny.

All of which comes to the same thing: man is not intended for this world *only*. Secularism, not understanding this, attempts in various ways to reconcile man to his finitude. But man, as Pascal says, is not "consoled." Christianity, on the other hand, sees the true implications of man's finitude. It traces his misery to its proper source—man's alienation from God—and its doctrine of a future life is a rational recognition of the fact that man in this life is dependent and incomplete. And so for Pascal and Johnson the only rational "choice of life" is the "choice of eternity." [18]

---

[18] "To me," said the princess, "the choice of life is become less important; I hope hereafter to think only on the choice of eternity" (*Rasselas,* ch. 48).

Johnson's copy of the *Miscellanies* of the Anglican divine
John Norris (1657–1711), now at Yale University (see Johnson,
Diaries, Prayers, and Annals, p. 100), is extensively underscored
and otherwise marked, indicating that he had read it carefully in
preparing the *Dictionary.* It is worth noting that certain of Norris's opinions are precisely those I have ascribed to Johnson. Thus
all men, according to Norris, "are as much agreed as they are in
the *Idea* of a *Triangle"* that perfect happiness is "such a State
than which a better cannot be conceiv'd: In which there is no Evil
you can fear, no Good which you desire and have not; That which
fully and constantly satisfies the Demand of every Appetite, *and
leaves no possibility for a desire of Change"* (italics mine). We are
unhappy in this world because "we do not rightly consider the nature of things, but promise our *selves* infinite Satisfactions in the
enjoyment of finite Objects." But finite objects can never satisfy
"since to a full satisfaction and *acquiescence* of Mind 'tis required
that our Faculties be always *entertained* and we ever *enjoying:*
it is impossible a *finite Object* should afford this Satisfaction, because all the good that is in it (being finite) is at length run over,
and then the *enjoyment* is at an end, The flower is suck'd dry, and
we necessarily desire a Change." But Norris insists that although
men may recognize their condition they are never able to reconcile
themselves to it:

The rest of our Passions are much at our own Disposal; yield either
to Reason or Time; we either Argue our selves out of them, or at least
outlive them. We are not always in Love with Pomp and Grandeur,
nor always dazzled with the glittering of Riches; and there is a Season
when Pleasure itself shall Court in vain: But the desire of perfect Happiness has no Intervals, no Vicissitudes, it outlasts the Motion of the
Pulse, and survives the Ruins of the Grave.

And this is an argument for man's transcendent destiny, for "certainly God would never have planted such an Ardent, such an im-
portunate Appetite in our Souls, and as it were *interwoven* it with
our very Natures, had he not been able to satisfie it." [19]

[19] Norris, *A Collection of Miscellanies: consisting of Poems, Essays, Dis-
courses, and Letters* (3d ed. corrected, London, 1699), pp. 316–23.

Johnson then, like Norris and Pascal, is aware of a psychological argument for the existence of God and the supernatural. Although Johnson believes in the cogency of the historical arguments for revelation, he does not rest his faith "almost exclusively" upon these arguments. On the contrary, Johnson finds in Christianity the one body of thought and doctrine which truly understands *la condition des hommes*. Christianity is psychologically perceptive; it understands man for what he really is, a finite being yearning for infinite satisfactions, and so far as Johnson is able to discover, its findings are supported by the hard facts of human experience.

ARTHUR H. CASH

Sterne as a Judge in the Spiritual Courts: The Groundwork of *A Political Romance*

IN 1759 *A Political Romance* was burned by the Church of York. It could hardly have had a greater compliment. The occasion of this little satire, Sterne's only work in the mode of Swift, was an unseemly pamphlet war, or skirmish, between Dr. Francis Topham, the leading lawyer of York, and Dr. John Fountayne, Dean of the Minster. The titles of their productions are as quaint as the contents were uncharitable: *A Letter Address'd to the Reverend the Dean of York, An Answer to a Letter Address'd to the Dean of York, A Reply to the Answer to a Letter Lately Addressed to the Dean of York*. Then Sterne stepped in with the *Romance* and so neatly severed Dr. Topham's head as to leave it standing upon his shoulders. Using the neoclassical device of reducing the great to the small, Sterne represented the Diocese of York as a rural parish. The Archbishop became a parson; the Dean, John, the parish clerk; the Chapter became churchwardens.

With amusing reference to Dr. Topham's many offices, Sterne displayed him as Trim, the sexton, dog-whipper, clock-winder, bailiff, and mole-catcher to the parish. The embarrassed churchmen of York quickly persuaded Sterne to suppress the book. But they could not stop his pen. The success of *A Political Romance* only inspired him to write *Tristram Shandy*.[1]

There is no need to review here Dr. Topham's maneuvers to gain preferment, the story allegorized in the *Romance,* for Wilbur Cross has reconstructed that history accurately.[2] Cross's account, however, reflects the limitations of the documents he used, the Topham-Fountayne pamphlets. Doctors Topham and Fountayne shared a world of understanding about the preferments in question upon which they had no need to comment. It is this unmentioned, rudimentary knowledge which has been lost to us. Twentieth-century students of Sterne are unaware that the appointments over which the two men quarreled were judgeships in the spiritual courts. The Commissaryship of the Peculiar Court of Pickering and Pocklington, which Sterne won from Dr. Topham, gave to Sterne the presidency of one of the largest spirituals associated with the cathedral. In other courts, Sterne served as a judge for twenty-five years.

We have missed the poignancy of the satire, not knowing that the toplofty dignitaries of York were bickering over the right to sit in judgment upon illiterate country girls who had unluckily given birth to bastards. Yet every one of the original readers had most certainly witnessed the common penance ordered by the church courts—some forlorn girl standing on a chair before a church congregation, dressed in a white sheet and carrying a white wand, confessing the detestable sin of fornication with some yokel who was probably sitting in the church and whom she was forced to name. Dealing out this punishment was the chief function of Dr. Francis Topham and Laurence Sterne as ecclesiastical judges.

---

[1] An accurate and complete modern edition of the *Romance* by Ian Jack is bound with his editions of *A Sentimental Journey* and *Journal to Eliza* (Oxford, 1968).

[2] *Life and Times of Laurence Sterne* (New Haven, 1929), I, 165–88.

The spiritual (or ecclesiastical) courts of this time were the weak remnants of what had once been a terrifying Protestant inquisition. The Tudors, having endowed these ancient institutions with new powers under Civil Law, used them to suppress religious dissent. But the attrition of monarchical power and the retreat of the Civil before the Common Law had weakened them again. They eventually were abandoned in 1860.[3] In Sterne's day, they were still a major instrument for church administration and discipline, an eventful part of community life, and an important source of honor and income to the servants of God.

Much of their work was what we would call administrative. They proved wills. They granted licences for meetings of dissenters. They disciplined barbers for practicing their trade on the Sabbath, farmers for neglecting to pay their church assessments, clergy for performing illegal marriages, and squires for not keeping the church in repair.

Primarily, however, they handled sexual offences in a manner which still had the aspect of a criminal trial. True, the spirituals no longer would "signify" the condemned to a temporal court for incarceration or corporal punishment. They punished by humiliation and excommunication, but these were persuasive threats to the common people.

I. COURTS AND COMMISSARIES: THE SATIRE ON AMBITION [4]

The high clergy who were ultimately responsible for the spiritual courts usually delegated their authority to a "Commissary or Official" (synonyms which almost always appear together). The qualifications for a commissary were set forth in Canon 127. He was supposed to be at least age twenty-six, "Learned in the civil

[3] See G. F. A. Best, *Temporal Pillars* (Cambridge, England, 1964); Ronald A. Marchant, *The Puritans and the Church Courts in the Diocese of York, 1560–1642* (London, 1960); Carson I. A. Ritchie, *The Ecclesiastical Courts of York* (Arbroath, 1956).

[4] Depending as I do upon the records of the spiritual courts now in the archives of York, I wish to thank the librarians and archivists who have so patiently sorted and organized them. I am especially grateful to Elizabeth Brunskill, formerly Librarian of the York Minster Library, and her succes-

and ecclesiastical laws," "well affected and zealously bent to religion," "touching whose life and manners no evil example is had." If Sterne fell a bit short of the last qualification, he was probably not the only one who did. On the whole, however, the commissaries were competent men. Many, of course, were clergymen; but a surprising number were laymen. There were many laymen also among the "surrogates," the substitute judges which the commissaries could appoint to preside at any particular session—for a fee. By Sterne's time, all the lay commissaries and surrogates were professional lawyers, better trained for the job than their clerical colleagues.

Since a commissaryship was usually held on a life patent, the security of the income made these preferments attractive even when the income was small. A few courts took a great many fees, and the commissaries of these might turn over most of the work to surrogates and still receive a handsome living. At York a handful of lawyers vied for and won most of the posts, which they could look after while maintaining their private practices. A few were wealthy and socially prominent. In the generation before Sterne's, Dr. William Ward had far outstripped the other lawyers. Dr. Topham had early aspired to be Dr. Ward's heir in all his preferments, though the competition offered by William Stables and Laurence Sterne prevented the perfect accomplishment of his ambition.

For all that, Dr. Topham did become the chief church lawyer at York, and the list of titles drawn up for him by Dean Fountayne gives us a just sense of his importance:

Commissary to the Archbishop of *York*—Official [Commissary] to the Archdeacon of *York*—Official to the Archdeacon of the *East-Riding*—Official to the Archdeacon of *Cleveland*—Official to the Peculiar Jurisdiction of *Howdenshire*—Official to the Precentor—Official to the Chancellor of the Church of *York*—and Official to several of the Prebendaries thereof.

sor, C. B. L. Barr, for their help and advice. I am much indebted to Norah K. Gurney, Ann Rycraft, and Neville Webb of the Borthwick Institute for Historical Research, which now houses the records of the Archepiscopacy.

This list may also serve to introduce us to particular courts and types of courts in the hierarchy which were allegorized in *A Political Romance*.

We must pause for a moment over the archdeaconry courts mentioned in this list even though Dr. Topham's ambitions in that direction do not figure in Sterne's satire. These courts were fundamental to the whole system, and it was in them that Sterne had his first and most prolonged exposure to Dr. Topham. Each of the four archdeacons, the administrative assistants to the Archbishops of York, was in charge of a large subdivision of the Diocese. Each made an annual "visitation," taking his court on a circuit of a few central villages to which were called all the parish officers. Topham, by performing this work for three archdeacons, was chief administrator and judge for at least two-thirds of the Diocese. From the time he first became a parson, Sterne and his churchwardens had to report annually to the visitation of the Archdeaconry of Cleveland, which almost always was presided over by Dr. Topham, first as Dr. Ward's surrogate and then as the commissary. Sterne was certainly hard on the doctor when he represented him as Trim, a "dirty, pimping, pettifogging, ambidextrous Fellow," but the original readers of *A Political Romance* were well aware that Sterne had stood before Topham's spiritual bench for twenty years and would stand there again the following year.

Dr. Topham had yet a higher post, which is represented in the *Romance* as the great warm watch-coat. This is the preferment which the Dean listed inadequately as "Commissary to the Archbishop of York." It was the highest judgeship to which a layman could aspire, and its full, impressive title was Commissary and Keeper General of the Exchequer and Prerogative Court of York. It was one of three courts, on a legal par, which topped the York hierarchy,[5] but because it handled no moral crimes was regarded as the least of those three. The others, the Archbishop's Chancery

[5] These three did not review each other's cases. Appeals from any of them went to the highest spiritual in England, the Court of Delegates, which met in London and had to be appointed *ad hoc* by the Crown for each individual case.

Court and his Consistory Court, were headed by Sterne's close associate, Dr. William Herring, the "grave, knowing old Man" of the *Romance,* who by virtue of these commissaryships was the Diocesan Chancellor and Vicar General of Spirituals.[6] Dr. Topham's court was confined to wills and administrations, hearing all appeals in this category from lower courts and handling immediately all cases involving *bona notabilia.*[7] It was the plum of the spiritual courts because it took more and higher fees than any other—"the most comfortable Part of the Place," as Sterne said of the watchcoat.

Sterne's satire does not call to question Topham's conduct in this court, but attacks his ambitions to attain the post and to keep it in his family. Trim's demeaning services to the parson, blacking his shoes, rubbing down his horse, fetching him a closestool, refer to the lawyer's undignified ministrations to a succession of archbishops. But the central allegory, Trim's cutting up the watch-coat to make an underpetticoat for his wife and a jerkin for himself, laughs at Topham's audacious attempt to rewrite his patent for two lives, enabling his son to inherit the commissaryship.

Another major episode concerns Trim's covetousness for a green pulpit cloth and old velvet cushion. These ancient but sacred items stand for the highest of a second system of courts known as "peculiars."

The peculiar courts can be explained only historically. During the Middle Ages, the archbishops had bartered with the various cathedral organizations to gain a measure of control over them. The bargain reached at York gave to each canon the use of and profit from certain lands. Since he now received a "prebend"

---

[6] Dr. Herring was not, as Sterne scholars have assumed, Chancellor of the Minster. That was another, relatively minor post. The identification of him as the "grave, knowing old Man" was recently made by Edward Simmen of Pan American College, who kindly informed me of his discovery.

[7] The goods of a deceased who had owned property outside his own diocese, had died outside it, or (in the case of clergy) had more than one living. In effect, therefore, the court handled the wills of all the prosperous clergy and gentry.

(a share of church income), he was called a "prebendary" as well as a canon. The name of his particular prebendaryship was taken from the parish encompassing his "prebendal estate." The lands of the ordinary prebendary lay within a single parish, whereas the higher officers had estates spread over several parishes. Were the prebendaryship one "with dignity," the man had the right to appoint the parish priest, and he had complete control over the parish (or parishes) in a "peculiar court," a term meaning no more than a spiritual outside the control of the archbishop or his officers.[8]

The pulpit cloth and velvet cushion represent the highest and largest York peculiar, the Court of the Dean and Chapter. This court, belonging to the Dean and Chapter as a collective body, had immediate jurisdiction over a sizable group of parishes in and near the city and heard appeals from lower peculiars. Dr. Topham wanted it less for its wealth, which was not exceptional, than for the honor. The Dean and Chapter, however, voted it to William Stables (William Doe of the *Romance*), one of the most able and conscientious lawyers of York. Although Topham accused the Dean of manipulating the preferment away from him by stacking the Chapter meeting when the vote was taken, he was being unjust. A reading of *Chapter Acts* over this period shows that the regular group made the decision. Topham may have been galled that Laurence Sterne happened to be present.

A third episode describes Trim's quarrel with John, the parish clerk, over whether or not John had promised Trim a pair of worn, black-plush breeches. The breeches stand for the Court of the Dean. The preferment belonged to Fountayne alone, for this

[8] There was confusion enough about these matters in the eighteenth century, though Sterne would have understood them from the impressive two-volume folio he is known to have borrowed from the Minster Library, Edmund Gibson's *Codex Juris Ecclesiastici Anglicani* . . . (London, 1713). A more helpful explanation to us may be found in the admirable law dictionary of Richard Burn, *Ecclesiastical Law* (London, 1763, 2 vols). Another contemporary source, though a badly written one, is Henry Conset, *The Practice of the Spiritual or Ecclesiastical Courts* (London, 1708).

court had jurisdiction over the parishes associated with the Dean's individual prebendal estates. As might be expected, it was the largest peculiar other than that of the corporate Dean and Chapter. It was commonly, though improperly, called, after the two villages where it met, the Peculiar Court of Pickering and Pocklington. One must read the Topham-Fountayne pamphlets to appreciate fully in what minute, accurate detail Sterne allegorized their argument over this preferment. John, of course, gave the breeches to an "unlucky Wight," of "a light heart," named Lorry Slim.

Had we nothing to judge by except the pamphlets, Dr. Topham's angry stutterings might convince us that Sterne's satire was just. A study of the actual court records at York modifies the conclusion. The judges of the spiritual courts may have been ambitious, but they were also honest and professional. During the middle years of the century, the spirituals were free of the corruption which had poisoned them for sixty or more years after the Restoration. In those earlier times almost anyone might have been made a commissary. Sterne's great-grandfather, Archbishop Richard Sterne, had not hesitated to give his son the best preferment, the Commissaryship of the Exchequer and Prerogative Court, even though he did not have the requisite university degree. Earlier officials had sold licenses to physicians, midwives, and notaries for fees which were elevated inversely to the qualifications of the applicant. They hid their dealings by neglecting to register deeds; they accepted bribes for suppressing presentments, and commuted sentences for those who could pay the price. There had been sweeping reforms during the second quarter of the century, including a Parliamentary investigation. The Dean and Chapter had cleaned up their courts in 1730; one supposes the Archbishop of York did so too. By the time of Topham and Sterne, the spiritual courts of York were honest.[9]

[9] My information about abuses and reforms is taken from William Bohun, *A Brief View of Ecclesiastical Jurisdiction, as it is this Day practiced in England* (London, 1733, reprinted at Boston, 1765); and from

Sterne himself eventually decided that he had been unfair. The laughter at lawyers and dignitaries in *Tristram Shandy* stops after Volume IV, which appeared in January 1761, only two years after the *Romance*. In December of that year, when he was preparing to go abroad, Sterne wrote a note to his wife in which he asked her not to republish *A Political Romance* after his death: "I have hung up Dr Topham, in the Romance—in a ridiculous light—w^{ch}, upon my Soul I now doubt, whether he deserves it." [10]

II. COURT SCENES: STERNE AS A JUDGE

A legalistic description of the spiritual courts can give us only a hollow understanding of *A Political Romance*. The ironies of a satire constructed upon the small, colorful details of parish life become apparent only when we look at the performances of the courts at the parish level. I shall turn to the scenes of Sterne as a judge, pointing out that he shared these experiences with Dr. Topham and all judges of the spiritual courts.

How curious to think of Laurence Sterne sitting in judgment upon men and women who had committed "the detestable sin of fornication." That was, however, his major job as a judge, for in this period the church courts had evolved a primary, unspoken purpose of holding down the incidence of illegitimate birth among the mass of laborers and peasants. Gentry were exempted from the charge, not by canon law, but by the system of "presentments." The churchwardens, who had to bring in the formal charges, were more often than not illiterates who could not sign their names. Such humble men could never think to accuse a gentleman of personal misconduct, much less a gentlewoman. They were guarding their own world, and they presented people of their own station. Women were presented far more often than men for the simple reason that the evidence of childbirth was irrefutable.

Aside from the offense to God, bastardy was a serious of-

Chapter Acts, 13 November 1730, at the York Minster Library. My thanks to C. B. L. Barr for calling my attention to this entry.

[10] *Letters of Laurence Sterne,* ed. L. P. Curtis (Oxford, 1965), p. 147.

fense to the community, which would have to support a child if the mother could not. Consequently, before they made a charge the churchwardens tried to discover the father. An unwed mother was required by civil law to name the father—a law which must have been the terror of bachelors. They then tried to badger the couple into a "knobstock wedding," so named from their staves of office. Failing a wedding, they tried to get the man to post bond guaranteeing support of the child or to buy his freedom for a fixed sum. Local officers had a frightening weapon at their disposal, a set of civil statutes called the "bastardy laws," which made it legally possible to have the couple fined, whipped, or even sent to the house of correction. But these harsh laws were seldom invoked.[11] Instead, offenders were more charitably presented in the spiritual courts. A wedding would not absolve them, for they would still be charged with "antenuptial fornication." We cannot tell which of these couples had been forced into marriage by the parish. Possibly some had married for love only to be cursed by the too early birth of a child.

More single people were presented than couples, and far more women than men. Many accused fathers simply vanished. A good many women were either so depraved they could not name the father, or so heroic they would not name him.

If found guilty, these venereal criminals were ordered to do penance by making public confession. If they refused, they faced excommunication. Notations in the court records show that most did the penance. The confession was a curious ritual, probably of medieval origin. Obviously, it was heavy with folk symbolism, the meaning of which is now lost completely. As single women or, more rarely, men, or as couples, they came to divine service bareheaded, bare-footed, wrapped in a white sheet, and carrying a wand. When directed, they mounted a chair and repeated their confession after the minister, who read it from an instruction sheet. Printed "Penances" were produced wholesale by the arch-

[11] W. E. Tate, *The Parish Chest: A Study of the Records of Parochial Administration in England* (Cambridge, England, 1946), pp. 213–20.

bishops and the Dean and Chapter, who sold them for a fee. There were appropriate blanks to be filled in with the name of the penitent, the partner in sin, etc. The archives of York contain thousands of these documents, all filled in.

PENANCE ENJOINED TO BE DONE BY _____
of the Parish of _____

THE said _____ shall be present in the parish church of _____ aforesaid, upon Sunday being the ____ Day of ____ in the time of divine Service, between the Hours of Nine and Eleven of the Clock in the Forenoon of the same Day, in the Presence of the whole Congregation then Assembled, being bare-headed, bare-footed, and bare-legged, having a White Sheet wrapped about ____ from the Shoulders to the Feet, and a white Wand in ____ Hand, where immediately after the Reading the Gospel shall stand upon some Form or Seat before the Pulpit, or Place where the Minister readeth Prayers, and say after him as followeth

WHEREAS, I good People forgetting my Duty to Almighty God have committed the Detestable Sin of Fornication with _____
and thereby have justly provoked the heavy Wrath of God against me, to the great Danger of my own Soul, and evil Example of others, I do earnestly repent, and am heartily sorry for the same, desiring Almighty God for the Merits of Jesus Christ, to forgive me both this and all other my Offences, and also ever hereafter, so to assist me with his Holy Spirit, that I never fall into the like Offence again, and for that End and Purpose, I desire you all here Present, to pray with me, and for me, saying,

OUR FATHER WHICH ART IN HEAVEN, *and so forth.*

Sterne frequently ministered this dire ritual as a parish priest. As we know from the records of the Cleveland Archdeaconry Court, hardly a year passed without some hapless girl doing her penance at Sutton-on-the-Forest. A number of times he was forced to excommunicate parishioners who refused to come to court when presented.

Sterne's experience as a judge of such trials began in 1742, when he was twenty-nine years old and the *Political Romance* was yet seventeen years away. The previous winter he had exchanged his first prebendaryship for that of North Newbald, becoming thus a "Dignitary" with the right to preside at the tiny prebendal Court of North Newbald. His services in this capacity have not before been noticed, for no actual court records survive from the years he presided. There are some records, however, from the period 1760–1767,[12] when he had turned the court over to the Curate of North Newbald, Rev. Anthony Almond. Sterne was probably careless in turning in his records to the Dean and Chapter, as he was required. Nevertheless, there can be no doubt he held court in the parish of North Newbald: the first four or five years after Mr. Almond took charge, the churchwardens, accustomed to Sterne's presence, continued to address their written presentments to Laurence Sterne. So we know that for many years Sterne made an annual trip to the village of North Newbald to hold a little court attended only by the minister and churchwardens—and a few poor women and men presented for fornication. If another kind of case arose, it would almost certainly have been appealed to Mr. Stable's Court of the Dean and Chapter.

We can see the sort of thing which went on at North Newbald from the records of the Prebendal Court of Stillington,[13] to which Sterne, as the Vicar of Stillington, annually reported. James Worsley, who became Prebendary of Stillington in 1750, was a conscientious man, and he faithfully turned in his records. Most of the offenses tried were sexual, and most were concluded with the inevitable penance. However, neither the community nor the judges were harsh, as we see from the touching case of Jane Harbotle, discovered by Lewis Curtis. The case is of special concern to us because it is the only one where Sterne's personal feelings are in part recorded. Jane Harbotle, impoverished and probably moronic, was presented in 1753 following the birth of her third bastard. After her trial before Mr. Worsley, when she started off toward York to pay her fine, Sterne gave her the following note:

---

[12] Loose sheets at York Minster Library, Box C3a.   [13] *Ibid.*

Mr Clough

the Bearer is the poor Woman who was presented at Stillington Visitation, and has left her Child to go & get these said Penances, wch I
& Mr Mosely [a neighboring parson] talked so much about. She is as
poor as a Church Mouse & cannot absolutely raise a Shilling, To save
her Life. so pray let her have the Penance—and so far as the Stamps,
I will take care to discharge. If not above 3 or 4 Shillings—

Y^{rs} L. Sterne [14]

The fine Sterne offered to pay—no small sum then—was never
demanded. The Church could be merciful, as Register Clough's
note on the presentment sheet reveals:

Mr Sternes certifying her poverty she only paid 4^d for the penance /
which was ret^d with a Certificate of due performance.

Five years later, we learn from the parish register, Jane Harbotle,
spinster, died, leaving two children on the parish.

The accused father, Robert Jepson, married and father of a
legitimate family, refused to come to court. Mr. Worsley was away
the day Jepson was cited to appear. Sterne presided. He had no
choice but to excommunicate the man. Sterne and Worsley, however, doubted Jane Harbotle's word, though it appears they had a
hard time getting Jepson to act in his own behalf. It has not been
known heretofore, but six years later the case was appealed to the
Court of the Dean and Chapter at York, where on February 14,
1760, Jepson was found not guilty and absolved.[15]

Sterne's status as an ecclesiastical judge rose considerably
with his two commissaryships. In 1750 Lord Fauconberg preferred him to the Peculiar Court of Alne and Tollerton. The following year John Fountayne named him to the Peculiar Court of
the Dean of York (the breeches of *A Political Romance*).

Alne and Tollerton had been the prebendal court of the
Treasurer of the Minster and was on a par with the courts of the

[14] *Letters*, pp. 47–48.
[15] *Dean and Chapter Abstract Book, 1739–1774*, Borthwick Institute,
shelf mark R.As.90.

Chancellor and Precentor, both handled by Dr. Topham. The office of Treasurer, however, had been abolished under Henry VIII, and the estates and associated rights had passed to an ancestor of Lord Fauconberg. By this accident of history, his Lordship was a hereditary judge of a spiritual court, though he had no intention of presiding. Upon the death of the previous commissary, he gave the post to his amusing and companionable neighbor, Laurence Sterne. It brought Sterne only about two pounds a year. Since he often traveled to York to do substitute preaching at the Minster for a fee of one pound, he must have been happy to get two pounds at Alne. Neither did it bring much honor, because it was a neighborhood affair. It always met at Alne, close by Sutton-on-the-Forest, and it embraced only three parishes, the parsons of which were his cronies.[16]

By contrast, the Deanery Court was the largest prebendal court of York, embracing nineteen parishes and chapelries. Among peculiars, only the Court of the Dean and Chapter was larger. It was divided into two sections which met on separate days in the large, handsome churches of Pickering and Pocklington.[17] The two communities were comparatively remote from York, and each served as the cultural and economic center for a large area. Sterne, who was otherwise a stranger, must have been received into Pickering and Pocklington with a great deal of deference as the dignitary who would preside at their most impressive annual church affair. No doubt he was put up in a local inn where, after the visitation, he was feted at a visitation dinner. Whether or not chestnuts were served, we cannot know.[18] Al-

---

[16] A remarkably complete record of Alne and Tollerton Court survives at the Borthwick Institute under the shelf mark R.VI.C. There are a *Court Book,* a *Subscription Book,* a record of the fees collected from the year 1765, and a set of loose papers.

[17] A good set of records of the Deanery Court remains. At the Borthwick Institute is the *Court Book,* shelf number RAs 87. At the Minster Library is the *Exhibition Book* (S3 [5] .d) and numerous loose papers (C3a).

[18] The visitation dinner, no longer mandatory, was a well-established custom for clergy coming from afar. I surmise, however, that the visitation

though Sterne did not grow rich on this preferment (he received only about four pounds a year) the honor must have been gratifying.[19]

As with all spirituals, the meetings of Alne and Tollerton Court and the Deanery Court were of two types, called the "visitation" and the "court." The initial annual meeting was a large affair held in a church to which were summoned all parish officers and presented offenders. It was called the "visitation." If any difficult case arose here, one which could be resolved only with the aid of lawyers—a contested will, for instance, a quarrel over tithes, or a suit for slander—Sterne would immediately defer the case for later, special attention. The parties would then be called to a special meeting, usually in the chambers of a lawyer, where the case would be given a full, formal trial. The judge was always one of Sterne's surrogates, better trained in law than he. The series of such special trials was popularly known as the "court," as distinct from the "visitation." This special, colloquial meaning of *court* must be distinguished from the word in its general meaning, which denotes the entire institution including both the visitation and the special "court."

---

dinner of *Tristram Shandy* followed a "primary visitation" of an archbishop. In a primary visitation, an archbishop went on circuit throughout the diocese, personally confronting the parishes and thus "inhibiting" for that year most of the courts I have mentioned. (The reports Sterne made for the Primary Visitations of Archbishops Herring and Drummond were described by Canon S. L. Ollard, *TLS*, March 18, 1926, May 25, 1933, and June 1, 1933). The prodigious number of lawyers and churchmen at the visitation dinner of *Tristram Shandy* strongly suggests a primary visitation. Furthermore, Sterne indicated the location with four asterisks, which contemporaries would have taken to mean "York." Previous to his writing of that scene, Sterne had been required to attend only one ecclesiastical court session held in York—the Primary Visitation of Archbishop Herring of 1743.

[19] Topham and Fountayne in their pamphlets agree that the position was worth about five pounds, but Sterne himself took less than the total of the judge's fees. Only one precise record survives—a note in Sterne's hand on the call sheet for Pickering in 1752, where we learn that in this first half of the visitation he had received less than two pounds.

Sterne always made his own visitations, but never—with one exception—appeared at the "court." In this respect, his experience differed from that of Dr. Topham, who, as a lawyer, naturally handled his own "courts."

In effect, Sterne as a judge was required to make decisions only in simple cases. Most of them were presentations for fornication or antenuptial fornication. A few others were disciplinary. Once, for instance, he tried a churchwarden who failed of his duty. If his ruling were contested, he would send the case to the special "court."

It is this last point which makes a study of the "court" records significant even though Sterne did not take part in these special trials. We can search them for cases of a simple sort, assuming that these would not have appeared here unless the accused had contested Sterne's ruling. So brief are the entries that no certain conclusion is possible. Nevertheless, I shall venture to say that only two entries *might* fall into this category. Both were trials of women in 1753 upon charges not recorded. Both failed to appear and were excommunicated. So we can know this much at least: out of the sixty or more trials for sexual offenses heard by Sterne, only two accused *may* have contested his ruling; and *if* they did, they were not serious about it since they failed to defend themselves when given a chance. I conclude, therefore, that Laurence Sterne was a very fair judge.

What customary pomp was followed at Sterne's visitations we do not know, but the "process" sent to the churches some weeks before his arrival indicates the ceremonious nature of the proceedings. This was always written in a beautiful hand by the Register of the Dean and Chapter and used the most formal language. The process sent to Pocklington for 1753, for instance, styles Laurence Sterne, "Clerk Master of Arts Commissary or Official of the Peculiar and Spiritual Jurisdiction of the Deanery of the Cathedral and Metropolitical Church of Saint Peter of York lawfully Authorized," and he is thereafter referred to by the noble first-person plural pronoun. He orders all rectors, vicars, curates, churchwardens, chapelwardens, and persons whose names are hereunder written,

humbly to undergo such our Visitation in this behalf to be exercised and celebrated and also to hear do and receive what shall be then and there expounded and administered to them and further to do and receive what the nature and Quality of our said Visitation require of them.

Beneath are listed the parishes and chapelries cited, followed by a list of "all and singular persons":

Cite Robert Atkinson and his wife of Pocklington for the Crime of Antenuptial fornication
Cite Mary Bernard of the same place for the Crime of fornication she having born a Bastard Child
Cite Timothy Sowersby of Givendale for neglecting to make up his Church wardens Accounts
Cite Ann Haxby of Kilham for the Crime of fornication with Thomas Creaser (since absconded) she having born a Bastard Child

A note by the curate of Pocklington tells us that the process was "published" in time of divine service. After it was read in church, the process was given to Mr. Sparke, the Apparitor, who attempted to serve it upon the accused cited. Since most of the teeth had been drawn from the spiritual courts, the apparitors were no longer hated as spies and turncoats, though they were not much liked.

When Sterne appeared for a visitation, he found a large group at the church. There were the parsons with their curates; the parish clerks; many awkward farmers, the church-wardens, ready to make presentments or, if they were new, to be sworn in; and such physicians, midwives, and masters of schools or hospitals as were required to exhibit the documents which gave them the right to practice. Sitting quietly at the back were the accused, women mostly, who had been presented the year before.

Sterne may or may not have opened ceremonies with a sermon. It was an old custom, but no longer mandatory. Once open, the visitation was conducted primarily by the Register (also called variously the Actuary, Recorder, or Scribe). Registers of this period were licensed notaries public. So highly was this profession regarded that in any court, spiritual or temporal, the single testimony of a notary was taken to be worth that of any two other witnesses. This august person had a "call," or roll, of all who had been summoned. As the day moved on, he jotted down notes beside the names, "sworn" by new churchwardens, "excused" or "failed to appear" by absent clergy. He took up a written presentment sheet from each set of outgoing churchwardens. For every step of the proceeding, he collected a fee—the income of the court. Only about a third of it would go to the judge. The Register, though he had fewer responsibilities, was permitted to keep the rest.

Finally came the actual trials. If they turned out to be difficult, Sterne deferred them for the special "court." But most were for sexual offenses, and these Sterne gave a "summary" (informal) trial. After questioning the parson and churchwardens and hearing what the accused had to say, Sterne would declare for guilt or innocence. If the person were found guilty, Sterne would order the penance. As judicial decisions, most were cut and dried. Typical is the case of Elizabeth Cook of Barnby Moor, who was tried at Pocklington in 1758: "Cook app[d] and confess'd the Crime, the Commissary admonish'd her to extract the usual pen[ce] at four o'Clock." The human drama of every case must have been intense, though it shows through the bare record only for a few. There was Robert Milburn, tried at Alne in 1753 for antenuptial fornication "with Jane his wife, now dead."

A small minority of accused would not acknowledge their guilt or do the penance. They simply stayed away from the visitation. The result, of course, was predetermined. The call for Pickering visitation of 1761 (Sterne's last appearance there) informs us that the three women cited for fornication,

were thrice publicly and openly called . . . and in no wise appearing or excusing their Contumacy, the said Commissary pronounced them and every of them to be Contumacious and in penalty of such their

Contumacy he Decreed the Lay persons to be Excommunicated and did Excommunicate such Lay persons within the said Jurisdiction.[20]

Notes added later show that two of the women eventually confessed, did penance, and were absolved.

Sterne made his visitations regularly—until he turned writer. His first appearance at Alne was in the summer of 1751; his first at the Deanery Court a year later. He never failed to show up until 1759, the summer following the *Political Romance* when he was furiously writing the first version of *Tristram Shandy*. Thereafter, he appeared at Alne and Tollerton three times and once at Pickering (but not Pocklington). These were his years of fame. He was out of the country a good deal, and often he was dangerously ill. In this period he left the courts to his surrogates, a respectable group of lawyers and clerics. The fact that Sterne made any visitations at all in these years implies that he enjoyed them.

Since we have evidence that Sterne himself was guilty of the crime of fornication,[21] some readers of this account may be tempted to revert to the Victorian view and summarily condemn him for hypocrisy. His peers at York would not have seen the matter so—not even Dr. Topham. They would have pointed out that he performed services inadequately recompensed by the small honor and income; that he tried the peasantry, not for unchastity, but for engendering homeless infants; and that he sheltered the unfortunate from the cruel temporal courts. Sterne was indeed a humane and conscientious judge, and Dr. Topham's pamphlets never give the least hint that the lawyer thought his rival unfit for the position. Were Sterne's indiscretions known, they would have attracted little attention in a city which was used to Archdeacon

[20] The judge pronounced the "lesser excommunication," cutting the criminal off from the sacraments. After a stipulated period, the parish priest pronounced in church the "greater excommunication" or "denunciation," supposedly cutting him off from all commerce and conversation.

[21] James M. Kuist, "New Light on Sterne: An Old Man's Recollections of the Young Vicar," *PMLA*, LXXX (1965), 549–53.

Jaques Sterne and Archbishop Lancelot Blackburn. Indeed Sterne did offend the church with what he wrote, but he never was called to account for how he lived.

Although Dr. Samuel Johnson had little respect for "the man Sterne," his balanced wisdom may help us to a just opinion. When Boswell told him about a Scotsman whose ordination in the church was opposed upon the grounds that he had been guilty of fornication, Johnson replied, "Why, Sir, if he has repented, it is not a sufficient objection. A man who is good enough to go to heaven, is good enough to be a clergyman."

DONALD J. GREENE

Samuel Johnson and the Great War for Empire

BITTER HOSTILITY and resistance by a large segment of a country's population to a war which its government is conducting is not a new phenomenon in the history of the English-speaking world. John Adams calculated that a third of the inhabitants of the Thirteen Colonies were opposed to the War of American Independence; the tarrings and featherings, the confiscations, eventually the exile inflicted on tens of thousands of objectors to that war were the basic cause of a persistent anti-Americanism in Canada that is still far from extinct. At the same time there existed in Britain a vigorous opposition to British participation in that war: as well as powerful political leaders like Shelburne and Fox, who eventually forced the pro-war administration of Lord North out of office and made peace by conceding American independence, there were high military officers who endangered their professional careers by refusing to accept commands in the American theater of operations. Britain fought the

Napoleonic wars to the accompaniment of determined obstruction-
ism by the Foxite Whigs, who made no secret of their admiration
for Napoleon. It was at least as much American internal hostility
to the War of 1812–1814 as external military opposition which
brought that war to a close. And so on, up to the Vietnam adventure of the 1960s and beyond.

Perhaps the most notable example of successful internal opposition to a British or American war was that directed against
the War of the Spanish Succession, 1702–1713. Marlborough's
spectacular victories over the might of Louis XIV's France did not
prevent his being recalled and dismissed for over-aggressiveness,
and peace was negotiated with the French on terms much less
stringent than Marlborough and his supporters wished to enforce.
If the opposition at that time was so effective, it was largely because the chief of propaganda of the peace party, the Tories, was
a consummate literary artist, the Reverend Jonathan Swift—it
seems appropriate to mention his clerical calling in connection
with an anti-war protest movement. The essence of his many anti-
war writings is distilled in his parting shot, long after the war was
over—his epitaph on his old enemy Marlborough, whose casualty
lists in the 1702–1713 war are said to have reached a figure
higher than the combined total of the casualties in all earlier British wars:

> Nor widow's sighs, nor orphan's tears,
> Wont at such times each heart to pierce,
> Attend the progress of his hearse.
> But what of that, his friends may say;
> He had those honours in his day.
> True to his profit and his pride,
> He made them weep before he died.

One is tempted to assert that strenuous internal opposition to
waging an aggressive war has been the rule rather than the exception in British and American history. There *is,* however, one conspicuous exception to this generalization—the Seven Years' War
of 1756 to 1763, which its most distinguished historian, L. H.

Gipson, has proposed renaming "the Great War for the Empire."
It did indeed bring the British Empire into being, adding the two
great subcontinents of Canada and India to Britain's territorial
possessions, and it provided Britain with easy access to markets
and sources of raw materials throughout the world and so laid the
foundations of Britain's amazing commercial prosperity in the
nineteenth century. Moreover, it made it possible for the future
United States to take the shape it did: had the Ohio Valley, where
the war actually started in 1754, not been wrested from France,
the Thirteen Colonies would have been restricted to a narrow strip
of land along the Atlantic seaboard, and in time not improbably
eliminated by the French power to the north and west. Gipson
sums it up well in his moving dedication of the three volumes entitled *The Great War for the Empire* in his monumental history:
to "the thousands of soldiers from the British Isles who lie buried
in unknown graves here in the New World" as casualties in that
war, whose sacrifice "helped to provide a future without parallel
for the English-speaking people here on the continent of North
America." [1]

This being so, it is understandable that nineteenth-century
historians, for whom the material prosperity of the English speaking peoples and their hegemony over the rest of the world seemed
the ultimate political value, should have spoken of the Seven
Years' War in terms of unquestioning approval, almost of reverence. "Never had England played so great a part in the history of
mankind as in the year 1759," says John Richard Green, whose
immensely popular *Short History of the English People* (1874)
shaped the views of English and American readers for decades.
"It is no exaggeration to say that three of its many victories determined for ages to come the destinies of mankind." As well as its
effects on the history of Europe and Asia, Green stresses that
"with the triumph of Wolfe on the Heights of Abraham began the

---

[1] L. H. Gipson, *The British Empire Before the American Revolution*
(Caldwell, Idaho, and New York, 1936–70), VI, [v].

history of the United States. . . . Pitt laid the foundation of the great republic of the west." [2]

For many decades, this attitude was embalmed in school textbooks of British history. It is a little surprising, however, to find historians still uncritically accepting it in the middle of the twentieth century, when Pitt's Empire is seen to have been only a fleeting episode in the two thousand years of British history, when it is beginning to be suspected that the "unparalleled future" of the English-speaking people in North America may contain some radical flaws, and when the way the destinies of mankind have been shaped for the past two hundred years may no longer seem to have been the completely ideal one. V. H. H. Green, for instance, in *The Hanoverians* (1948), begins his account of the war with a promising expression of skepticism: "National historians are rarely honest in their estimates of the causes that lead to war, because they are the victims and sometimes the perpetrators of the legends that mould history to suit national prejudice." Very true. But this healthy skepticism is never actually applied to Green's treatment of the war itself—Pitt headed "the most distinguished ministry in the annals of eighteenth-century history. . . . And, happily for the country, he had very great abilities"—and he concludes by approvingly quoting Horace Walpole: "Lord Chatham's first administration had secured the most real and substantial benefits of his country. . . . Even the shameful Peace of Paris—" shameful because it treated France and Spain somewhat more generously than Britain's military power made necessary—"could not rob the nation of all that he had acquired, nor could George III resign so much as Pitt had gained for George II. Half the Empire of Hindostan, conquered under his administration by the spirit he had infused, still pours its treasures into the Thames." [3] Nothing could be franker. The conquest of territory and the subsequent gain of material wealth are automatically praiseworthy, and their relinquishment, whatever its ultimate results in terms of world

[2] Chap. X, sec. II.   [3] V. H. H. Green, pp. 219, 220.

peace, is shameful. When one analyzes the moral values implicit in many of the judgments that historians have passed on the events they deal with, one is sometimes sadly inclined to agree with Samuel Johnson, "There is but a shallow stream of thought in history."

As remarkable as the uncritical approbation later historians have given to the Seven Years' War and its outcome is what appears to have been the near-unanimity of the British general public, including the literary world, that Pitt's enterprise was a cause for unqualified rejoicing. At the outset of the war, when military defeats were frequent, there was of course complaint; and when, toward its end, the question arose of whether to make a "hard" or a "soft" peace with France and Spain, there was bitter controversy between the supporters of the two positions. But to the fact of the war itself, notwithstanding its heavy price in British lives and money, an astonishingly small amount of objection seems to have been raised. Robert D. Spector's recent detailed study of the content of dozens of the British periodicals flourishing at the time demonstrates this unanimity. Even the two great literary journals of the eighteenth century, the *Critical Review* and the *Monthly Review,* normally given to taking opposing stands on most issues, saw eye to eye: "While the weight of magazine opinion favoring Pitt is impressive [that is, of periodicals bearing the title "Magazine"], perhaps nothing better describes the extent of the periodical writers' allegiance to the minister at this time than the complete agreement in the two reviews," and "Pitt's ability to remain above criticism in the periodicals . . . indicates how successful his efforts had been in unifying the nation. Politics had become a subdued issue during his conduct of the war, and the periodical writers in 1759 suppressed their political emotions for the sake of the country and its popular minister." [4]

[4] Robert Donald Spector, *English Literary Periodicals and the Climate of Opinion During the Seven Years' War* (The Hague and Paris, 1966), pp. 52–53, 61.

From this general chorus of journalistic and popular support there was one conspicuous note of dissent, one editor who took a longer view and questioned whether the success of the "popular minister" and his war was necessarily to be equated with what was "happy for the country." The *Literary Magazine, or Universal Review* began publication in the month in which Britain formally declared war on France, May 1756, and indeed carried in its first number the full text of the declaration—and much else concerning the war. Its opening article was a long and rigorously objective analysis by the editor himself of the historical and economic background of the conflict. He begins by raising a question concerning the whole rationale of European imperialist expansion: of British overseas possessions, he remarks, "We seem to have snatched them into our hands upon no very just principles or policy, only because every state, according to a prejudice of long continuance, concludes itself more powerful as its territories become larger." If, of course, this basic premise of nationalistic expansion is challenged, there is no telling into what heresy such a skeptic may be led. He cannot see what advantage the French expected from the colonization of Canada, "a cold uninviting region, from which nothing but furs and fish were to be had." [5] As it is, however, the French have managed their American colonies with more astuteness than the British:

Their great security is the friendship of the natives, and to this advantage they have certainly an indubitable right, because it is the consequence of their virtue. It is ridiculous to imagine that the friendship of nations, whether civil or barbarous, can be gained and kept but by kind treatment; and surely they who intrude, uncalled, upon the country of a distant people ought to consider the natives as worthy of common kindness and content themselves to rob without insulting them. The French admit the Indians, by intermarriage, to an equality with

[5] The parallel with Voltaire's "quelques arpents de neige" in *Candide* (1759) is worth noting. Johnson may seem unique among English writers in his bitter anti-colonialism, but he may well owe something to Continental criticism, from Bartolomé de Las Casas on, of the European adventure in the New World and its attendant atrocities.

themselves, and those nations with which they have no such near intercourse, they gain over to their interest by honesty in their dealings. . . . Our traders hourly alienate the Indians by their tricks and oppressions, and we continue every day to show by new proofs that no people can be great who have ceased to be virtuous.[6]

Samuel Johnson was permitted for some four months to use the *Literary Magazine* as a platform for delivering sentiments so unpatriotic and potentially subversive of the British "war effort" as these, and he used it vigorously. But in the fifth number a very different hand takes over the political commentary, one which pays tribute to those "eminent patriots . . . the hon. Mr. Pitt . . . the hon. Charles Townshend, esq.," and praises their "glorious example." Clearly, enough was enough for the proprietors of the *Magazine,* and Johnson, though allowed to contribute sporadically to subsequent numbers, was no longer in control of its editorial policy. The *Magazine* became violently patriotic, printed as its frontispiece a representation of Britannia stabbing with her spear the loathsome dragon of France, adopted the fatuous designation of the *Literary and Antigallican Magazine,* and presently expired.[7]

The Seven Years' War was the most important event in British, indeed world, history during Johnson's lifetime. It concerned him deeply, and it is instructive to study in some detail his attitude toward it. He was as uniformly and bitterly hostile to the whole of Pitt's ambitious enterprise as Swift had been to Marlborough's. Swift, however, wrote as a member of a powerful political party working together to discredit the morality and expediency of the conduct of the earlier war and achieved striking success. John-

[6] *Literary Magazine,* I, 1 (April 15–May 15, 1756), 1–9 ("An Introduction to the Political State of Great-Britain"). This and the majority of the writings by Johnson quoted below are easily accessible in the various nineteenth-century editions of Johnson's *Works* found in most large libraries, and can be located by title in their tables of contents. In future, footnote references will be given only for pieces not included in these editions or with special problems of identification.

[7] For a detailed study of Johnson's connection with the *Literary Magazine,* see D. J. Greene, *Review of English Studies,* n. s. VII (October 1956), 367–92.

son's was a one-man crusade; yet he never seems to have been swerved from his position by the thought of his isolation and his failure to achieve any results whatever.[8]

Johnson's views on the immorality of European intervention in other parts of the world had been expressed early in his career. In the preface to his earliest book, published when he was twenty-five, his translation and adaptation of Joachim Le Grand's version of the Portuguese Jesuit Jeronymo Lobo's *Voyage to Abyssinia,* 1735, he congratulates Lobo for reporting, contrary to the custom of other travelers to remote regions, that the natives of Ethiopia are fairly ordinary, run-of-the-mill members of the human race: "Nor are the nations here described either devoid of all sense of humanity, or consummate in all private and social virtues. . . . [The reader] will discover what will always be discovered by a diligent and impartial inquirer, that wherever human nature is to be found, there is a mixture of vice and virtue, a contest of passion and reason. . . ." That is, Ethiopians are basically no better and no worse human beings than Portuguese or English, and there is no reason for the latter to adopt an attitude of superiority to them. Johnson goes on to condemn the Jesuit mission in Ethiopia, whose leader, the Patriarch Oviedo, "was continually importuning the Portuguese to beat up their drums for missionaries who might preach the gospel with swords in their hands, and propagate by desolation and slaughter the true worship of the God of Peace," and continues with bitter denunciation of the history of European missionary activity generally, such as that in Mexico and South America, as the handmaid of imperial and commercial expansion.

As with so much of Johnson's social and political thinking, his attitude here is based on his religious convictions: it stems from the fundamental Christian tenet of the essential equality of

---

[8] Unless, of course, Bute's later success in making a "soft" peace was to some degree aided by Johnson's having kept alive a small spark of opposition to Pitt's policy of aggressiveness. The reason for Bute's awarding Johnson a government pension in 1762 has never been wholly satisfactorily explained.

all human beings, their parity of value in the eyes of their Creator, whatever their language, their culture, the color of their skin. This has always been a most radical doctrine: its political implications are tremendous, and when political and social institutions of the Western world are confronted with it, the effects may be revolutionary. Few writers on political matters have held more tenaciously to that doctrine, whatever the consequences, than Samuel Johnson—the Johnson who unceasingly denounced Negro slavery, and at Oxford horrified the dons by toasting the next insurrection of the Negroes in the West Indies; who virtually adopted as his son the young Negro slave from Jamaica, Frank Barber, did his best to give him a liberal education, and, to the distress of his chief executor, made him residuary legatee to his estate.

In some of the fierce invective that the young Johnson was given to composing at this time, he seems to have been modeling himself on Swift, then at the height of his power and fame. Johnson's first pronouncement on the question of specifically English colonial enterprise was in fact a purported continuation of the first book of *Gulliver's Travels,* and owes much to Swift's mordant satire there of English political principles and practices. This is the introduction to the *Gentleman's Magazine*'s series of reports of the debates of the British parliament, disguised, to evade the ban on reporting them, as debates in the senate of Lilliput—not a designation very complimentary to the wisdom of the British legislators.[9] "The people of Degulia, or the Lilliputian Europe," says Gulliver junior, the narrator of the piece,

are, above those of the other parts of the world, famous for arts, arms, and navigation, and, in consequence of this superiority, have made conquests and settled colonies in very distant regions, the in-

[9] The device is believed, plausibly, to have been Johnson's. The introduction appeared in the *Gentleman's Magazine,* VIII (June, 1738), 283–87, and is conveniently reprinted in Benjamin B. Hoover, *Samuel Johnson's Parliamentary Reporting* (Berkeley and Los Angeles, 1953), pp. 172–81. Every scholar who has made a careful study of the Parliamentary reporting in the *Gentleman's Magazine* has been convinced that it is Johnson's (for a detailed argument from style, see Hoover, pp. 144–45), and I know of no published challenge to the attribution.

habitants of which they look upon as barbarous, though in simplicity of manners, probity, and temperance superior to themselves; and seem to think that they have a right to treat them as passion, interest, or caprice shall direct, without much regard to the rules of justice or humanity; they have carried this imaginary sovereignty so far that they have sometimes proceeded to rapine, bloodshed, and desolation. If you endeavour to examine the foundation of this authority, they neither produce any grant from a superior jurisdiction, nor plead the consent of the people whom they govern in this tyrannical manner; but either threaten you with punishment for abridging the Emperor's sovereignty, or pity your stupidity, or tell you in positive terms, that "Power is right."

Gulliver questions whether "their conquests and acquisitions in Columbia (which is the Lilliputian name for the country that answers our America)" have in the end added to their own welfare: not even "Iberia," which "secured to herself by the most dreadful massacres and devastations . . . the richest and most fertile part of that quarter of the world," has become more prosperous as a result. As for the activities of the English in North America, he says sardonically,

It must be observed to the honour of the Lilliputians, who have in all ages been famous for their politics, that they have the art of civilizing their remote dominions without doing much injury to their native country; for when any of their people have forfeited the rights of society, by robberies, seditions, or any other crimes which make it not safe to suffer them to live, and yet are esteemed scarce heinous enough to be punished with death, they send them to some distant colony for a certain number of years proportionate to their crimes. Of these Mr. Gulliver, during his stay, saw ten thousand conveyed from the prisons of Mildendo [London] in close lighters to ships that lay at anchor in the river to carry them to Columbia, where they were disposed among the inhabitants, undoubtedly very much to the propagation of knowledge and virtue, and no less to the honour of their native country.

Moreover, "Another inconvenience of these new claims is that they are a constant source of discord and debate among the Degulian powers, some of which are perpetually disputing their titles to countries which neither has a right to."

This "Appendix to Gulliver's Account of Lilliput" was published in 1738, and in it are found the basic positions which account for Johnson's objections to the war of two decades later. Swift's tale satirizes the folly and immorality of aggressive war against a neighboring European country; in the "Appendix" Johnson effectively extends the satire to imperialistic aggression in the non-European part of the world. It was written as, among other things, a comment on the dispute between Britain and Spain over trading rights in the Caribbean, which was presently to develop into the so-called War of Jenkins' Ear and lead to the downfall of the pacific Prime Minister Sir Robert Walpole. Johnson at the time was engaged in writing violently anti-Walpole propaganda, and in the "appendix" he goes on to a somewhat chauvinistic and illogical appeal for great resistance to the Spanish claims. It was not long, however, before he changed his mind about Walpole, of whom he was later to say, "He was the best minister this country ever had; and if we would have let him, he would have kept the country in perpetual peace." The War of Jenkins' Ear presently escalated into the War of the Austrian Succession, a milder forerunner of the Seven Years' War, nominally terminated by the Peace of Aix-la-Chapelle in 1748. In India and the strategic Ohio Valley, however, French and English troops remained on a warlike footing, and actual hostilities broke out again in 1754.

During these years Johnson was making a precarious living by various literary projects. He did not, however, lose touch with the international scene. He seems to have frequently reported on it for the monthly feature of the *Gentleman's Magazine* entitled "Foreign History." [10] His contributions can be identified only by internal evidence, but it seems unlikely that such a passage as this, from the August 1741 number of the *Magazine,* could be by any of its other contributors. The reference is to Dutch colonial activ-

[10] For recent work devoted to tracing Johnson's (substantial) part in this, see D. J. Greene, *PMLA,* LXXIV (March, 1959), 81–83; Gwin J. Kolb, *Studies in English Literature,* I (Summer, 1961), 79; Gunther Rothenberg, *Notes and Queries,* CCIX (August, 1964), 296–98; F. V. Bernard, *ibid.* (November, 1964), 432–33.

ity in the East Indies, specifically to the horrifying massacre the previous year of some 10,000 Chinese immigrants to Java, whose presence had been making the Dutch administrators nervous: [11]

In the East, the Dutch are now dividing the plunder of a nation newly extirpated, and, as it is said, celebrating the success of the dreadful butchery which, at best, could be no longer necessary than till the numbers of the Chinese were reduced below the possibility of ever becoming dangerous, and which can surely admit of no excuse, when exercised upon prisoners, suppliants, and fugitives. It is scarcely to be supposed that it was not equally practicable to have expelled as to have murdered them, and in Christian or human breasts, it might have been expected that compassion would have overbalanced the sense of any slight apprehensions of danger. But what cannot cruelty commit, inflamed by the lust of money and dominion. . . .[12]

The "Foreign History" closely followed the military campaigns on the Continent involving Prussia under Frederick the Second, later called the Great, Maria Theresa's Austria-Hungary, and Bavaria under the Elector Charles Albert. When the Austrian War was concluded, Johnson delivered himself of a sardonic outburst against the famous fireworks display in London—that for which Handel wrote his Royal Fireworks Music—to celebrate the rickety Peace of Aix-la-Chapelle: "In this will consist the only propriety of this transient show, that it will resemble the war of which it celebrates the period. The powers of this part of the world, after long preparations, deep intrigues, and subtle schemes, have set Europe in a flame, and after having gazed a while at their fireworks, have laid themselves down where they rose, to inquire for what they had been contending." [13] But for several years, Johnson was too closely engaged with his *Dictionary* and the *Rambler* to have time for much journalistic work on the contemporary scene.

With the completion of the *Dictionary* in 1755, however,

[11] *New Cambridge Modern History* (Cambridge, 1957), VII, 587–88.

[12] *Gentleman's Magazine,* XI (August, 1741), 444.

[13] *Ibid.,* XIX (January 1749), 8. Signed "O. N." Reprinted in editions of Johnson's *Works* from 1823 on as "Letter on Fireworks."

something like an outburst of pent-up energy and concern took place, manifesting itself in the remarkable four-months production in 1756 when he edited and almost singlehandedly wrote the *Literary Magazine*. Comprehending the immense importance of the war on which Britain had just embarked, Johnson seems to have determined, in a spirit of the most highly responsible journalism, to provide his contemporaries and posterity with the fullest possible record of the transactions of that war. "The time is now come," he declares at the beginning of his most powerful article —ironically, the one that probably led to his efforts being suppressed—"in which every Englishman expects to be informed of the national affairs, and in which he has a right to have that expectation gratified," and he goes on to rebut the perennial contention of "ministers, or those whom vanity or interest make the followers of ministers, concerning the necessity of confidence in our governors, and the presumption of prying with profane eyes into the recesses of policy." [14] He prints in full the texts of important documents as they are released—declarations of war, official diplomatic exchanges, military dispatches, relevant legislation, proceedings of court martial. A monthly feature, "Historical Memoirs," provides a lucid and comprehensive survey of current events at home and abroad. His leading articles are pungent, blunt, well-informed and well-argued pleas for clearing the mind of cant about the causes and consequences of the war—such as the opening blast mentioned above, "An Introduction to the Political State of Great Britain," in which the fundamental question is raised, why European nations should seek territorial acquisitions in other parts of the world at all.

The book review section gives much space to publications dealing with the war. It had opened, as British wars so often have, with a series of military fiascos, the most spectacular of which was the loss of the island of Minorca to a French expedition from

[14] *Literary Magazine*, I, 4 (July 15–August 15, 1756), [161]. ("Observations on the Present State of Affairs"; reprinted in *Works* as "Observations on the State of Affairs in 1756.")

Toulon. A British naval task force under Admiral John Byng had been dispatched to intercept the French attackers; Byng, provided with inferior forces, let them get through. There was a great public outcry, and the administration defended itself by putting all the blame on Byng, who was court-martialed for cowardice and shot —"pour encourager les autres," as Voltaire put it. As to the loss of Minorca, Johnson, reviewing a history of the island in the first number of the *Literary Magazine,* and calculating what it has cost Britain to maintain possession of it, coolly observes,

I am not able to image to myself any [advantages] that in forty-eight years have been equivalent to so much money and so many lives. It is said to increase our reputation in the Levant, but that reputation neither makes us richer nor much happier. If the distribution of empire were in my hands, I should indeed rather give up Gibraltar, the possession of which will always keep us at variance with Spain, than Minorca, which may be less invidiously retained. But I know not whether either is worth its charge, and by losing them, I am not sure that we shall suffer anything more than that vexation which accompanies disgrace, and the pain of doing that against our will which we should have been glad to do if no violence had compelled us.[15]

As for Byng, Johnson agrees with Voltaire and many others that his execution was a piece of grossly cynical injustice perpetrated in the hope of saving the administration from the consequences of its own incompetence: "Mr. Byng is stigmatized with infamy and pursued with clamours artfully excited to divert the public attention from the crimes and blunders of other men; and . . . while he is thus vehemently pursued for imaginary guilt, the real criminals are hoping to escape." [16]

Because of such military reverses, there was one of the invasion scares recurrent in British history, which government pam-

[15] *Ibid.,* I, 1 (April 15–May 15, 1756), 11–14 ("The History of Minorca extracted from the history written in the form of letters by Mr. Armstrong in 1740").
[16] *Ibid.,* I, 6 (September 15–October 15, 1756), 299 (review of *A Letter to a Member of Parliament . . . relative to the case of Admiral Byng* and *An Appeal to the People*). Other reviews of pamphlets on the Byng affair in the *Literary Magazine* take the same anti-administration line.

phleteers were doing their best to foster for governmental purposes. Johnson lustily pooh-poohs it: "Surely he [the author of the pamphlet under review] would not have us forget the alarm which frighted some of our women to strong waters, and our parliament to Hanoverian troops. Let us not forget the flat-bottomed boats, built, I suppose, in the clouds, and now lost in the clouds again. Again, let us not forget that when any nation is to be fleeced, it is first to be frighted." [17]

In Johnson's review of Armstrong's *History of Minorca* he reverts to the question of the treatment by an imperial power of the indigenous peoples of the territories they annex. Armstrong laments that the natives of Minorca remain strangely unfriendly toward their British conquerors, and regrets that they "fatally missed a favourable opportunity of becoming partakers of all the various benefits of the mildest constitution of government upon earth." This chauvinism is examined coolly by Johnson:

It was natural for a people little acquainted with the state of other countries, and conquered by men whom they considered as heretics, and had been taught to dread and hate as the most mischievous of the human race, to prefer any condition, of which they knew all the good and bad, before that which the caprice of a conqueror might prescribe. . . . The time is now come when it will appear that oppression is folly as well as wickedness. . . . A people taxed, harassed, and insulted will always be desirous of changing their condition.

In the monthly feature "Historical Memoirs," he preaches the same doctrine: "Let us not, because we owe much to the generosity of our Indian friends, be so unreasonably covetous as not to be contented with less than all they had to give"; and "While the French have been endeavouring by every artifice that human pol-

---

[17] *Ibid.*, I, 7 (October 15–November 15, 1756), 351 (review of *The Conduct of the Ministry Impartially Examined*). See also I, 4 (July 15–August 15), 186–87 (review of Charles Parkin, *An Impartial Account of the Invasion under William, Duke of Normandy*): "This pamphlet is published to prove what nobody can deny, that we shall be less happy if we were conquered by the French. . . . There is no great danger of invasions while we have the sea covered with our ships, and maintain fifty thousand men in arms on our coasts."

icy could suggest to establish an interest among them [the Indians], our Governors there . . . have for a series of years past taken no care to cultivate new friendships with the ancient inhabitants." [18]

In the sixth number of the *Magazine,* Johnson reviews a work by Lewis Evans describing the Ohio region and emphasizing its strategic and economic importance. "He concludes his pamphlet," says Johnson, "with some observations which may be of great use in the present system of European policy, but which will not prove that this system is right; or in other words, that it is more productive than any other of universal happiness"—a criterion not too often applied by journalistic commentators to so impressive a body of dogma as "the present system of European policy." Evans urges that Britain make a great effort to obtain and secure possession of the Ohio Valley. Johnson throws cold water on his enthusiasm:

This great country, for which we are so warmly incited to contend, will not be honestly our own though we keep it from the French. . . . An increase of lands without increase of people gives no increase of power or of wealth. . . . Since the end of all human actions is happiness, why should any number of our inhabitants be banished from their trades and their homes to a trackless desert, where life is to begin anew? [19]

Johnson, it will be seen, was behind his times (or perhaps much ahead of them) in refusing to endorse a Turnerian view of the virtues of the frontier.

Among Johnson's independent contributions to the early numbers of the *Literary Magazine* dealing with problems of the war are analyses of a bill to reorganize the English militia on a more efficient basis, and of treaties concluded with Russia and Hesse-Cassel whereby those countries agree to defend Hanover.

[18] *Ibid.,* I, 2, 105–06 and I, 3, 153.
[19] *Ibid.,* I, 6, 293–99 (review of *Geographical . . . Essays . . . Containing an Analysis of a General Map of the Middle British Colonies in America*).

As a staunch "little Englander," he is in favor of strengthening the native militia and refusing to become involved in "entangling alliances" on the Continent. But his masterpiece of denunciation of the war appeared in the fourth number, 15 July–15 August 1756, under the title "Observations on the Present State of Affairs." The war between the French and the English in America, he says flatly, is about "grounds and rivers to which, I am afraid, neither can show any other right than that of power, and which neither can occupy but by usurpation and the dispossession of the natural lords and original inhabitants. Such is the contest that no honest man can heartily wish success to either party." He continues with several paragraphs of invective about how the European invaders have cheated or robbed the Indians of their lands. True, it is alleged that the Indian tribes voluntarily surrendered huge tracts to the invaders; but this is cant: the fact is that in all cases the Indians were the victims of *force majeure:*

When we see men acting thus against the precepts of reason and the instincts of nature, we cannot hesitate to determine that by some means or other they were debarred from choice   They yielded to us as to beings of another and higher race, sent among them from some unknown regions, with power which naked Indians could not resist, and which they were therefore, by every act of humility, to propitiate that they who could so easily destroy might be induced to spare.

What it comes down to then, Johnson says, is that "The American dispute between the French and us is . . . only the quarrel of two robbers for the spoils of a passenger"; and now to hear these two robber nations declaiming against each other in lofty language about "infractions of limits, violation of treaties, open usurpation, insidious artifices, and breach of faith" he finds little less than nauseating.

Johnson's apparent removal as editor of the *Literary Magazine* did not put an end to his criticism of the war. Other media remained available for the man who was starting to win recognition as the greatest literary figure of his time. During the same year, 1756, he contributed a number of articles to his friend

Christopher Smart's monthly, the *Universal Visiter,* one of which, "Further Thoughts on Agriculture," gives his economic reasons for objecting to the war, as his piece in the *Literary Magazine* gives his moral and political reasons. Johnson makes the article a criticism, by implication, of the purpose of Pitt, the representative of British trading interests, in seeking imperial and commercial expansion that would transform Britain from what she has been in the past—a self-contained economy, with agriculture and industry carefully balanced and controlled by government regulation, able to feed her own population—into a world-wide commercial enterprise, bringing raw materials to Britain from all over the world, manufacturing them, and then selling them back to the rest of the world at a profit large enough to ensure British prosperity. Johnson predicts that when the rest of the world has caught up with and surpassed British superiority in technology and navigation, the basis for that prosperity will vanish: "The natives of Lombardy might easily resolve to retain their silk at home, and employ workmen of their own to weave it. And this will certainly be done when they grow wise and industrious, when they have sagacity to discern their true interest, and vigour to pursue it." (History seems to have proved Johnson an accurate prophet.) The transformation Pitt and his business men wish to bring about is therefore, in the long run, folly, and the expansionist war which is his instrument to bring about that transformation is wilder folly.

The abortive military expedition to the French stronghold of Rochefort the next year gave Johnson an opportunity for vigorous censure of the conduct of British military affairs. This was in a speech he was reported (after his death) to have furnished for delivery at "a certain respectable talking society." It was vigorous:

They went out, and they are come back again, not only without doing, but without attempting to do anything. . . . It is fit that this miscarriage, whether it be the effect of treachery or cowardice, be detected and punished, that those whom, for the future, we shall employ and pay may know they are the servants of a people that expect duty for their money, that will not be mocked with idle expeditions or satisfied with an account of walls that were never seen and ditches that were never tried.

Even old King George II is not spared: "It is said, an objection expresses some distrust of the king, or may tend to disturb his quiet. An English king, Mr. President, has no great right to quiet when his people are in misery." [20]

In 1758 Johnson found a new platform in Payne's weekly, the *Universal Chronicle*. In April he began publishing in it his *Idler* essays, which were to continue for two years, several of them dealing with the war, some more than glancingly. In August he adopted more direct tactics, beginning a weekly column, as we should now call it, of "Observations" specifically on the progress of the war.[21] It lasted exactly four numbers. In the first three he comments on a British raid on Cherbourg (rather like that on Dieppe in 1943), using it as another opportunity to heckle the military—"What [do] we propose to gain by invading France with seven thousand men; a force which . . . must appear contemptible as a troop of wolves descending from the mountains?" —on the state of the war on the Continent (he takes a gloomy view of Frederick of Prussia's military prospects), and the capture of Louisbourg in Cape Breton, which, though it roused wild enthusiasm in Britain, Johnson dismisses with "Louisbourg is not useful to us in the same degree as its loss is detrimental to our enemies."

These detached, judicious analyses were probably not much to the taste of the *Universal Chronicle*'s patriotic readers, but could be tolerated. With his fourth set of "Observations," how-

[20] First printed (presumably by John Nichols) in the *Gentleman's Magazine*, LV (October, 1785), 764–65. The reference to "a certain respectable *talking* society" sounds as though Nichols thought it was to be delivered in Parliament. But this seems unlikely; it may have been the London Common Council.

[21] *Universal Chronicle*, Nos. 20 to 23 (August 19 to September 9, 1758). Reprinted by Boylston Green (who first ascribed them to Johnson) in *Yale University Library Gazette*, April, 1942, p. 70.

ever, Johnson again overstepped the mark. A few days earlier the government had organized a triumphal procession at which the French colours captured at Louisbourg were paraded before the King, and then marched to St. Paul's Cathedral, where the Bishops of Oxford and Bristol conducted a thanksgiving service over them. It was no doubt this blasphemous use of religion in the service of war propaganda that made Johnson lose his temper, but in his comment he confines himself to the secular argument that in fact the capture of Louisbourg, though enormously costly, was not a strategically important victory and that the ministry are deliberately deceiving the people by pretending that it is: the celebration approaches "the grossest stratagem of political fraud." The colors thus exalted were not won at a battle like those of Blenheim and Ramillies, or taken from Paris or Toulon: "They came from a place so obscure and inconsiderable that its name is known only to the French and English, and are purchased at an expense which would be barely countervailed by the conquest of a province on the Continent or the defeat of a royal army."

This was too much to endure, and in the next issue the *Chronicle* printed a long protest from an outraged patriotic reader. The capture of Louisbourg is, he insists, immensely important—"the whole continent of North America now lies open to our army"—and he pays a glowing tribute to

those to whose wisdom and spirit in forming the plan of this conquest and to whose resolution and integrity in the execution of it we owe the only means of establishing our trade and power in North America . . . those Patriot Ministers . . . that, by "setting a just value on this conquest" . . . "convinced every understanding" . . . how highly qualified they are to conduct the business of this kingdom, in the most critical and dangerous situation.[22]

This protest brought an end to the "Observations," but two weeks later Johnson published in the *Universal Chronicle* a letter in reply to his critic which is a masterpiece of polemics:

Sir: It was often said by the Earl of Oxford that "a knot of idle fellows made a noise in one another's ears at a coffee-house, and imag-

[22] *Ibid.*, No. 24 (September 16, 1758).

ined the nation to be filled with the same clamour." This seems to have been lately the case of the English rabble; they have drank to the conquest of Louisbourg, till they take Louisbourg to be the seat of the Empire.

He quotes such extravagant statements of the objector as "Louisbourg is of ten times more importance than Paris," and on the assertion "The whole continent of North America now lies open to our army," observes caustically, "Surely not the whole wide continent. Ticonderoga must at least be excepted." The allusion is to the British disaster at Fort Ticonderoga, at the same time as the capture of Louisbourg, in which over 500 British soldiers were killed and over 1,300 wounded. In the rejoicings over Louisbourg, the slaughter at Ticonderoga has been conveniently forgotten.[23]

For the second time a publication of Johnson's designed to subject the war to uncanting analysis had been abruptly terminated. In the *Idler,* however, he was still able to give it the occasional shrewd blow. In Number 5 (May 13, 1758), he printed a mock proposal that the army should include women as well as men: "Our masculine squadrons will not suppose themselves disgraced by their auxiliaries, till they have done something which women could not have done. The troops of Braddock never saw their enemies, and perhaps were defeated by women. . . ." In *Idler* 20, published in the same number of the *Universal Chronicle* as his first "Observation" on the capture of Louisbourg, he concocts two contrasting imaginary accounts of that event, such as an English and a French historian may give in the future, and makes sombre fun of the nationalistic bias and distortion in each account.

Much more serious is *Idler* No. 22 (of the original numbering),[24] which appeared in the same *Chronicle* as the biting fourth and last "Observation" on the thanksgiving service for the capture

[23] *Ibid.,* No. 26 (September 30, 1758).

[24] When the *Idlers* were first published as a collected volume in 1761, No. 22 was omitted and the subsequent ones renumbered. Presumably the reason for its exclusion was its intense bitterness of tone, but whether the decision was Johnson's or the publisher's we have no means of knowing. In later collections, it was reintroduced, being placed after the last *Idler* (originally No. 104; renumbered 103).

of Louisbourg. The essay undoubtedly had its source in the same emotional revulsion from the hypocrisy of the warmakers as that "Observation." Its mordant force is as great as some of his model Swift's denunciations of human folly. A mother vulture is instructing her young in the ways of life. They know how to snatch up a kid or a hare in their talons and bring it home to the nest to feed on. But the flesh of man is even more delicious. How can it be obtained, the young vultures ask, since man is so much bigger, and stronger than a vulture? Nature has kindly provided a way, the mother points out: from time to time two herds of men confront each other, slay each other with flashes of fire, and leave the ground covered with smoking corpses, to regale the vultures. But, asks one young vulture, when men have killed their prey, why do *they* not eat it? 'Man,' replies the mother, 'is the only beast who kills that which he does not devour, and this quality makes him so much a benefactor to our species.' . . . 'But still,' said the young one, 'I would gladly know the reason of this mutual slaughter; I could never kill what I could not eat.'" The mother does not know, and can only refer to the hypothesis of one old philosophic vulture: Men are not really sensible beings, like vultures, but merely mechanical automata, whose activities a benevolent Providence has arranged to provide food for vultures.

Such was Johnson's response to the butchery at Ticonderoga and the conquest of Louisbourg, which, in spite of his arguments to the contrary, was in fact the beginning of the end of French military power in North America. The end came the next year with Wolfe's capture of Quebec. And Johnson's reaction to the news of this great victory was equally remarkable—*Idler* No. 81, of November 3, 1759. An Indian chief sombrely watches the British army advance up the St. Lawrence toward Quebec, observes its discipline and efficiency, turns to his companions and delivers a bitter recapitulation of the treachery, cruelty, and tyranny of the white men toward the Indians—and Negroes:

Those invaders ranged over the continent, slaughtering in their rage those that resisted, and those that submitted, in their mirth. Of those that remained, some were buried in caverns, and condemned to dig metals for their masters; some were employed in tilling the ground, of which foreign tyrants devour the produce; and when the sword and the mines have destroyed the natives, they supply their place by human beings of another colour, brought from some distant country to perish here under toil and torture. . . . Their arts they have studiously concealed from us. Their treaties are only to deceive, and their traffick only to defraud us.[25]

With the events of 1759, the war was in effect over in America. Pitt and the "future without parallel for the English-speaking people on the continent of North America" had won; Johnson—and the Indians and the Negroes—had lost. He at last fell silent about the Great War for the Empire, though in 1775 there was one final emotional outburst—*Taxation No Tyranny*—directed this time against the high-sounding resolutions of the Continental Congress, proclaiming its independence of Britain in the sacred names of liberty and self-determination; things not, of course, to be accorded to inferior beings like Indians and Negroes, but reserved for the virtuous white newcomers. There is nothing hard to understand about Johnson's opposition to the movement for American independence. That movement was merely the logical extension —as historians have frequently pointed out—of the Great War of 1756 to 1763. For Johnson, both stemmed from the same immoral assumption, that the white European has a God-given right, a manifest destiny, to overrun any part of the world he can seize by means of his superior weapons and techniques, and to exploit it to his material advantage in whatever way he wishes, without regard

[25] Johnson's introduction to Rolt's collection of travel accounts, *The World Displayed,* published a few weeks later (December 1), has much more to say along the same lines: for example, "We are openly told that they [early Portuguese explorers of Africa] had the less scruple concerning their treatment of the savage people, because they scarcely considered them as distinct from beasts; and indeed the practice of all the European nations, and among others of the English barbarians that cultivate the southern islands of America, proves that this opinion, however absurd and foolish, however wicked and injurious, still continues to prevail. Interest and pride harden the heart, and it is in vain to dispute against avarice and power."

to any possible rights of indigenous peoples; and while he does so, to feel himself actuated by the most lofty ideals and an acute sense of his superiority to those on whom he intrudes. To Johnson the noble sentiments of the Declaration of Independence seemed the most hypocritical cant, and his stinging question to its slave-owning signers, "How is it that we hear the loudest yelps for liberty from the drivers of Negroes?" remains unanswerable. The great Empires of the English-speaking peoples, both British and American, which the war of 1756–1763 brought into being are founded on the denial of the radical social and political principle Johnson's religion had taught him, that all human beings, whatever the color of their skin or the nature of their culture, are of equal worth before God and have equal rights. The Europeans, the Indian chief continues in Johnson's final comment on the war,

have a written law among them, of which they boast as derived from Him who made the earth and sea, and by which they profess to believe that man will be made happy when life shall forsake him. Why is not this law communicated to us? It is concealed because it is violated. For how can they preach it to an Indian nation, when I am told that one of its first precepts forbids them to do to others what they would not that others should do to them?

Pitt has won his war; Johnson and the Indian chief have lost theirs. But it would be a mistake to think that the final recommendation of Johnson, the pupil of Swift, might be to adopt and recommend a posture of resignation and acquiescence in the face of triumphant wrong. Far from it. Here is the Indian chief's peroration, Johnson's last word on the war:

But the time perhaps is now approaching when the pride of usurpation shall be crushed, and the cruelties of invasion shall be revenged. The sons of rapacity have now drawn their swords upon each other . . . let us look unconcerned upon the slaughter, and remember that the death of every European delivers the country from a tyrant and a robber. . . . Let us endeavour, in the mean time, to learn their discipline, and to forge their weapons; and, when they shall be weakened with mutual slaughter, let us rush down upon them, force their remains to take shelter in their ships, and reign once more in our native country.

Counsels approximating these in violence were beginning to be heard from the more extremist spokesmen of non-European minority groups in North America in the 1960s, often to the surprise and bewilderment of the dominant white-skinned, European-descended population. Samuel Johnson, who penned the earliest and most violent of such protests, would not have been surprised at this logical outcome of the principles on which the "future without parallel for the English-speaking people here on the continent of North America" had been founded—Johnson who, at the outset of the war which was to establish that future, had remarked, "We continue every day to show by new proofs that no people can be great who have ceased to be virtuous." His only wonder might have been at the two-hundred-years lapse of time between his own protest and the later ones.

It is pleasant to record that Johnson's last two appearances in print on subjects connected with the war (though no longer dealing directly with the war itself) are milder in spirit, though in no way compromising the intransigence of his position on the injustice and immorality of that war. The overwhelming British military victories of 1759—"this wonderful year," as Johnson's friend Garrick ecstatically put it in his popular patriotic song, "Heart of Oak"—caused Johnson to pause and contemplate "the bravery of the English common soldiers," [26] who, slaughtered in thousands at Ticonderoga and Quebec and Minden, often led by bungling generals in operations conceived by incompetent strategists, miserably fed, clothed, and paid, and subjected to a brutal code of military law, had brought about those victories. For the army and the "military mind" generally, Johnson had in the past shown little but the traditional contempt of the intellectual (especially the Tory intel-

---

[26] The piece bearing this title seems to have been first published in the January, 1760, number of the *British Magazine*—a somewhat mysterious incident, since Johnson is not known to have had any other connection with the periodical. But no earlier printing of it has yet been discovered. It is about the length of the average *Idler* and was perhaps a by-product of that enterprise.

lectual), as his frequent sarcasms in the *Idler* and elsewhere testi-
fied. Like his friend Goldsmith, however, whose touching account
of the hard life of a simple English private appeared about the
same time,[27] Johnson is led to look at the war from the point of
view of such a participant, and to ponder the "epidemic bravery,"
the "plebeian magnanimity" of "a peasantry of heroes." Whence
does it come, he wonders? Not from rigid discipline like that in
which the Prussian army is trained; not from admiration and awe
for the beings of higher rank who lead them, as it is said French
soldiers feel for their officers; certainly not from their concern for
the "stake" they have in the welfare of their country or their devotion to the British constitutional principles of "Life, liberty, and
property"—"Property they are . . . commonly without. Liberty
is, to the lowest rank of every nation, little more than the choice
of working or starving. . . . The English soldier seldom has his
head very full of the constitution; nor has there been, for more
than a century, any war that put the property or liberty of a single
Englishman in danger." Johnson concludes—though without com-
mitting himself to unqualified praise of that system—that it must
be the result of British economic and social individualism, "that
dissolution of dependance which obliges every man to regard his
own character." This independence, this "neglect of insubordina-
tion," may produce "inconveniences," in the form of public tur-
moil, of "want of reverence" for authority: "but good and evil will
grow up in this world together; and they who complain, in peace,
of the insolence of the populace, must remember that their insolence in peace is bravery in war."

By the end of 1759 also, British military success had resulted
in the capture of several thousand French prisoners, now interned
in Britain. There were of course at this time no such international
conventions as were later adopted for the custody of prisoners of

[27] "The Distresses of a Common Soldier," *British Magazine,* June, 1760.
Later included (with changes) in *The Citizen of the World* under the title
"On the Distresses of the Poor, Exemplified in the Life of a Private Centi-
nel."

war, nor any provision in the national budget for maintaining them, and their condition was miserable. Johnson's friend John Wesley recorded his emotions on seeing their plight:

I walked up to Knowle, a mile from Bristol, to see the French prisoners. Above eleven hundred of them, we were informed, were confined in that little place, without anything to lie on but a little dirty straw, or anything to cover them but a few foul, thin rags, either by day or night, so that they died like rotten sheep. I was much affected, and preached in the evening on Exodus xxiii, 9 ["Also thou shalt not oppress a stranger: for ye know the heart of a stranger, seeing ye were strangers in the land of Egypt"].[28]

As so often happened in eighteenth-century England, private charity rose to the occasion. A group of well-to-do citizens met at a London tavern in December 1759 and organized a committee to take charge of collecting funds and expending them for the relief of the French captives. By the following June, over £4,000 had been collected and expended; more than 3,000 greatcoats, 6,000 shirts, and 3,00 pairs of shoes, to mention some of the items, had been distributed [29]

In the same month, June 1760, the committee decided to prepare and publish a report giving a detailed accounting of its receipts and expenditures, and it also resolved—possibly because of criticism of the committee's activities—to print a short preface in explanation and justification of them. Johnson was commissioned to write this ("Introduction to the Proceedings . . . for cloathing French prisoners"), and the result was one of Johnson's most masterly pieces of prose—economical, precise, carrying complete emotional conviction. "Charity would lose its name [he begins], were it influenced by so mean a motive as human praise: it is, therefore, not intended to celebrate, by any particular memorial,

[28] *Journal,* October 15, 1759, quoted by G. B. Hill, ed., Boswell's *Life of Johnson,* I, 353, n. 2.

[29] Information from the *Proceedings* themselves. See also James L. Clifford, "Some Problems of Johnson's Obscure Middle Years," in *Johnson, Boswell, and Their Circle: Essays Presented to L. F. Powell* (Oxford, 1965).

the liberality of single persons, or distinct societies: it is sufficient that their works praise them."

He then turns to the objections which have been made to the work of the society, objections which one suspects (though Johnson scrupulously refrains from saying so directly) stem from "patriotic" hostility to the idea of giving aid to "the enemy." They are put, Johnson says, in the form of urging "that while we are relieving Frenchmen, there remain many Englishmen unrelieved; that while we lavish pity on our enemies, we forget the misery of our friends." This is easily answered:

Grant this argument all it can prove, and what is the conclusion?— That to relieve the French is a good action, but that a better may be conceived. . . . To do the best can seldom be the lot of man; it is sufficient if, when opportunities are presented, he is ready to do good. . . . It is far from certain that a single Englishman will suffer by the charity to the French. New scenes of misery make new impressions; and much of the charity which produced these donations may be supposed to have been generated by a species of calamity never known among us before. . . . We know that for the prisoners of war there is no legal provision; we see their distress, and are certain of its cause; we know that they are poor and naked, and poor and naked without a crime.

But it is not necessary to make concessions to the objectors' arguments, Johnson continues. This charity can be proved to be good in itself—perhaps even "the best":

That charity is best of which the consequences are most extensive: the relief of enemies has a tendency to unite mankind in fraternal affection; to soften the acrimony of adverse nations, and dispose them to peace and amity: in the meantime, it alleviates captivity, and takes away something from the miseries of war. The rage of war, however mitigated, will always fill the world with calamity and horror: let it not then be unnecessarily extended; let animosity and hostility cease together; and no man be longer deemed an enemy than while his sword is drawn against us.

The effects of these contributions may, perhaps, reach still further. Truth is best supported by virtue: we may hope from those who feel or who see our charity, that they shall no longer detest as heresy that religion which makes its professors the followers of HIM who has commanded us to "do good to them that hate us."

No better testimony to the impressiveness—and prescience —of this plea could be found than the fact that two centuries later the official journal of the International Red Cross reprinted it in French translation,[30] praising it as an early expression of the ideal which was to come to realization, through the efforts of Henri Dunant, only in the later nineteenth century. It makes a fitting conclusion to the story of Johnson's long and troubled involvement with the Great War for the Empire.

[30] Under the significant heading "Un Siècle avant Solférino," the battle of 1859 in which the horrible suffering of the men on both sides inspired Dunant to begin the movement that led to the founding of the International Red Cross: *Revue Internationale de la Croix Rouge* (Geneva), XXXIII (December 1951), 969–71.

Publishing and Journalism

EDWARD L. RUHE

Edmund Curll and His Early Associates

"I HAD LONG a design upon the Ears of that Curl," Swift wrote in 1716, "but the rogue would never allow me a fair stroke at them, though my penknife was ready and sharp." [1] Earlier, Edmund Curll had earned, at most, only a small reputation as one of the London booksellers of relatively colorful character. But in the year of Swift's remark he rose to remarkable notoriety. Pope, having perpetrated the famous practical joke of the drugged wine, published his *Full and True Account of a Horrid and Barbarous Revenge by Poison, on the Body of Mr. Edmund Curll, Bookseller.* For publishing without permission a student poem, the boys of Westminster School lured Curll to the schoolyard and tossed him in a blanket. In the same year he received a reprimand before the bar of the House of Lords for unauthorized publication of a Lords' proceeding, and Defoe attacked him in print. By the time Pope enshrined him in *The Dunciad,* 1728, he had achieved

[1] *The Correspondence of Jonathan Swift,* ed. Harold Williams (Oxford, 1963–1965), II, 214.

a notoriety perhaps never surpassed as a paragon of disreputable book publishers. Given his odd appearance (tall, ungainly figure, white face, bulging eyes), his constant commerce with other booksellers, his frequent public appearances as a book auctioneer, and his love of taverns, he must have become widely known by an early date in his career. Since the facts of literary life in Pope's day often prove more interesting than the myths, we need not fear any deflation of interest in probing for the less dramatic facts of Curll's early years.

The present study will attempt to define Curll's relationship with his earliest bookseller-associates. It will illustrate both the extensive normality and the occasional but indicative irregularities of his professional conduct as he made his way in the trade. And it will confront a central problem in Curll studies: how to distinguish the books for which Curll was primarily responsible as undertaker or principal in a group of partners from those in which he "had a hand," as his biographer Ralph Straus has it,[2] whether as partner to another bookseller acting as undertaker or in a looser association formed prior to publication, and from those which he purchased at wholesale from any member of such an association without being himself a member. The fact that Curll sometimes advertised books in the last category does not mean that Curll "had a hand" in their publication. Knowledge of some basic conventions will usually clarify an Augustan bookseller's connection to a given book.

The most common and reliable evidence of such a connection for the early years of Curll's career (1706–1714) is to be found in

---

[2] *The Unspeakable Curll* (London, 1927), *passim*. The other significant biographical studies are W. J. Thoms, *Curll Papers* (London, 1879), and H. R. Tedder's article in the *Dictionary of National Biography*. Robert L. Haig's short article, " 'The Unspeakable Curll': Prolegomena," *Studies in Bibliography*, XIII (1960), 220–23, has substantially supplemented our heretofore thin knowledge of Curll's early career. Henry Plomer's unsatisfactory *Dictionary of the Printers and Booksellers . . . 1668 to 1725* is cited casually in the text of the present study for his dating of various booksellers' careers.

the imprint, that is, the publication statement of the title-page: "Place, printed by P, for A, B, and C, and sold by X, Y, and Z, date." Any of these elements may be missing in an actual imprint; anonymously published works may use forms like "London, Printed in the Year MDCCXII." Generally, the booksellers A, B, and C, may be understood to be the principals, X, Y, and Z, co-operating booksellers with whom an agreement had been reached before the time of printing to act as retail agents and thus partial guarantors of the venture. While a strictly equal partnership was possible between A, B, and C, in nearly all cases A was the true undertaker, supplying copy to the printer, seeing the book through the press, registering agreements with his author and with other booksellers, and managing the stocks of printed books. B and C might perform some of these functions, but their important role was to share costs, profits, and copyright. When A, B, and C were retail booksellers, they would, like X, Y, and Z, offer their book in their shops at the advertised price. The reliability of an Augustan imprint as so interpreted has not, so far as I know, been firmly demonstrated. But in the preparation of the present study it has been supported quite generally by cross-reference between imprints and related materials—Curll's advertisements, particularly, and such random manuscript sources as legal documents involving Curll's books, registers of the Stationers' Company, and Curll's receipts from printers, authors, and others. In this process, inconsistencies nearly always yield instructive fresh information. Throughout the present essay, nearly all imprint data will be presented by formula, within single quotes, with strict attention to the spelling and order of booksellers' names. The place of publication, London in all cases, will be omitted; and publication date (usually from newspaper notices) will appear outside the quotes, being preferred to the imprint date.

Common sense tells us that the imprint was a useful but not indispensable convention to the Augustans, since many books and pamphlets were published anonymously. In general, it was a truth-

ful shorthand statement of some use to the trade and to retail cus-
tomers. Since Curll in his early years seemed most concerned to
develop a clientele of genteel book-buyers—on the evidence of his
strong interest in theology, travel, English antiquities, Tory tracts,
classics and French works in translation, and important contemporary poetry—he rarely had evident occasion for falsifying data in
his imprints. Curll was, at the start, conservative in his practices
and, within his circle, unexceptional although promising enough in
his energy, ambition, and ingenuity. The imprints carrying his
name have been assumed reliable in nearly all cases; when they
are not, they may have exceptional interest.

Curll was born July 14, 1683, probably in the vicinity of
Maidenhead, Berkshire, if his claim of an early friendship with
the theologian Henry Dodwell may be believed. In May 1706 he
was "recently out of the service and apprenticeship" of the bookseller Richard Smith, who had just declared bankruptcy.[3] We may
guess that his apprenticeship ran from about 1698 to 1705,
whereupon he went on his own. By January 1, 1706, he was issuing catalogues of book auctions conducted by himself along Fleet
Street and the Strand. The first three catalogues, listed as available
from designated booksellers in several quarters of London—
Holborn, Cornhill, Cheapside, St. Paul's Churchyard, Westminster, and (Curll's neighborhood) Temple Bar—did not specify an
address for Curll. But the third catalogue, that of the library of a
Dr. Harrison (*Bibliotheca Harrisoniana*), was advertised in the

---

[3] Curll's birth date is indicated in an addendum to his will, partly quoted
in Straus (p. 190): "Written and Signed by me this 14th day of July—
1742/Ent^g my 60th Year/Edmund Curll." For confirmation of the birth-
day, July 14, see Norma Hodgson and Cyprian Blagden, *The Notebook of
Thomas Bennet and Henry Clements* (N.S. VI Oxford Bibliographical Society Publications, 1956), p. 89. Curll claimed a twenty-year "intimate Correspondence" with Henry Dodwell, died 1711, in his *Apology for the Writings of Walter Moyle, Esq;* (London, 1728), p. 17; Dodwell resided at
Cookham, near Maidenhead, after losing his Oxford professorship in 1691.
The material on Richard Smith is from Smith's Bill of Complaint, 1708, in
which Curll figures (Haig, p. 221).

Daily Courant of February 27, 1706, as sold by "Mr. Curl at the Peacock" near St. Clement's Church in the Strand. Since auctioned libraries were sold book by book in nightly sessions, often at coffeehouses, over a period of several days or weeks, Curll perhaps became a familiar figure to many book buyers in very short order.

From the Peacock two weeks later, Curll advertised "The Second Edition" of an expensive little book of 326 pages called *The Athenian Spy,* 'sold by J. Baker and Edm. Curll' at 2s. 6d. (information from the *Daily Courant* notice, March 14, presented by formula). The book had first been issued by Curll's quondam partner, the young bookseller Robert Halsey, in 1704, in time for a flattering notice of Halsey in *The Life and Errors of John Dunton,* 1705: "He is one of good Judgment and knows how to bid for a saleable Copy, or had never printed the *Athenian Spy*." [4] But if the book actually exists in a distinguishable 1706 'second edition' (presumably a second issue with cancel title page), no copies have been located. Baker and Curll presumably bought their stocks from Halsey, and disposed of them with or without fresh title pages. Curll might well have followed standard practice by using most of his copies to barter for a variety of current books stocked by other booksellers.

We hear next of Curll's participation in proceedings arising from the bankruptcy of his former master, Richard Smith, on May 3. At this time Curll and Halsey acted as appraisers of books recently seized from Smith by his creditors. In a Bill of Complaint two years later, Smith claimed incidentally that Curll had knowingly undervalued certain books. Perhaps he did. By the middle of June one of Smith's books, Martin Bladen's translation of Caesar's *Commentaries of his Wars in Gaul,* 1705, was reissued as the "Second Edition Improv'd," 'printed for R. Smith, sold by Cha. Smith and E. Curll.' With the names of two Smiths preceding Curll's on the title page, it is impossible to know whether or not

---

[4] John Dunton, *Life and Errors of John Dunton* (London, 1705), p. 294.

Richard Smith was able to share in the profits through some arrangement with the creditors, or whether Curll had some private advantage, shared with the other Smith, by reason of the low appraisal figure. Smith's seized book stocks will come up several times again. Meanwhile, on June 18 appeared an anonymous eight-page folio poem called *A Letter to Mr. Prior, Occasion'd by the Duke of Marlborough's Late Victory at Ramilly, and Glorious Successes in Brabant* "written in Milton's Stile," and 'printed by W.D. for Edmund Curll and sold by Benj. Bragge.' Then, July 10,[5] was published *The Miscellaneous Works of the Right Honourable the Late Earls of Rochester and Roscommon,* "London printed: and sold by B. Bragge" according to the title page, but reissued a few weeks later as *The Works of the Right Honourable the Late Earls of Rochester and Roscommon,* 'second edition,' "Printed for Edmund Curll," with Bragge's name omitted. These volumes have some importance in Rochester studies,[6] and will come up again in connection with the edition of Matthew Prior's *Poems on Several Occasions,* 1707.

In the first months Curll seems to have moved from a state of impecuniosity to a position of strong promise and some distinction. His first books should all have been quite negotiable within the trade and serviceable therefore in building his shop stocks. The auctioneering, which he was to continue for years, probably supplied him with the necessary funds for a beginning. Whether or not he was in any unusual way indebted for help to younger booksellers like Halsey and Charles Smith, or to older ones like Baker, Bragge, and Richard Smith, it is easy to believe that his energy and enterprise and his sense for plausible book ventures quickly built for him a small, sound reputation in the trade. What of his subsequent relations with the five

[5] Date from the *Post Man,* July 8–10, 1706, a "This Day Publish'd" notice; the later date in a biweekly newspaper masthead, i.e., July 10 in the above, is the date of publication for the paper.

[6] For a general discussion, see David M. Vieth, *Attribution in Restoration Poetry: A Study of Rochester's Poems of 1680* (New Haven, 1963), pp. 12–13, 373–74.

booksellers with whom he had associated himself in these early months?

After the Smith bankruptcy Curll and Halsey parted company, perhaps dropping their association mainly because Curll's place of business, near Temple Bar, was inconveniently far from Halsey's in Cornhill. In most cases Curll found his partners closer to home. Bragge, according to John Dunton, was in serious trouble in 1705: "He has been unhappy, but his Soul is too great to be crush'd under the weight of *adverse storms.*" [7] Perhaps he could offer little help to Curll, unless as a front for the Rochester volume; perhaps Curll in fact helped him by offering partnership as a low-risk opportunity. We know that he stayed in business until 1709 or later, but without further noteworthy connections to Curll. It may be significant that he was prominent among publishers of tracts by Dissenters, for Curll was a High-Churchman and a Tory.

Charles Smith, Curll's near neighbor at the Buck, between the two Temple Gates in Fleet Street, had handled Curll's auction catalogues early in 1706 and was his partner in the Caesar volume in June. With Curll he enjoyed one more happy partnership in the publication of Robert Warren's *The Devout Christian's Companion,* three editions between November 1706 and May 1708. Curll certainly continued the association in smaller ways. Thus in December 1707 Curll advertised Joseph Harrison's *Exposition of the Church-Catechism* (*Daily Courant,* December 20), 'printed for A. Barker and C. Smith' according to the title page. We may guess that Curll now and again stocked books of Charles Smith whether he advertised them or not.

The connection to Richard Smith must remain enigmatic. Smith's Bill of Complaint against his creditors, June 3, 1708, contained an accusation against the appraisers Curll and Halsey, as already noted. Curll may have had special arrangements with the creditors. In May 1708 he and Egbert Sanger advertised *A Paraphrase and Annotations Upon All the Epistles of St. Paul* by

[7] Dunton, p. 297.

Abraham Woodhead, Richard Allestry, and Obadiah Walker, "The third Edition" with lives of the authors prefixed. The volume has not been located. But there was an earlier 'third edition,' 'printed for Richard Smith,' 1702 (not to mention a 'third edition,' "London, Printed in the Year, 1703"). Curll's notice of 1708 evidently denotes another issue of the 1702 item, distinguished by the addition of the authors' lives. Another Smith item of 1702 was the second folio volume of Sir Orlando Bridgman's *Conveyances: Being Select Precedents of Deeds and Instruments* (etc.), reissued in May 1710 or later with a cancel title page 'printed for E. Curll, E. Sanger, and R. Gosling.' Two auction catalogues of 1710 and 1711 again show Curll collaborating with Smith. The *Bibliotheca Wichiana* could be purchased at six-pence from the auctioneer, Edmund Curll, and "at *R. Smith's* Ware-House the Place of Sale." And Smith was similarly associated with Curll in the auction of a Dr. Dillingham's library in 1711. The library had been on sale in Curll's shop in late August; the auction catalogue appeared November 1 at six-pence, and the *Daily Courant* notices of November 5 and 7 list Curll and Smith alone as agents for it. In view of Smith's charge against Curll in 1708, we may see evidence of deviousness in this series of associations. It seems equally likely, however, that Curll had a reasonable defense against the charges of 1708. Appraising the book stocks at a low figure on behalf of the creditors, he offended Smith, but whether Smith should have been offended, we can hardly tell. Smith seems to have been reconciled either to chicanery on the part of his former apprentice, or to the hard lot of a bankrupt.

The older bookseller John Baker joined with Curll in issuing *The Athenian Spy,* "second edition," 1706, when his shop was at Mercers Chapel. From about January 1707 to July 1708 or later Baker seems to have been the junior partner, sharing a shop with Richard Burrough "at the Sun and Moon in Cornhill." In 1709 he was in a stall or shop "near the Bank, in the Poultry." And late in 1709 he moved to the Black Boy in Paternoster Row, continuing sporadic associations with Curll to the spring of 1712. A very prominent Dissenting tradesman, he was to earn his most permanent reputation through his connection with Defoe. Nearly all the partnership arrangements involving Curll and Baker have distinct interest. During Baker's Sun and Moon period, Curll and a partner (usually Egbert Sanger) plus the Burrough-Baker combination amounted to a small conger, capable of launching ambitious and promising books for the Francophiles, like Grandchamps, *Memoirs of the Marquess de Langallerie* (October 1707), Mme. Aulnoy's *Secret Memoirs* (February 1708), and Boileau's *Lutrin* (May 1708). Burrough and Baker as partners seem to have been undertakers of the first two of these, Sanger of the Boileau. Partnerships incorporating the same quartet but evidently led by outside booksellers account for the edition of Josephus, *Jewish History,* July 1708, 'printed for S. Briscoe, Burrough-Baker, Curll, and Sanger,' and of John Conant, *Sermons on Several Subjects,* vol. V, November 1707, 'printed for J. Clarke, Burrough-Baker, Sanger, and N. Cliffe,' but with Curll's name regularly appearing after Sanger's in the *Daily Courant* notices, and regularly misspelled.

On his own again, in March 1709, Baker retained some connections with Curll. Philip Horneck's *Ode. Inscribed to His Excellency the Earl of Wharton,* was 'printed for J. Baker, sold by Sanger and Curll.' The following July Baker seems to have transferred to Curll his interest in an edition of the poems of Shakespeare, as will be noted later. We may assume that Baker consented to be a front for Curll in publishing Curll's Sacheverellian tract, the *Letter to His Grace the Duke of Beaufort* (a reissue of Curll's *The Case of Dr. Sacheverell*) in October 1710; the title page uses the form "Printed, and sold by J. Baker." Finally, in the paper war over the witchcraft trial of Jane Wenham in the spring of 1712, Curll published three credulous tracts by Francis Bragge, and Baker countered with three more arguing in her favor and attacking the doctrine of witches. That Baker and Curll may have been partners rather than antagonists is suggested by the *Post Boy* notice of Bragge's *Witchcraft Farther Display'd,* 'This day published,' April 15, by Curll and Baker; Curll's name alone appears in the imprint. [8] After this affair Curll and Baker went separate ways.

The foregoing account of Curll's five earliest significant associations in the trade suggests interesting patterns. Curll seems to have entered the trade from the bottom, finding his first friends among extremely marginal booksellers. Richard Smith and Benjamin Bragge were in financial difficulties; Robert Halsey was a beginner; John Baker was about to join forces with another bookseller in a way that suggests weakness; Charles Smith's short career began about the same time as Curll's and ended in 1709, according to Plomer. One guesses that Curll chose these five because he could not choose better. This group of booksellers typically produced tracts, broadsides, and other modest pieces, seeking partnerships when more expensive items were to be published. The treatment of Curll's more showy publications in the present essay may accordingly mislead, for Curll published many three-penny and six-penny pamphlets without help from partners. In politics Curll had unusually strong Tory and High-Church leanings, a circumstance reflected in his writings in the Sacheverell affair and in nearly all the controversial political and religious materials he published, including the fascinating and silly witchcraft pamphlets. His trade associates were, in general, moderates or men of his own persuasion; the association with the Whiggish John Baker had almost evaporated before the Sacheverell trial. As a partner Baker was exceptional in another way, keeping shop near the Royal Exchange, a long walk from Temple Bar. Nearly all of Curll's friends in the trade were, as might be expected, rather close neighbors. Rather quickly Curll moved into the middle range of booksellers. His thwarted aspiration to rise higher is strongly suggested

---

[8] Curll-Baker relations were resumed briefly in February 1712, when Curll advertised two poems in Baker's tri-weekly, *The Protestant Post-Boy.* The seven other Curll notices in this paper all concerned the witchcraft trial, and appeared between March 22 and May 22. At the beginning of June, Baker advertised "the Tryal of the Hertfordshire Witch and all other Tracts for and against Witchcraft," i.e., Curll's pamphlets as well as his own.

by his interesting early associations with the prince of the book trade, Jacob Tonson.

In January 1707 was published the unauthorized first collection of works by Matthew Prior, the *Poems on Several Occasions,* 'printed for Burrough, Baker, and Curll' according to the title page, but in all likelihood a Curll undertaking, as tradition has always had it. The advertisement leaf facing the title page lists both Curll and Burrough-Baker books. But newspaper notices use formulas suggesting that Curll had primary control of the Prior book stocks. Thus the volume was advertised on January 31 as sold by Burrough, Baker, Curll, Place, and Egbert Sanger, in that order (*Daily Courant*); Sanger was to become an important associate of Curll's before the year was over. Again, Curll, Charles Smith, and Baker *solus* were named in that order in a notice of March 28 (*Daily Courant*); here we reduce to Curll plus two of his important early associates. In addition, the character of the collection points to Curll's probable leadership, especially if the project is compared to Curll's Rochester volume of a few months earlier. The latter contains a Preface which establishes a genuine claim for Curll as the earliest editor of Rochester; and like the Prior, it represents a definite achievement in the compilation of theretofore uncollected poems from various sources.[9] The Rochester edition, while it successfully avoided the use of poems printed earlier in Tonson's editions of that poet, may have seemed risky, for, as noted, Curll's name was withheld from the imprint in the earlier of the two issues. When the Prior collection was announced, Tonson addressed a letter to the *Daily Courant,* January 24, affirming his claim to be Prior's sole authorized publisher; a little later Prior supported him, condemning the volume, which had been published in the meanwhile. Whether Curll successfully concealed his hand from Tonson, or whether the matter was less important than it seems, we find Curll advertising Tonson's edition of Prior two years later. And, surprisingly, Tonson acquiesced in Curll's

[9] Vieth, p. 279, n. 2, for evidence on Curll's editorial labors.

edition of Shakespeare's Poems (first announced in July 1709), designed and widely advertised as a seventh volume suitable to complete Tonson's six-volume collection of the plays. Other booksellers had had the same idea, including John Baker. The fact that Baker's proposal was dropped just before Curll's was first advertised suggests that Curll took over the other man's idea, probably by agreement. Curll's second venture in this realm, a ninth volume to complete Tonson's eight-volume Shakespeare in April 1714, actually listed Tonson first among the associated retail booksellers named in the imprint. In 1709 Curll enlisted and advertised Tonson's services as printer of an elegant small volume of Latin poems under the title *Nundinæ Sturbrigienses,* by Thomas Hill, two editions. Curll's open involvements with the principal men of the trade were minimal, but in the case of Tonson no bad feeling is evident after the Prior affair of 1707.

The second phase of Curll's career involved him with active, solvent partners, two of whom added color to his life and perhaps helped to steer his career in the direction of notoriety. Down to 1714, four more booksellers worked with Curll often enough to be regarded as partners. These were Robert Gosling, Egbert Sanger, John Harding, and John Morphew. Of Gosling, little need be said. Between May 1710 and June 1713 Curll and Gosling collaborated in at least twenty-five publications. Gosling's shop was close to Curll's, in Fleet Street, and the pair must have enjoyed each other's company. The British Museum copy of Curll's *A Search After Principles* has a note in the author's hand: "This I wrote at Farmer Lambert's at Banstead, in Surrey, whither I went with Mr. Gosling. E Curll." Books published by the partnership have a miscellaneous character, and Gosling had no special flavor to contribute; further, his name precedes Curll's in only two of the imprints (Charles Gildon's *Life of Mr. Thomas Betterton,* 1710, and a work by a Dr. Adams, *A Poem Dedicated to the Queen, and Presented to the Congress at Utrecht,* 1713). Among Curll's early partners, Gosling alone may have had high standing in the trade, for he was apparently a member of the wholesaling conger, led by Tonson, in 1716.[10]

Egbert Sanger may have been equally respectable. He was associated with Curll in the Prior volume, 1707, and their partnership began that fall. The fact that they freely advertised and sold each other's books (as well as those published in partnership) led to many confusions in Straus's Handlist of Curll's publications. Their partnership books come to thirty-nine or more titles before Sanger's death and several more later involving Sanger's widow, Katherine Sanger. The two were close neighbors, Sanger conducting his business at the post-house at the Middle Temple Gate in Fleet Street. They strongly shared an interest in antiquarian studies, Sanger taking the lead in a new edition of Bulstrode Whitlocke's *Memorials of the English Affairs,* 1709, and Jodocus Crull's *The Antiquities of St. Peter's,* 1711.[11] Sanger, like John Baker, brought to the partnership an interest in French literature, demonstrated in such Sanger-Curll productions as the first volume of Boileau's *Works,* 1712 (the set was completed after Sanger's death), and a translation of Quillet's *Callipædia,* 1712; the two booksellers, Curll apparently in the lead, purchased five hundred copies of La Bruyère's *Characters* from the printer Dryden Leach in September 1708 and announced publication the following January.[12] Sanger also led the partnership in publishing stage items— William Taverner's *The Maid the Mistress,* 1708, and Rowe's *Epilogue Spoken by Mrs. Barry,* 1709. Curll's independent interest in theatre was nearly nonexistent, or so it seems.[13] The interest in

[10] Hodgson and Blagden, p. 81. The conger purchased several lots of books from Curll in 1712, 1713, and 1714.

[11] Westminster Abbey. The title-page statement is incomplete: "Printed by J. N. and Sold by JOHN MORPHEW." The *London Gazette,* February 3–6, 1711, supplies missing data with a tell-tale misspelling of Curll's name: 'printed for Egbert Sanger, E. Curle, and R. Gosling, sold by J. Morphew.'

[12] British Museum, Upcott manuscripts, Add. 38730, f. 116.

[13] With one or two exceptions, the few theatrical items in which Curll "had a hand" were undertakings of one or another of his partners.

belles-lettres was far stronger in Curll, who published with Sanger the items by Shakespeare and Thomas Hill already mentioned, Edward Holdsworth's popular *Muscipula* in the authorized edition, 1709, the *Musae Britannicae,* 1711, and collected poems of Samuel Cobb, 1709; Sanger's principal contribution in this area was Richard Blackmore's *The Kit-Cats,* 1708 (an attack on Jacob Tonson for which Curll was evidently not blamed), and his *Instructions to Vanderbank,* 1709. All the religious titles produced by the partnership were Curll's. The association reached its peak in 1708 (ten titles) and 1709 (fourteen titles through September), then dwindled rapidly to the time of Sanger's death in the summer or fall of 1712.

John Harding was an older bookseller who regularly gave his place of business as the Post Office, upon the Pavement in St. Martin's Lane. Plomer dates his bookselling career from 1678 to 1712. In November and December 1709 Harding was managing the sale by auction of Sir Henry Spelman's library. For the sale of Spelman's manuscripts beginning December 20, he employed Curll as his auctioneer; and from January 26 to February 6 Curll was auctioning the second half of the library in nightly sessions. The associated catalogue, entitled *Bibliotheca Selectissima: Pars Altera,* contained a notice of two interesting books published by the pair in some kind of partnership, to be discussed in the next paragraph. From this date until early 1714, Curll and Harding had occasional associations of the usual kind, collaborating in the publication of four books and participating together twice in partnerships with other booksellers. But book auctions remained prominent. For Harding, Curll auctioned the *Bibliotheca Cotterelliana,* January 1711. Harding listed Curll among purveyors of the sale catalogues entitled *Bibliotheca Streterriana,* November-December 1711, and the *Bibliotheca Biggeana,* March 1713,[14] and

---

[14] Harding was an agent for the *Bibliotheca Wichiana* catalog (Curll and Richard Smith) in 1710. A *Post-Boy* advertisement of January 1714 lists Doriack Chancel's *New Journey Over Europe* as 'printed for John Harding, sold by W. Taylor, B. Barker, and E. Curll.' Plomer's wrong date for the termination of Harding's career is typical.

may again in these two sales have used Curll's services as auctioneer since no other person is so specified.

At the time of the Spelman auction, Curll, in company with Harding and John Morphew, launched a project of the kind which was to blacken his name for all time. One advertisement, already mentioned, in the *Bibliotheca Selectissima* named *The Case of John Atherton,* "Printed for *E. Curll* . . . and Sold by *J. Harding* . . . At either of which places is to be had, The Tryal and Conviction of *Mervin* Lord *Audley."* These pamphlets were reprints of distasteful publications of the early seventeenth century. Audley had been condemned for sodomy, Bishop Atherton for "the Sin of *Uncleanness* with a *Cow."* Curll's name alone appeared in the imprint of the Audley item; the Atherton was 'printed for E. Curll, sold by J. Harding.' There is more to the case than Straus realized.

The Case of Sodomy, in the Tryal of Mervin Lord Audley, "The Second Edition," 1710, reprinted Morphew's 1708 edition (published November 1707), which had been promptly advertised by Curll. In the paper war of 1710, Curll, Harding, and Morphew were all open enough in their behavior, even if the affair seems contrived; and the project had the familiar vices of lurid title pages with rather innocent contents and a specious atmosphere of high-mindedness. When Curll published *The Case of John Atherton,* January 5, 1710, Morphew, as if by prearrangement, immediately became his antagonist with an answer entitled *The Case of John Atherton . . . Fairly Represented,* 'printed for Luke Stokoe, sold by Morphew.' Curll turned out to have more material for more tracts which he later issued as composite publications under the titles *The Cases of Unnatural Lewdness* and *Some Memorials of the Life and Penitent Death of John Atherton.* In Curll's *Case of John Atherton* and *Bishop Atherton's Case Discuss'd,* the editor and principal author signed himself "D. L." Straus guessed that D. L. was Curll himself. There is an equal probability, or improbability, that D. L. was Dryden Leach, the printer and despised "cousin" of Jonathan Swift, who had been involved with

Curll in the publication of LaBruyere's *Characters* in 1708. His newspaper the *Post Man* contained notices of the Audley and Atherton tracts (January 5), a matter worth mentioning because Curll in 1710 was placing most of his advertising in the *Daily Courant* and the *Tatler* published by Morphew. Not long after, Curll, again with Harding, blundered into the dangerous world of Jonathan Swift with his publication, by early April, of *A Meditation Upon a Broom-Stick,* 'printed by Curll and sold by Harding' without the author's permission, not that Swift had acknowledged authorship. In the following four years Curll's literary ambition led him to further trespasses against Swift, none of which seem at all serious. But Curll and Swift can not be treated here, although the topic has some cryptic relevance to the remainder of the present discussion.

John Morphew, the most interesting of Curll's early partners, was every bit as active and resourceful as Curll, and perhaps more worthy of study, everything considered. Plomer pronounces him "one of the principal booksellers of the period" and dates his career from 1706 to 1720 or later. He does not seem to have had a shop sign, locating himself regularly in his title pages as "near Stationers Hall," a good walk from Curll's shop. The association with Curll began in March 1707 with a trifling broadside *List of the Horsematches to be Run at Newmarket,* advertised as sold by Morphew, "Curl," and John Deard. In November of that year, as noted, he published, and Curll advertised, *The Case of Sodomy;* then on December 4, Morphew advertised "A Warning to Great Britain, or the Shame and Danger to this Nation from the Sodomites" (*Daily Courant*). Curll seems not to have been interested in the second item, but he reprinted the first and advertised it in Morphew's *Tatler* in 1710; and Morphew, like John Baker in the witchcraft controversy, no doubt sold Curll's tracts as freely as his own contributions to the controversy. The partnership also collaborated in *The Case of Insufficiency Discuss'd,* 'printed for Curll, sold by Morphew' according to the *Daily Courant* notice (August 11, 1711); Curll's name appears by itself on the title page. This was the first of a number of volumes published by Curll which dealt with the divorce scandals of the eminent; like the Atherton and Audley tracts, it was antiquarian in character, speciously high-minded, and distasteful.

The Curll-Morphew association ran strong from the beginning of 1710 to the end of 1713. Many of its productions come in large groups, as if the two booksellers thought regularly in terms of complex projects. While the Atherton-Audley affair continued, Curll responded to the Sacheverell controversy with a number of sober attacks of his own authorship against Bishop Burnet. His tracts were anonymous, and he perhaps wanted the "front" which Morphew gave him. *Some Considerations Humbly Offer'd to the Right Reverend the Ld. Bp. of Salisbury,* two editions, April and May 1710, *A Search After Principles,* May, and *An Impartial Examination of the Right Reverend the Lord Bishop of Salisbury's, Oxford's, Lincoln's, and Norwich's Speeches,* October, were all 'printed for Morphew.' One of several Sacheverellian pamphlets originating within Curll's circle of booksellers was *Some Account of the Family of Sacheverell,* October 1710, 'printed for Morphew.' A Stationers Company register has this entry: "Sept. 13, 1710. Edmund Curll then entered for his copy, a book entitled, 'Some Account of the Family of Sacheverell, from its original to this time'." [15] Morphew's edition of the work (there may be another, unlocated, by Curll) contains at the end a two-page list of "Books lately Printed and Sold by E. Curll." The Curll-Morphew association was not only close; it was, in terms of trade practice, downright promiscuous.

In 1712 and 1713 Curll had ever-increasing traffic with a poet and hack named Dr. George Sewell. He seems to have shared him at the start with Morphew, thereby discovering his special talent for attacking Bishop Burnet. Sewell's *The Clergy and the Present Ministry Defended* (in a letter to Burnet) went through four editions between January and May, 1713, the first three 'printed

[15] Thoms, p. 12, for this and other register entries.

for Morphew,' the fourth 'printed for Morphew, sold by Curll.' A *Second Letter to the Bishop of Salisbury,* April 1713, was 'printed for Curll, sold by Morphew.' Sewell's *Remarks Upon a Pamphlet Intitul'd Observations Upon the State of the Nation,* published February 21, was 'printed for Morphew'; very soon after, the second edition was 'printed for Curll, sold by Morphew.' It is possible that in this close relationship each partner was free to represent himself as undertaker; their practices obviously tended to obscure distinctions and to reduce the information value of an imprint. By the middle of May 1713 the Curll-Morphew association was all but dead, and Sewell seems to have been adopted as Curll's very own hack writer about this time, starting with the successful *Observations Upon Cato.*

Apparently aware of and happy to cultivate a public taste for sensationalism, Curll and Morphew were partners in the publicizing of several current and historic events of a scandalous or violent cast, usually with political and religious overtones. *The Perjur'd Fanatick,* July 1710, was an account of a conspiracy in 1668 against one Robert Hawkins by a group of religious zealots including an Anabaptist preacher; *Fanatical Moderation,* January 1711, recounted the murder of Archbishop Sharpe in 1679 by Presbyterian fanatics; *A True Account of . . . the Tryal of Richard Thornhill,* May 1711, concerned a duel early in the month; *A Vindication of His Grace the Duke of Leeds, from the Aspersions of Some Late Fanatical Libellers,* July 1711, revived a scandal of 1678; *The Medal,* October 1711, told of a crass Jacobite gesture by the Faculty of Advocates in Edinburgh during the preceding summer. The Thornhill pamphlet was 'printed for Morphew,' according to the imprint, but registered at Stationers Hall by Curll and Gosling.

In late May 1711, Morphew assisted Curll in launching a long series of two-penny tracts reproducing the preambles to a number of recently granted patents of nobility. The first, *Reasons which Induc'd Her Majesty to Create the Right Honourable Robert Harley, Esq; a Peer of Great Britain,* was 'printed for Morphew' (imprint) in two separate editions, but, again, entered at Stationers Hall by Curll and Gosling. From the following September to March 1712 *Reasons* or *Preambles* titles with Curll's or Morphew's imprint and, in at least one other case, Curll's copyright registry, presented preambles relating to the creation or elevation of the new Lords Harcourt, Lewisham, Wentworth, Tamworth, Orrery, Hamilton, Bolingbroke, and others. At least three times during the period Curll assembled the items in print and sold them under the title *A Collection of Preambles*. Throughout the affair, the initiative seems to have been Curll's, with Morphew, a veritable agent of the Tory ministry at the time, acting as a front in what may have been a moderately dangerous venture. But in intrigues of this kind we are reduced to guessing games.

In the context of Curll's total activity during the period, the Morphew partnership was notable for abundant publications centering in a small number of shared interests and coherent schemes. The joint ventures do not seem to have been based upon considerations of finance, for nearly all involved inexpensive items. We may suspect that Curll in general worked harder in the partner ship than Morphew, who perhaps gave himself little trouble over the Sacheverellian tracts or the *Reasons* and *Preambles*. Morphew's total activity as a bookseller is hard to assess. There was as much variety in his publications as in Curll's. But one must suspect that from 1710 to 1714 his life largely centered in political intrigue. For his numerous clandestine services to Swift, so richly registered in Teerinck's bibliography, he almost certainly deserves a high position among minor Augustans. In his relation to Curll we may suspect several principles of attraction: shared political convictions, similar tastes, comparable energy and ingenuity. Possibly Morphew had an influence in developing the opportunism and shiftiness for which Curll was not yet famous. Quite probably Curll, with his seven rather innocent and unimportant Swift publications during these years, lusted after a genuine connection to the great man. A Morphew axis with Curll at one pole and Swift at the other suggests the ultimate in the elaborate, devious, fascinating games which the principal Augustans played so well. "And who are all these enemies you hint at?" Swift asked Pope, in the letter of 1716 quoted at the outset. "I can only think of Curl, Gildon, Squire Burnet, Blackmore, and a few others whose fame I have forgot: Tools in my opinion as necessary for a good writer, as pen, ink, and paper." The background noise of black and blackened Augustan pots and kettles is hard to miss. But how did Morphew contrive to escape the wider notice he plainly deserved?

At the start of his career Curll appears to have flourished happily and with little friction within a definable community of booksellers. Aside from the minor links with Tonson and the dull ones with Gosling, he was unconnected to the respectable upper stratum of the trade as defined by membership in the congers, by significant partnership with Knaptons, Churchills, or any of the other better-known figures of the book world, by book, rather than pamphlet production, and so on. The ten partnership associations described here account for only about 150 of the nearly 400 Curll titles (including pamphlets and more modest items) published before 1715. That he was clever and dauntless cannot be doubted: we must never forget Pope's extraordinary footnote tribute to him in the 1743 *Dunciad* or his consistent preeminence in all editions of Book II of that poem. The Rochester and Prior publications at the start of his career showed him to be remarkable enough. That he had high, if frustrated, ambitions to publish excellent work in fine editions, and perhaps sufficient taste and literary judgment to support them, is nevertheless not well known. Like Swift, he was a Tory, and his culture, like Swift's, linked him to the pragmatic, earthy world of the Restoration rather than to the pre-Victorianism of such contemporaries as Addison and Steele. More than any other early association, the contact with John Morphew seems to have enlarged his scope (for better and worse), lessened the drive he probably had toward respectability, and whetted his appetite for intrigue. His exceptional vitality and his willingness to intrude into worlds where he found no welcome made him a rascal and a whipping boy to certain influential contemporaries whose power to make and destroy reputations has never been equalled. But it would be wrong to conclude with this oversimplification, however salutary. Curll's early career was for the most part unexciting, but it had enough interesting passages to demonstrate that Curll the man could never have been dull.

BERTRAM H. DAVIS

The Rival *Angler* Editors:
Moses Browne and John Hawkins

I

THE EIGHTEENTH-CENTURY revival of *The Compleat Angler* owes its success to two ardent anglers. It owes its inspiration to Samuel Johnson, who perhaps never cast a fishing rod in his life. One of the two anglers, John Hawkins, has left a record of Johnson's first meeting with the other, probably in the year 1737—not on the banks of a trout stream, but inauspiciously in a Clerkenwell tavern where Johnson, still fresh from the midlands, had his curiosity gratified by the sight of Moses Browne "at the upper end of a long table" and "in a cloud of tobacco-smoke." [1]

As Hawkins tells us, the meeting was arranged by that indefatigable editor of the *Gentleman's Magazine,* Edward Cave, for the purpose of dazzling the neophyte Johnson with a glimpse of the magazine's chief poetical luminary. The well-intentioned Cave is engagingly naive in Hawkins's account; yet it is worth remembering that by the late 1730s Moses Browne, who was five years

---

[1] Sir John Hawkins, *The Life of Samuel Johnson, LL.D.* (London, 1787), pp. 49–50.

Johnson's senior, had achieved a literary eminence which Johnson
was still finding elusive. Browne's poem *The Richmond Beauties*
had been published in 1722, when Browne was only eighteen, and
his tragedy *Polidus* in 1723. His *Piscatory Eclogues* appeared in
1729, prefaced by an "Essay in Defence of Piscatory Eclogue," in
which he warmly commended *The Compleat Angler* to his readers. He was a constant contributor to the *Gentleman's Magazine,*
which as Hawkins notes "he fed with many a nourishing
morsel." [2] Most notable was his poem on "Life, Death, Judgment,
Heaven, and Hell," which in 1736 won him the fifty-pound prize
offered by Edward Cave for the best poem on those subjects. By
1739 he had proved sufficiently prolific to publish a volume of
collected verse, which he accurately if unimaginatively entitled
Poems on Various Subjects; but for verses which probed heaven
and hell and the waters in between perhaps no title adequately
suggestive was to be found.

In 1739 John Hawkins reached the age of twenty and completed his second year of clerkship to the attorney John Scott in
Devonshire Street, near Bishopsgate. With the assistance of some
ephemeral contributions to the *Gentleman's Magazine,* he was
probably becoming known to the thirty-year-old Johnson, but unfortunately he has left no similar record of his own first meeting
with the man whose biographer he was destined to be. A record
does exist, however, of his introduction to Moses Browne, who
seems to have made just such an impression upon Hawkins as
Cave must have assumed he had made upon Johnson only a few
years earlier.

Most of the hours the young Hawkins could steal from his
clerkship were devoted to literary endeavors. He rose each morning at four to ponder some of the authors who had no place in
John Scott's curriculum. At other times he busied himself with the
writing of moral essays and poems, several of which made their
way into the *Gentleman's Magazine* and other periodicals. And he

[2] *Ibid.,* p. 46n.

found a satisfying literary companionship in Foster Webb, who was to die in 1744 before reaching the age of twenty-two, and Thomas Phillibrown, who admiringly entered the effusions of his two friends in a manuscript now preserved in the Bodleian Library.[3]

In November 1741 Hawkins and Foster Webb directed their efforts to the kind of poetical imitation made popular by Dryden, Pope, and others, and they chose as their subject "The Canonization" of John Donne. Insofar as their choice reflected an admiration for Donne's poem, it was hardly open to question. The difficulty was that they had chosen to imitate the inimitable—that however they exerted themselves their imitations would appear pale in comparison with Donne's full-blooded original. In actual fact, one can only wonder if the two young poetasters did not mistake their role and take in their hands not the quill of the poet but the leech of the barber-surgeon.

It would be asking too much of patience to quote the full texts of the Hawkins imitation in twenty-four lines and the Webb imitation in thirty, even though the *Gentleman's Magazine* did so in 1761, when Thomas Phillibrown disinterred them from his manuscript and sent them to the magazine's editor.[4] Yet some selection is necessary. Donne's vigorous opening lines, for example,

> For God's sake hold your tongue, and let me love,
> Or chide my palsy, or my gout;

are pallid enough in Foster Webb's version:

> Forbear thy grave advice, and let me love,
> Or lay on nature, not on me, the blame:

---

[3] Bodleian Ms. Eng. Poet. C. 9. The ms. is described by Dr. L. F. Powell in Percy A. Scholes, *The Life and Activities of Sir John Hawkins* (London, 1953), pp. 258–67.

[4] *Gent. Mag.*, Oct. 1761, p. 472. The opening stanzas of the imitations have been reprinted by Earl R. Wasserman in *Elizabethan Poetry in the Eighteenth Century* (Urbana, Ill., 1947), pp. 186–87.

In Hawkins' they seem to fall from the lips of an undernourished dandy:

> I Prithee cease to chide my guiltless love,
>   Nor tire my patience with thy loath'd advice.

The opening lines of Donne's second stanza,

> Alas! alas! who's injur'd by my love?
>   What merchant ships have my sighs drown'd?
> Who says my tears have overflow'd his ground?
>   When did my colds a forward spring remove?

are stripped of their startling imagery in both the Webb version:

> But how can evils from my passion rise?
>   When did my sorrows drown the fruitful year?
> Have I e'er caused a tempest by my sighs,
>   Or did they ever taint the wholesome air?

and the Hawkins:

> Alas! what evils from my passion spring!
>   When did my sighs contageous taint the air?
> My tears retard the beauties of the spring
>   Or drown the rip'ning produce of the year? [5]

Pleased with their accomplishments and stirred by the spirit of contest, Hawkins and Webb looked about them for a critic qualified to determine the laurels. Ambitiously, they turned to that bulwark of the *Gentleman's Magazine,* Moses Browne, to whom Hawkins forwarded the two poems with a covering letter. On November 23, 1741—referring to Webb's version as No. 1 and Hawkins's as No. 2—Moses Browne obligingly rendered his judgment:

Sʳ. I have considerately read over the enclosed Peices & compared them with Dʳ Donnes Cannonization from whence they appear to be imitated. In my Opinion they have both their Merit & are each of them Improvements of the Dʳˢ. . . . To be plain there are great Marks of Genius in both and I could single out distinguishing Beau-

[5] The texts of the poems are taken from the *Gentleman's Magazine.*

ties. I am at a loss where to give my Approbation but upon the whole
I believe N° 2 to be the most finished peice which I hope as I know
neither of the Gentlemen will not give Offence when I give it, if the
mistaken, yet as the unprejudiced Judgment of S^r Y^r very humble
Servt.

Moses Browne [6]

II

The author of an imitation adjudged superior to John
Donne's original might have been expected to seek out the critic
who had discovered great marks of genius in his work. Perhaps
Hawkins and Moses Browne were brought together at the *Gentleman's Magazine* offices in St. John's Gate, as Hawkins and Johnson apparently were, but there is nothing in existing records to
suggest that their paths crossed for almost two decades after the
November 1741 judgment. Johnson and Browne, on the other
hand, were probably frequently in each other's company, and they
were certainly aware of each other's work. In 1749, for example,
when Browne published his *Sunday Thoughts,* "Johnson, who
often expressed his dislike of religious poetry, and who, for the
purpose of religious meditation, seemed to think one day as
proper as another, read them with cold approbation, and said, he
had a great mind to write and publish Monday Thoughts." [7]

Perhaps Johnson thought the time had come to divert
Browne's attention from such unsettling matters as life, death,
judgment, heaven, and hell. With Browne's qualifications for the
work established by both his *Piscatory Eclogues* and his "Essay in
Defence of Piscatory Eclogue," Johnson commended to his friend
the editing of Izaak Walton's *Compleat Angler,* which had quickly
gone through five editions in the seventeenth century but had not
been republished since 1676. Browne seems to have fallen to his
task with a will. His small volume appeared in 1750, with the text

---

[6] Bodleian Ms. Eng. Poet. C. 9, f. 12. The singularities of spelling and
punctuation may be Phillibrown's responsibility rather than Browne's. The
manuscript does not contain Hawkins's letter enclosing the two imitations.

[7] Hawkins's *Life of Johnson,* p. 46n.

of Walton's fourth edition and the Charles Cotton supplement to the fifth. It contained also an appropriate acknowledgment of Johnson's suggestion (the book was undertaken, wrote Browne, "at the Instigation of an ingenious and learned Friend") and a notice to the reader that Johnson might some day "oblige the Publick" with a life of Izaak Walton.[8]

This sixth edition, as Browne later called it, was an attractive book, charmingly illustrated with a number of copper plates by H. Burgh and with more than a dozen woodcuts of freshwater fish. Whether or not Browne's approach to his editorial responsibilities also proved an attraction to his contemporaries is not clear, for not until nine years after the book's publication is there any evidence of a reaction to his efforts. What strikes the modern reader, as it struck John Hawkins in 1759, is that Moses Browne took extraordinary liberties with Walton's text, not merely by omitting parts of it but, more seriously, by occasionally altering passages —including the poetry—to suit the editor's rather than the author's taste. Walton, wrote Browne, had permitted inaccuracies and redundancies to insinuate themselves into the text

which I should be injurious to him as his Editor, not to retrench and prune away. I have been modest and used great Deliberation in these Retouches, and have supplied some Deficiencies I found in him, by the Notes and Appendix, which I have added from later Experience. My Aim was, but to file off that Rust, which Time fixes on the most curious and finished Things. . . .

These Variations are so conducted as not to be discerned but by an inquisitive Eye, and I have the Presumption to think will always be adjudged in my Favour. . . .[9]

By and large perhaps Browne's presumption was justified, but, as has been suggested, at least one person with an inquisitive eye was not inclined to adjudge in Browne's favor. Having learned

[8] Izaak Walton and Charles Cotton, *The Compleat Angler: or, Contemplative Man's Recreation,* ed. Moses Browne (London, 1750), pp. iv–v.

[9] *Ibid.,* pp. viii-ix. The text, which in both editions is largely italicized, is taken from the 1759 edition, pp. xiii–xiv.

in the spring of 1759 that another edition of *The Compleat Angler* was in preparation, John Hawkins sent off a letter to Browne offering to make available a number of Walton materials in his possession. He suggested also that Browne base his text upon Walton's fifth edition, which contained the author's final additions and corrections, instead of the fourth edition, from which Browne had worked in 1750. In a subsequent meeting of the two men, Hawkins communicated several facts of Walton's life, which Browne incorporated in the preface to his new edition.

Browne's second edition, which he not unreasonably called the seventh, was advertised for sale beginning with the October 4–6, 1759, issue of the *London Chronicle*. For all Hawkins's urging, it was based largely upon Walton's fourth edition, although some of the additional material of the fifth edition was stuffed into an unsightly postscript. Even more disconcerting to a man of scholarly and aesthetic sensitivities, it took the same liberties with Walton's text as its predecessor and justified them to the public in almost identical language.

To Hawkins, these deficiencies in the new edition were the signal to move ahead in conformity with his own ideas of an editor's function. Exactly when he first resolved to edit *The Compleat Angler* cannot be determined, but in all likelihood he had been assembling materials for a new edition long before he became aware of Browne's intentions in the spring of 1759. His considered suggestions to Browne, and his possession of hitherto unknown information about Walton's life, point to a scholar's interest in a sound scholarly work. And it would have been no easy matter for the busy London attorney to put together a carefully annotated edition, as Hawkins's proved to be, between early October, 1759, and April 10, 1760, when his manuscript appears to have been completed. On that day he signed the dedication to Edward Popham, a Wiltshire member of parliament who seems to have been one of his fishing companions. Hawkins, in short, appears to have interrupted his own plans in the hope that Browne, with the help that Hawkins could provide him, might yet repair the damage of his 1750 edition. When he did not, Hawkins felt free to resume his own project, and he quickly brought it to fruition. By June 19, 1760, his edition was far enough along in the press for the publisher, Thomas Hope, to announce that it would be published on July 1, and it was made available to the public according to promise.[10]

III

Numerous advertisements placed by Thomas Hope in the *London Evening-Post, Lloyd's Evening Post,* and the *General Evening Post* reflect his awareness of a rival publication which might seriously limit the sale of his own. Although he avoided any direct reference to Browne's edition, anyone informed of the different approaches of the two editors would have recognized immediately that the very heading of each advertisement—"A New and Correct Edition"—was intended to suggest an invidious comparison. The conclusion of the advertisements was rather less subtle. After giving an assurance that the cuts, designed by Samuel Wale and engraved by William Ryland, cost "upwards of One Hundred Pounds," Hope cautioned the public to "Be careful to ask for the Edition with the Lives of Mr. *Isaac Walton* and *Charles Cotton, Esq;* (never before done) being the only correct and complete Edition."

Such puffs were a bookseller's stock-in-trade, and Hope, who had some reason to justify the publication of Hawkins's edition only nine months after Moses Browne's, can hardly be accused of unfairness to a rival who was at liberty to extol the virtues of his own edition. At most one would have expected Browne or his publisher, Henry Kent, to respond with advertisements similar to those that had announced publication of the book in October, 1759. But the poet who could look upon the Hawkins and Webb imitations as improvements upon John Donne's original was not

---

[10] Izaak Walton and Charles Cotton, *The Complete Angler: or, Contemplative Man's Recreation* (London, 1760). The book was advertised in the *London Evening-Post,* June 17–19 and June 28–July 1, 1760.

readily predictable. To an advertisement published in at least two newspapers on August 16, he appended a lengthy statement which was at once a defense of his own edition and an attack upon his rival's.[11]

Browne's opening comments were probably not displeasing to Hawkins and Thomas Hope, for, although Browne accused them of pretending that theirs was the only correct and complete edition, he at the same time invited the public to make "the closest, strictest, and most impartial Comparison" between the two editions. No doubt the rival editor and publisher would have liked nothing better. To support his invitation, Browne provided in parallel columns the texts of two poems as they appeared in each of the editions, although he neglected to inform the public that Hawkins's texts were true to their originals and his own were not. The final paragraph of Browne's statement charged that "the so much boasted Plates" in Hawkins's edition were "copied from the Designs in his" and that the life of Walton, "said by them to be never done before," was largely borrowed from the life of Walton in his own edition.

Hawkins did not himself reply to these charges, but, according to Browne, new advertisements blatantly ridiculing Browne's edition were "stuck all round the Windows" of Thomas Hope's shop at the Bible and Anchor in Threadneedle Street. Infuriated by the window display and perhaps by the effect which Hawkins's edition was having on the sale of his own, Browne returned to the controversy with a lengthy diatribe in the *Public Advertiser*s of September 25 and 29 and the *London Evening-Post* of September 28–30:

If the Conductor of a late self-applauded Edition of this Author, had been Master of Qualifications sufficient to have confined himself within the Bounds of Modesty, Truth, or even common Sense (to say nothing of his unprecedented Ill-manners and Scurrility) the Editor of

[11] *Public Advertiser,* August 16, 1760; *Whitehall Evening-Post,* August 14–16, 1760. The advertisement was repeated in the *Public Advertiser* of August 18.

this present one had suffered him silently to have sunk into Oblivion, and the Chaos of his own Stupidity; and to have left him quietly exulting in those many Blunders he has inserted and boasted of, and is only peculiar to his Edition.

The blunders, explained Browne, included the failure to excise those parts of Walton's text which directed his readers to a number of places which either were destroyed by the fire of 1666 or had otherwise disappeared—Dr. Nowel's monument in St. Paul's Church, John Tradescant's house at Lambeth, and a coffee house in King Street, Westminster, where Walton had seen on display an eel a yard and three quarters long. These, said Browne, and a few other similar passages—including fifteen verses by Du Bartas which Hawkins himself called "execrable bombast"—common sense directed him to omit, and they are "the only Cause of all that Outcry made by Mr. Hope's Editor, of 'whole Pages left out.' " Browne expressed his willingness to have them read "in none but Mr. Hope's Edition."

As for the poetry, Browne offered no defense, except by implication, of his practice of rewriting the verses in Walton's book —"filing off the rust," as he called it in his preface. Instead he charged that Hawkins had failed to refine Walton's crudities out of his own "Laziness and Dulness." Again he insisted that the illustrations in Hawkins's edition were mere copies of his own; and, he added, Hawkins had actually applied to Browne's illustrator to prepare a set of fish for his edition, "but that Person had the Honour and something more (which himself is much a Stranger to) on such a Motion, to refuse him."

In "his last gasconading insolent Advertisement," continued Browne, Hawkins had the effrontery to affirm that the life of Walton "was never done before," whereas Browne had published it "(the same in every material Fact with his own, though he denies it)" before Hawkins's edition had made "its slow Appearance." Indeed, he noted, "It is really amazing he should treat this Editor with the Rudeness and Contempt he has done, when he had mentioned him with that Respect by Name in a Note at Page 235 of

his Edition." And as to Hawkins's charge that Browne was ignorant of Walton's fifth edition, "be it known to him, that he knew
of and was possessed of that Edition, before ever this conceited,
busy, rough-hewed Editor was born."

And now, he concluded, "it is neither him nor me" but the
public which must determine "to which of us the Slander he has
affixed of 'Meanness and Dishonesty,' most properly appertains."
Certainly it is clear just who has been practicing "the Artifices he
mentions in 'getting rid of a very sorry Edition.' " He himself will
reply no more, but will leave the other editor "to plague the Press,
tire the World, please himself, tell—, propagate Slander, and do
every Thing he can in his own little Heart, to make himself (if
that is to be done) more offensive, detested, and ridiculous."

Although Hawkins held his peace in August, he found it impossible to ignore the late September outburst. Catching up
Browne's concluding appeal to the public, his reply in the October
6 issue of the *Public Advertiser* and the October 9–11 issue of the
London Evening-Post points out a way for the public to determine
both "the Merits of . . . [Browne's] Book, and the Candor and
Honesty of its Editor." Browne, for example, has asserted that he
possessed a copy of Walton's fifth edition "many Years before he
undertook his Work." Yet his book follows, with all its errors,
Walton's fourth edition until the 185th page, after which it follows
the fifth edition; [12] the editor has inserted the omissions from the
first 185 pages in a Postscript—only fifty lines, however, when
"above five times that Number" were actually omitted—and has
attributed the omissions to his printer, "who, he tells you, misun-
derstood his Copy." "But to put the Matter out of Dispute," said
Hawkins, the reader is invited to peruse, at Thomas Hope's shop,
a letter from Browne dated April 28, 1759, in which he confesses
that the fifth edition "had not then fallen into his Hands," and a
second letter in which he defends the word *poesies* (instead of

[12] So Hawkins thought, no doubt because the final pages of Walton's
fifth edition are largely identical with those of the fourth. Actually Browne
continued to follow the fourth edition.

posies) in Christopher Marlowe's "Come Live with Me" on the ground that *poesies* was the word in the edition he was using— that is, the fourth edition.

His own life of Walton—forty pages, compared to Browne's five—continued Hawkins, was compiled "from authentic Memorials in his Custody only, and Authorities cited in the Margin of the Book." [13] In a conversation about June, 1759, he communicated two or three of these particulars to Browne,

who has not only inserted what he could recollect in his Preface, without confessing whence he had his Information, but with an Assurance that none can reflect on without Astonishment, this strictly conscientious Divine, the pious Author of Sunday Thoughts forsooth! . . . in his Advertisement of the 16th of August last has asserted that our Life of Walton is "the chief Part borrowed from them!"

True to his August 16 promise, Browne issued no reply to Hawkins's statement. It was well for him, of course, that he did not, for he was engaged in a controversy which could only make him appear increasingly ridiculous. He should never, in fact, have allowed himself to be drawn into it in the first place, but to persist after his first volley had failed to draw fire was to tempt annihilation. The advertisements "stuck all round the Windows" of Thomas Hope's shop may, to be sure, have been offensive to him. At the Bible and Anchor, however, the display amused only a few book fanciers, window shoppers, and passersby, whereas by taking notice of it in the newspapers Browne was providing laughter at his own expense for much of the London reading public. Hope must have been gratified by the publicity, for he could never himself have spread the word so effectually that Browne's was "a very sorry Edition."

Hope, of course, was aided by his ally as well as by his enemy. In his edition of *The Compleat Angler,* Hawkins knew exactly what he was doing. He makes clear in his newspaper state-

---

[13] The life of Charles Cotton in the 1760 edition was written by William Oldys. Hawkins did not write his own life of Cotton until 1784.

ment that he knew what Browne was doing also. Browne had no such comprehensive view of their two roles. When he accused Hawkins of failing to make the necessary refinements in Walton out of his own "Laziness and Dulness," he displayed in fact an ignorance of Hawkins's methods which very nearly defies belief. "Great names," wrote Hawkins in his 1784 revision of the life of Walton, "are entitled to great respect." [14] Great books, he might have added, arc also entitled to great respect, particularly by their editors. One duty of the editor was to present to his readers the best text of the author that he could find, and Hawkins's choice of Walton's fifth edition was unassailable, as even Browne, in his bungling way, was compelled to admit when he gathered up some of his omissions from the fifth edition and bundled them together in a postscript. The author's text was not quite sacrosanct, of course. One might modernize spelling, punctuation, and capitalization, as Hawkins did even in the title (*The Complete Angler*), where his purpose was doubtless to distinguish his edition from Moses Browne's. But the text was beyond that tinkering which permitted either unheralded deletions or alterations of words and sentences which distorted the writer's meaning or obliterated his style. To do as Browne did was to convey to the public not the text which Walton wrote, but the text which Browne would have wished him to write had Walton been attempting to please a mid-eighteenth century audience such as Browne conceived it to be.

Hawkins thus succeeded in introducing Walton to his readers just about as he was. Browne too often stands between his readers and Walton. This is not to say that Browne's edition is without charm. Fortunately Browne was not so untidy an editor that he never left anything in order, and many of his changes would be noticeable only to someone with Walton's text before him—to "an inquisitive Eye," as Browne himself commented. His notes are often helpful. Burgh's illustrations, as has been mentioned, have unusual grace, and it is not surprising that Hawkins never replied to Browne's charge, rather too sweeping though it was, that he had

[14] *Complete Angler* (1784), p. xxxii.

sought out Burgh himself and that Samuel Wale's illustrations for the Hawkins edition were mere copies of Burgh's. Two of them —those of the Milkmaid's Song and of Venator and Piscator reclining on the river bank—bear such a marked resemblance to Burgh's illustrations as to leave Wale's originality suspect.

Understandably Browne's touch is most conspicuous in the poetry of Walton's volume; if he does not shatter it like glass, he almost always leaves a visible thumbprint. The second stanza, for example, of Henry Wotton's poem, "This day dame Nature seem'd in love," is transcribed by Hawkins with only minor changes in spelling, punctuation, and capitalization:

> There stood my friend with patient skill,
> Attending of his trembling quill.
> Already were the eaves possest
> With the swift Pilgrim's dawbed nest:
> The groves already did rejoice,
> In Philomel's triumphing voice.
>
> (*Complete Angler*, 1760, pp. 43–44) [15]

It comes through Browne's hands as follows:

> There stood my Friend, with patient Skill,
> Attentive o'er his trembling Quill.
> Already were the Eaves possest
> With the fleet Swallow's loomy Nest;
> The Groves, at Philomel's sweet Voice,
> From all their Echoes did rejoice;
>
> (*Compleat Angler*, 1759, p. 31)

Even Christopher Marlowe's "Come Live with Me" is not beyond Browne's desecration. Hawkins transcribes the third stanza with only the change of *Embroidered* to *Embroider'd:*

> And I will make thee beds of Roses,
> And then a thousand fragrant Posies,
> A Cap of flowers, and a Kirtle
> Embroider'd all with leaves of Mirtle.
>
> (*Complete Angler*, 1760, p. 76)

[15] The texts of these and the following verses are italicized in the various editions.

Browne, accepting the erroneous fourth edition *Poesies,* to which
Hawkins called attention during their controversy, submits the following refinement:

> Pleas'd will I make thee Beds of Roses,
> And Twine a thousand fragrant Poesies;
> A Cap of Flow'rs, and rural Kirtle,
> Embroider'd all with Leaves of Myrtle.
>
> *(Compleat Angler,* 1759, p. 59)

The last two stanzas of the poem were omitted from
Browne's 1750 edition. When they were restored to the text in
1759 they were scarcely recognizable. Marlowe's next-to-last
stanza, for example, was transcribed by Hawkins exactly as it appeared in Walton's fifth edition:

> Thy silver dishes for thy meat,
> As precious as the gods do eat,
> Shall on an Ivory table be
> Prepar'd each day for thee and me.
>
> *(Complete Angler,* 1760, p. 77)

Browne's flourishes are those of a love-struck schoolgirl:

> Impearl'd Shell-Dishes for thy Meat,
> Choice as is that th' Immortals eat,
> Shall on Earth's Flower-deck'd Table be
> Serv'd up, each Day, for Thee and Me.
>
> *(Compleat Angler,* 1759, p. 59)

No doubt Browne assumed that his contemporaries would
share his own tastes and thus reject the plain-speaking of Walton
and his poets. *Dawbed,* after all, was hardly a word for polite
company; and there were many other places where the rust would
yield readily to the editor's file. But Hawkins, who knew his duty
as an editor, had also a better feeling for his times. Browne, it is
true, managed another edition of his *Compleat Angler* in 1772,
but he made substantial concessions in it to Hawkins's point of
view. For Browne's *Angler,* however—except for an abortive revival in 1851—that was all, whereas by 1797 the sixth Hawkins
edition had been published and no one had the slightest question

as to who had carried the day. In Hawkins's editions the public had seen Walton plain, and it nodded its approval. Walton without rust was much less to its liking.

Moses Browne must be honored for reawakening interest in *The Compleat Angler* after a slumber of seventy-five years. But it was the work of Hawkins which found the book its proper niche as a classic of its kind and fixed it in the public's affections. The four editions of Hawkins's lifetime were succeeded, between 1791 and 1826, by ten editions under the direction of his son, John Sidney Hawkins, who retained all the materials of the 1784 edition and added his father's posthumous notes as well as a few of his own.[16] Between 1833 and 1857 James Rennie published twenty editions containing Hawkins's notes and his lives of Walton and Cotton. These nearly three dozen editions, spanning most of a century, bear eloquent testimony to the quality of Hawkins's work as an editor.

IV

Samuel Johnson's view of the Browne-Hawkins controversy has not been recorded, although as a friend of both men and the "instigator" of Browne's 1750 edition he could hardly have failed to take an interest in the progress of Izaak Walton at the hands of his editors. Johnson's own work makes clear that he shared Hawkins's editorial convictions rather than Moses Browne's, but he was much too sensitive a man to criticize openly an editor who to the best of his limited ability had carried out an assignment which Johnson himself had commended to him. If Johnson suffered any pangs of regret at being associated with the mangled Browne edition, he gave no evidence of that fact. Nor is it likely that Browne's execution of his assignment, or his dispute with Johnson's much closer friend John Hawkins, accounts in any way for his total disappearance from Johnson's subsequent biography or for Johnson's

[16] A manuscript in the Houghton Library, Harvard University, contains rough notes, apparently for the first John Sidney Hawkins edition, in the handwritings of Hawkins's children.

failure to mention him in any of the conversations recorded by James Boswell. Browne, of course, was even less Johnson's intellectual equal than he was Hawkins's; but Johnson never hesitated to associate with men whose intellectual attainments fell seriously short of his own. And he was particularly fond of old friends, whatever their intellectual abilities.

The likelihood is that, with his appointment as chaplain of Morden College in 1763, Browne completed the withdrawal from the London scene which he had begun in 1753 with his appointment as vicar of Olney. Perhaps Browne reached the height of his career when in 1736 Thomas Birch awarded him the *Gentleman's Magazine* prize for the best poem on Life, Death, Judgment, Heaven, and Hell.[17] A mind which had ranged the infinite, and to the extent of 506 lines, was perhaps not suited to sustain a Grub Street career. So Browne became the country vicar and chaplain, reissuing now and then some of his earlier works and publishing anew only occasional sermons and a translation of a religious work. No doubt between his clerical and family duties (he is said to have had thirteen children) he found time to live his own piscatory eclogue—to enjoy the "contemplative man's recreation," as Izaak Walton called it; and with the gentle Walton to minister to him, perhaps he steadily closed the wounds laid open by an upstart editor "conceited, busy, rough-hewed," and (alas!) once praised above John Donne.

But even Walton could not inspire enough philosophy for Browne to acknowledge Hawkins's achievement openly. Browne's 1750 and 1759 editions, it will be recalled, were the first to follow the five editions of Walton's lifetime, and Browne specifically designated the 1759 edition the seventh. Although Hawkins's first edition was published in 1760 (and sold with a new title page in 1766), Browne seems to have pretended that it had never existed. When he republished *The Compleat Angler* in 1772 he called it the eighth edition.

Hawkins could afford to be more generous, and was. Moses

---

[17] *Gentleman's Magazine,* February, 1736, pp. 59–60.

Browne, as we have seen, had himself referred to one of the notes in Hawkins's edition: ". . . a Gentleman now living, the Reverend Mr. *Moses Browne* has obliged the world with Piscatory Eclogues, which I would recommend to all lovers of Poetry and Angling; and am much mistaken if the fifth of them, entitled *Renock's Despair,* is not by far the best imitation of *Milton's Lycidas,* that has ever yet appeared." [18] After the hysterical attack upon him for what Browne called his "Stupidity," "Laziness," "Dulness," and "Rudeness," it would not have been surprising if Hawkins had either modified this generous tribute to a rival editor or withdrawn it completely. The note remained unchanged, however, not only in the second edition of 1766, which was merely the first edition with a canceled title page, but also in the third edition of 1775, when the type was reset, and in the fourth edition of 1784, which Hawkins substantially revised. In his *Life of Johnson,* published in 1787 when Browne at eighty-three was in the last year of his life, Hawkins overlooked their 1760 quarrel and again warmly commended Browne's poetry, which, he says, provides "proofs of an exuberant fancy and a happy invention " [19] Having read this passage, Horace Walpole was prompted to scribble a marginal note beside it: "It is handsome in Hawkins to say nothing uncandid of Browne who wrote against him." [20]

The subject of John Hawkins was one upon which Walpole and Johnson found themselves in general agreement. Given an advance copy of the 1760 *Angler,* Walpole wrote to Sir David Dalrymple on June 28, 1760: "There is a little book coming out that will amuse you; it is a new edition of Isaac Walton's *Complete Angler,* full of anecdotes and historic notes. It is published by Mr. Hawkins, a very worthy gentleman in my neighbourhood. . . ." [21] Johnson's first known comment upon the Hawkins edition dates

---

[18] *The Complete Angler* (1760), pp. 235–36n.

[19] *Life of Johnson,* p. 46n.

[20] Walpole's copy of the *Life of Johnson* was kindly made available to me by Mr. Wilmarth S. Lewis.

[21] *The Yale Edition of Horace Walpole's Correspondence,* ed. W. S. Lewis, (New Haven, 1951), XV, 70.

from 1774, when Johnson was corresponding with the Reverend Dr. George Horne, and it perhaps explains why Johnson never "obliged the Publick" with his own biography of Walton: "The Life of Walton has happily fallen into good hands. Sir John Hawkins has prefixed it to the late edition of the Angler, very diligently collected, and very elegantly composed. You will ask his leave to reprint it, and not wish for a better."

"I wish," continued Johnson, "that in the leisure of academical retirement more Men would think to review our stores of antiquated literature, and bring back into notice what is undeservedly forgotten." [22] Nowhere is the cogency of Johnson's wish better illustrated than in the eighteenth-century history of *The Compleat Angler*, with its foreword by Johnson, its initial chapters by Moses Browne, and its conclusion by John Hawkins. In the long run the unreconciled editors proved excellent collaborators.

[22] *The Letters of Samuel Johnson*, ed. R. W. Chapman (Oxford 1952), I, 405. Dr. Horne was projecting an edition of Walton's own biographies.

ROBERT DONALD SPECTOR

The *Connoisseur:* a Study of the Functions of a Persona

FOR LITERARY-PERIODICAL writers and editors in the eighteenth century, the persona was not an abstract problem giving rise to theoretical discussions—as it has done for twentieth-century scholars and critics—but rather a realistic fact of life upon which the success or failure of the journalistic venture might depend. It is clear, for example, that when the popular joke associated with the name of Isaac Bickerstaff had ceased to have currency and when Addison and Steele planned a periodical that would be taken more seriously, the authors terminated the *Tatler* in favor of the *Spectator* and created the more respectable figure of Mr. Spectator,[1] a man whose authority and commonsense could

[1] Richmond P. Bond, "Isaac Bickerstaff, Esq.," *Restoration and Eighteenth-Century Literature: Essays in Honor of Alan Dugald McKillop,* edited by Carroll Camden (Chicago, 1963), p. 124, makes the suggestion that the need to change the persona was at least one reason for the demise of the *Tatler* and the altered character of the subsequent periodical. As Bond

command the sober attention of the reading public.[2] In the same way, at mid-century with the outbreak of the Seven Years' War it proved fatal to have personae suggestive of frivolity or levity. New publishing ventures, like the *Old Maid* and the *Prater,* using inconsequential pseudo-editors named Mary Singleton and Nicholas Babble, were short-lived. Even the well-established *World,* under the persona of Mr. Fitz-Adam, had a spokesman inadequate to be heard above the din of warfare, the tumult of resounding defeats. Not until England was on its way to victory did the lighter personae of Goldsmith's *Bee* and *Busy Body* and Johnson's *Idler* return the less serious type of fictional author to the literary scene.[3]

The *Connoisseur,* which first appeared in 1754 and ceased publication in 1756, serves as a fine example of the relationship of the periodical persona to its audience. Like the *World,* the *Connoisseur* was a well-written essay-journal given to ironic treatment of taste, manners, and morals, but never intended to create a great disturbance in society. Midway through their periodical labors, the editors made clear the characteristics that they intended to impart to the *Connoisseur:*

I personally avoided the worn-out practice of retailing scraps of morality, and affecting to dogmatize on the common duties of life. . . . I have therefore contented myself with exposing vice and folly by paint-

---

(pp. 114–18) makes clear, attempts to broaden the character of Bickerstaff never quite succeeded, since "his connection with astrology, however softened by the grace of irony, was not an ideal professional affiliation, and the Partridge business lost its value. . . ." (p. 118) In the same way, essay-journals like the *Connoisseur* and *World* could not alter their personae to appeal to public interest during the Seven Years' War.

[2] Mr. Spectator presented a fine balance between the warmly human and yet distinctive characteristics necessary for a successful persona, who required the respect of his readers while he was interesting and different enough from them to hold their attention and carry out his functions as an inquirer into multiple areas of society. Bond (pp. 113–14) summarizes the necessary qualities of an effective periodical persona.

[3] See Robert Donald Spector, *English Literary Periodicals and the Climate of Opinion during the Seven Years' War* (The Hague, 1966), *passim.*

ing mankind in their natural colours, without assuming the rigid air of a preacher, or the moroseness of a philosopher. I have rather chose to undermine our fashionable excesses by secret sapping, than to storm them by open assault (II, 132).[4]

George Colman, a twenty-four-year-old law student, and Bonnell Thornton, a thirty-year-old Bachelor of Physic turned writer (III, 243), knew precisely the kind of persona that they needed for their type of criticism. Or, perhaps, personae would be a more suitable description. For Colman and Thornton the imaginary essayist they created was a composite figure. Part of his character was depicted in the title of his periodical; another was established in his name, Mr. Town; and yet another was characterized by his assumed role as Censor-General.[5]

The character of Connoisseur lent itself readily to ironic comment and permitted a kind of criticism that was witty without being unduly serious. If a periodical sought to denigrate fads and fashions, if it sought to scoff at minor flaws in taste and morals, it required a cover to allow it to make its points without seeming overly serious or grave. The role of Connoisseur, as Colman and Thornton recognized, could be a serious one if the term were interpreted, as the first two meanings in Johnson's *Dictionary* allowed, as "a judge; a critick." However, as Johnson's concluding definition stated, *connoisseur* was "often used of a pretended critick." The very play between the denotation and the popular connotation of the name permitted Colman and Thornton to create a mock-serious tone in their criticism of taste.

In their amplification of a passage from Horace that became

---

[4] References are to the three-volume edition in Chalmers's *British Essayists* (London, 1819). Citations to volume and page will appear at appropriate places in the text.

[5] This division of the persona roughly parallels that of the *Tatler*. The title of the earlier periodical creates a jest at the expense of the ladies; the persona of Bickerstaff recalls the popular joke in Swift's attack on Partridge, the astrologer; and the role of Censor, that adopted as well by the *Connoisseur*, represents an attempt—unsuccessful in both periodicals—to give some seriousness to the character.

their motto, the editors expressed an understanding of how they would use their persona:

> Who better knows to build, and who to dance,
> Or this from Italy, or that from France,
> Our Connoisseur will ne'er pretend to scan,
> But point the follies of mankind to man.
> Th' important knowledge of ourselves explain,
> Which not to know all knowledge is but vain.   (I,7)

There it was: the pretense that their Connoisseur stood above pettiness and triviality, concerning himself solely with important matters of mankind. And yet the juxtaposition with the pejorative associations of the name reminded the reader that the authors were not altogether serious in their use of the persona.

Almost immediately Colman and Thornton played upon this double meaning of *connoisseur* to gain the light humor that characterized their essay-journal. In response to "letters from several *Virtuosi*"—a term conveying the same denotative-connotative effect as *connoisseur*—the editors remarked that they were cognizant of the advantages to be accrued "by supporting the character of Connoisseur in its usual sense." There was money to be made from "auction-rooms, toy-shops, and repositories." It could bring "reputation as well as profit," appointment as keeper of a museum or to the Royal Society. In mock-serious tones the authors described the great discoveries that could be made by acting the role of the traditional Connoisseur. It would be a most noble endeavor to pursue the antiquarian interests of the "genuine" Connoisseur; it would be a mark of distinction "to shew . . . sagacity in conjectures on rusty coins and illegible marbles" or the "profound erudition . . . contained in an half-obliterated piece of copper!" (I, 8–9)

Throughout the journal the role of Connoisseur was played with tongue-in-cheek, allowing for satiric comment at the expense of Connoisseurs either by placing the persona above the generality of his kind or else by using him as typical. With great gravity the persona could proclaim his dismay at the weaknesses of his brethren. In all honesty he had to admit to their "known dishonesty" when their passions were aroused by their precious interests:

The moment they conceive a love for rarities, and antiques, their strict notions of honour disappear; and Taste, the more it establishes their veneration for *Virtù,* the more certainly destroys their integrity: as rust enhances the value of an old coin, by eating up the figure and inscription (I, 95).

Before describing his personal experiences abroad, his own integrity as a Connoisseur, the persona regretfully had to confess that "the Connoisseur enlarges his museum, and adds to his store of knowledge, by fraud and petty larceny." The abuses of medalists and of collectors of scarce editions and original manuscripts were detailed by him in order to set himself off from these corrupt virtuosos (I, 96).

Rather like a light-hearted Jonathan Swift, to whom they often referred,[6] the editors used the traits of the Connoisseur to undercut himself. He was a Connoisseur aware of the grossest practices of his kind. Speaking on the subject of taste, an appropriate province for his interests, he set himself off from his brothers without altogether forsaking them:

Should I attempt to define it [taste] in the style of a Connoisseur, I must run over the names of all the famous poets, painters, and sculptors, ancient and modern; and after having pompously harangued on the excellencies of Apelles, Phideas, Praxiteles, Angelo, Rubens, Poussin, and Dominichino, with a word or two on all tasteful compositions, such as those of Homer, Virgil, Tasso, Dante, and Ariosto, I should leave the reader in wonder of my profound erudition, and as little informed as before. But as deep learning, though more flaming and pompous, is perhaps not always so useful as common sense, I shall endeavour to get at the true meaning of the word taste, by considering what it usually imports in familiar writings and ordinary conversation (III, 138).[7]

The appeal to "common sense" immediately set off the character of the Connoisseur from the derogatory associations conjured up

---

[6] See, for example, I, 230; II, 45; III, 64, 76.   [7] See also III, 100–101.

by the title. Nevertheless, the persona was such that it allowed the essay-journal to use material that ironically criticized taste by pretending to the pejorative meaning of the term. The Connoisseur himself could express his feeling of having been "vastly entertained" by an acquaintance who had contributed to his learning by providing an estimate of the amount of bread, cheese, cakes, and ale consumed on Sundays in London's suburbs (I, 136). In somber tone he could pass on hare-brained proposals sent to him by a fellow projector (I, 140–41). Or the letters to the periodical could treat the persona as a Connoisseur in the finest tradition of pedantry and triviality.

It was to this pedantic Connoisseur that a reader could offer a ballad, discovered by an antiquary, because "it will do you more credit, as a Connoisseur, to draw this hidden treasure into light, than if you had discovered an Otho or a Niger" (I, 81). In this character he could not be opposed to printing a correspondent's notice of a nonsensical flower advertisement because it was likely to "oblige the virtuosi in flowers" (III, 88–89). Mr. Connoisseur (though that was his character rather than his name) could be rebuked for not writing sufficiently about eating habits, a subject, after all, not beneath the dignity of "Dr. Martin Lister, who was universally allowed to be a great Connoisseur, and published several learned treatises upon cockle shells" (I, 100).

Indeed, to the very conclusion of the periodical, the character of Connoisseur was carried on in playful fashion to comment on matters of taste and learning. As Connoisseur, the editors ironically lamented, they had unfortunately failed in their efforts to reform taste. There had been no election to the academies or societies, no recognition by the authors of the *Philosophical Transactions* or *Magazine of Arts and Sciences*. Neither material rewards nor spiritual satisfaction had been gained by playing the role of Connoisseur:

I am not worth a farthing in antique coins; nor have I so much as one single shell or butterfly. . . . with concern I still see the villas of our citizens fantastically adorned with Chinese palings, and our streets incumbered with superb colonnades, porticos, Gothic arches, and Venetian windows, the ordinary decorations of the shops of our tradesmen (III, 236).

If the pose of Connoisseur was intended to allow comment on taste, the name of the persona, Mr. Town, was devised to permit a particular kind of social criticism. Like *connoisseur,* the term *town* was ambiguous and created an ironic tension for the reader. Its metonymous definition meant simply the people who lived in the capital, London. As such it was a good descriptive word for a persona whose business it was to report on the habits, customs, and foibles of the general populace.

Such a figure had to give the impression of a man whose knowledge of the town derived from personal experience, a man who moved about in society.[8] Mr. Town might comment on his weariness after a night at "the coffee house, where I had just been reading the votes" (II, 91). In the interest of gathering information on mores and manners, he had to pass his time in good company "at White's, and the other coffee-houses about St. James's" (II, 60). The portrait that he presented of himself in this respect was intended to be that of a real human being, having the same desires and weaknesses—in many respects—as his readers:

I left the coffee-house pretty late; and as I came into the piazza, the fire in the Bedford-Arms kitchen blazed so cheerfully and invitingly before me, that I was easily persuaded by a friend who was with me, to end the evening at that house (I, 57).

Indeed, in his very first number, where he described his task as being "to mark the Manners of the Town" (I, 1), he had em-

[8] To broaden their coverage, the editors included correspondence from Mr. Town's cousin, Mr. Village, whose job was to combat "vice and folly" in the Country as his kinsman was doing in the City (I, 3). Like Mr. Town, the country cousin commented ironically, and in his final dispatch noted with sorrow the failure of their mission: "From your intelligence, some of our most polite ladies have learned, that it is highly genteel to have a rout; and have copied the fashion so exactly, as to play at cards on Sundays. Your papers upon dress set all our belles at work in following the mode . . ." (III, 234–35).

phasized the need for making the rounds of the coffee-houses, to
go to *all* places, even "a common porter-house" (I, 6). To "delineate and remark on mankind in general," he had need to play the
role of his company so that "I am a Scotchman at Forrest's, a
Frenchman at Slaughter's, and at the Cocoa-Tree I am—an Englishman" (I, 6). His quest for information, his "curiosity," led him
to examine the design for a pastry-cooking academy and allowed
him to remark on how the art of cookery was no longer a require-
ment for young ladies in the "polite world" (II, 71–72). In order
to be able to comment on the vagaries of fashion and conduct of
women—a popular subject for Mr. Town—he was required to attend "the opera, the playhouse, a lady's rout, or any other assembly" (III, 83). His interest in men's use of cosmetics necessitated
his "taking a survey of one of these male-toilettes . . ." (II, 97).

This human side of Mr. Town, this accounting for his access
to information, and this serious statement of purpose recall Mr.
Spectator. However, the persona created by Colman and Thornton
ultimately lacked the seriousness that Steele and Addison had
given to their fictive spokesman. To be sure, Mr. Town could announce his pleasure at receiving correspondence from the universi-
ties (III, 161), or he could be acknowledged by a reader as having
taken "the city under your immediate care" (I, 28). Nevertheless,
his business, unlike Mr. Spectator's, was not in bringing philosophy out of the closets and into the drawing room. He sought to
make his productions "an agreeable part of the equipage of the
tea-table" (I, 141). If Mr. Town had more substance than Mary
Singleton or Nicholas Babble (and thus the periodical more dura-
bility), he was not, after all, the kind of man to whom readers
might refer before forming their opinions for the day. The sober
and moral side of Mr. Spectator finally outweighed the lightness
and wit; for Mr. Town, it was the other way around.

The ambiguity in his name that detracted from his seriousness was well recognized by the editors. They themselves scoffed
at "the several tribes of play-house and coffee-house Critics, and
that collective body of them called the Town . . ." (II, 63). After

all, the "Town" was fashionable society, fickle and unstable in its opinions, unreliable in its judgment, and so lacking in taste that the contemporary *Critical Review* set as its specific task opposition to the point of view "of those gentlemen who call themselves the Town. . . ." [9] The decision to call the persona Mr. Town indicated that in their social criticism, as in their comments on taste, Colman and Thornton sought to amuse more than instruct their audience.

Actually, the treatment of Mr. Town and his own expressed attitude toward his work suggested the tone to be expected in his criticism of mores and manners. Discussing the ornament to preface his work, Mr. Town confessed that he had thought of his own profile as adornment, but he had been "mortified to see what a scurvy figure I made in wood . . ." (I, 40). At the same time, he scoffed at the frontispiece in the *World*, a "portrait of a philosopher poring on the globe," a bit of pretentiousness not suited to the role played by periodical writers (I, 41). On the characteristics of periodicals themselves, he was quite clear, not overvaluing their importance any more than his own:

We, whose business it is to write loose essays, and who never talk above a quarter of an hour together on any one subject, are not expected to enter into philosophical disquisitions, or engage in abstract speculations; but it is supposed to be our principal aim to amuse and instruct the reader, by a lively representation of what passes round about him. Thus, like those painters who delineate the scenes of familiar life, we sometimes give a sketch of a marriage *à la mode,* sometimes draw the outlines of a modern midnight conversation, at another time paint the comical distresses of itinerant tragedians in a barn, and at another give a full draught of the rake's or harlot's progress. Sometimes we divert the public by exhibiting single portraits; and when we meet with a subject where the features are strongly marked by nature, and there is something peculiarly characteristic in the whole manner, we employ ourselves in drawing the piece at full length. In a word, we consider all mankind as sitting for their pictures, and endeavour to work up our pieces with lively traits, and embellish them with beauti-

[9] *Critical Review,* IX (February, 1760), 133.

ful colouring: and though, perhaps, they are not always highly finished, yet they seldom fail of pleasing some few, at least, of the vast
multitude of Critics and Connoisseurs, if we are so happy as to hit off
a striking likeness (III, 218–19).

In descriptions of his person and his work, Mr. Town repeatedly reminded his readers that the business of periodical writing
should not be taken too gravely. He scoffed at the vanity of authors, himself included. He portrayed his own meanderings about
town to seek out praise on the mornings of publication and his uneasiness at discovering the common uses to which his paper was
put. Seeing his *Connoisseur* soaring into the air in the material of
a kite, he could imagine some small achievement of immortality,
only to have the string break and his high hopes, like the kite,
come plummeting to the ground (I, 151–55). Although he might
pride himself on his work, his lost copy had made its way into the
hands of "ignorant sailors . . . so regardless of its inestimable
contents" that they employed it to light their pipes (II, 61–62).
He wondered about his readers' impressions of him as a man and
laughed at those who fancied that his "satires on present modes in
dress" meant that he himself worked away in poverty in a garret
and wore nothing better than "a tattered night-gown"; or those
who believed that his attacks "against luxury and debauchery"
meant that he himself was starving (III, 109–10).

But nothing that Mr. Town wrote about himself was more
likely to indicate his intended light humor than his description of
how an author rose in the world. Using his own "experience" to
illustrate, he presented a biographical account of the Grub Street
writer. Beginning as a schoolboy who wrote themes to sell to
classmates, he progressed to making contributions to magazines
because he believed the world must know of his amazing powers.
An aunt's conversion to Methodism brought him naturally to
hymn-writing that terminated when she joined the Moravians, a
sect too crazy for him to follow. Next he turned to love poetry,
but failing to win a young lady, he followed with the bitter verse
of Juvenal. It was an easy step to the writing of verse for patrons,

travel books for publishers who worked by subscriptions, and pamphlets that brought a profit out of controversy. He would, if he could make his work sufficiently "pathetic for the modern taste," turn out a drama or, if he could find a producer, he would offer him a two-act comedy. These had the appeal of being profitable. But now, early in the life of his periodical, he was determined to make a success. So far he had gained little note at taverns, coffee-houses, and ambassadors' halls, but he had better be noticed or else, as he threatened, he would go off to the King of Prussia to replace Voltaire (I, 30ff.). This portrait of Mr. Town, linked with his satire on contemporary literature, was hardly intended to win the kind of respect for authority that Addison and Steele had sought to gain for Mr. Spectator.

And yet a certain amount of seriousness was necessary for the periodical to survive for almost three years. Colman and Thornton recognized the need for balance even in the first number of their essay-journal, where they extended the character of Mr. Town by having him assume the function of Censor-General. Although ultimately only slightly more serious than Mr. Town, the Censor-General— modelled as he declared on "the old Roman Censor, the first part of whose duty was to review the people" (I, 1)—could gain more serious attention than an old maid or a babbler. In such a role, too, the persona could combine the functions of a Connoisseur, who commented on taste, and of Mr. Town, who concerned himself with mores and manners.

Mr. Town himself proclaimed to the public that he was its servant (II, 7), and insisted on the seriousness with which he accepted his obligations (I, 183), as well as on his incorruptibility in conduct (I, 228). In turn, as they indicated in their letters to him, his readers demanded that he act in their behalf in his role as Censor-General. Complaining about his wife's excesses of generosity, one letter-writer commanded him to present his views because "Your office, Mr. Censor, requires and leads you to hear domestic occurrences . . ." (III, 24). Another correspondent, irate over the practice of dueling, reminded the essayist that "it is your duty, as Censor General, to attack the reigning follies: as it is for the clergy to preach different sermons on the same text" (I, 162).

In relation to ladies, especially, Mr. Town was called upon to play his part as Censor-General. He himself described his concern for the female sex and its improvement. As Censor-General he had taken "a survey of the female world . . ." (I, 231). The ladies, he was told by a reader, "are naturally become the immediate objects of your care . . ." (I, 70). He was "their professed patron" and it was his duty, with his "eloquence to recommend, and . . . authority to enforce," to lay out the rules for their conduct (II, 12).

A serious Censor-General had the opportunity to carry on the important job of instruction that had been carried over from the courtesy books into periodical literature by Eliza Haywood in her *Female Spectator.* The *Female Spectator* (1744–1746) attempted "to supply answers to the feminine problems of the mid-eighteenth century." Its pages informed women readers on such "subjects as love and marriage, parent-child relationships, female education, moral and social decorum. . . ." [10] With equal concern for the education of women, the contemporary *General Magazine of Arts and Science,* beginning in 1756, provided a program of study for young ladies as well as young gentlemen. The *Lady's Museum* (1760–1761) and the *Royal Female Magazine* (1760) made similar attempts at engaging women readers in discussions that were meaningful. [11]

For the Censor-General of the *Connoisseur,* however, the treatment of the ladies did not differ from the light and rather superficial criticism that generally characterized the journal. With his customary irony the persona announced that "his chief ambition [was] to please and instruct the ladies" and that he could

[10] James Hodges, "The *Female Spectator,* a Courtesy Periodical," *Studies in the Early English Periodical,* ed. Richmond P. Bond (Chapel Hill, 1957), p. 153.

[11] For all three periodicals, see Spector, *passim.*

"congratulate [himself] upon the happiness of living in an age, when the female part of the world are so studious to find employment for a Censor" (I, 6). The concern for women in the *Connoisseur* never extended beyond criticism of such matters as their use of cosmetics, their emotionalism, their interest in gambling and parties, their addiction to over-dressing and under-dressing—topics different in kind but not in significance from those that generally composed the ironic but light comment in the periodical.

If Colman and Thornton had chosen to make the *Connoisseur* a serious periodical, they would have developed the Censor-General function of Mr. Town. Clearly that was not their decision. Instead, even with the role of Censor-General, their treatment remained lightly ironic. Assessing their effectiveness as Censor-General, they playfully noted that they had had as much success in ending gambling and other vices as "justices of the quarter-sessions" (III, 237). Even in the days immediately preceding the outbreak of the Seven Years' War, the editors failed to develop the character of the Censor-General along serious lines. They saw the public interest in news events, but responded in the old ironic tone. Expressing a fear that "the public should be called off from the weighty concerns of these papers" by their interest in war news, Mr. Town in mock-serious terms reminded his readers that

I myself am acting (as it were) in a military capacity, and . . . Censor-General Town has done his country no less service as a valiant and skilful commander at home than Major-General Johnson in America. . . . It has been my province to repel the daily inroads and encroachments made by vice and folly, and to guard the nation from an invasion of foreign fopperies and French fashions (III, 2–3).

In his role of Censor-General, the persona remained a composite of Mr. Town and the Connoisseur, and his essays, while entertaining for an audience unoccupied by more serious matters, could not survive for another half-year in the new climate of opinion during the Seven Years' War.

ARTHUR SHERBO

Some Observations on Johnson's Prefaces and Dedications

PROFESSOR Allen Hazen's *Samuel Johnson's Prefaces and Dedications,* published in 1937, still remains the best book-length study of one part of the Johnson canon. Most of Professor Hazen's conclusions on these scattered and somewhat ephemeral bits and pieces from the pen of a very busy journalist have gained wide acceptance. I am in fullest accord with most of his attributions, and where I differ with him it is with no impregnable confidence. But perhaps some questions may be profitably raised again in a review of a number of those attributions. One general point that should be made initially is that even a work like Professor Hazen's is at a number of junctures based almost wholly on subjective criteria, usually in the form of his interpretation of internal evidence. Sometimes, too, the appeal is to external evidence of dubious worth. These are the hazards that face the attributor, yet the risks must not be avoided. The pieces under discussion are taken up in order of their appearance in Professor Hazen's work.

I

Professor Hazen writes, of Johnson's presumptive help in six works by Giuseppe Baretti, that "there is external evidence for only one, *Easy Phraseology;* the rest are attributed because of internal evidence confirmed by known facts of Johnson's interests and his acquaintance with Baretti" (p. 5), and he attributes most of the first five of the seven paragraphs of the Preface to the *Introduction to the Italian Language* to Johnson. My own answer to the problem of Johnson's part in the Preface is that only the first two paragraphs are Johnson's and the last five are Baretti's.[1] Professor Hazen (pp. 11–12) also attributes to Johnson the opening two sentences of what he labels an "introduction" to Baretti's *Guide Through the Royal Academy,* and I am fairly sure that most Johnsonians will continue to concur in the attribution. But two more sentences that make up the rest of the introduction are quoted as Johnson's in *Johnson and Baretti* by C. J. M. Lubbers-Van Der Brugge (p. 143). I wonder whether those two sentences are not Johnson's also, as they complete the introductory paragraph as well as sound like him:

The subsequent lists of the Casts in the Academy, with some kind of explanation to each, may therefore be useful to those that love the Arts and desire not to love them blindly. I am able to estimate better the deficiency of that kind of knowledge in others, by the difficulty I met in obtaining that information which I am now desirous to afford.

Nothing else in the pamphlet strikes me as Johnson's, with the possible exception of the last paragraph:

Such are the embellishments of this new Seminary of Arts, and such the Models it contains for its improvement, the Originals of which have long been the delight and wonder of Mankind. Let us confidently

[1] For the reasons for my conclusion and the full text of the Preface in Italian and English, see my article, "Samuel Johnson and Joseph Baretti: A Question of Translation," *RES,* N.S., XIX (1968), 405–10.

hope in the present hour of Royal Patronage, that productions of equal perfection will soon be added to them by the rising genius of the English School.

I would argue strongly for the acceptance of the last two sentences in the opening paragraph and am willing to abide by a contrary decision, if that should be its fate, on the last paragraph.

II

Professor Hazen accepts the word of William Shaw that Johnson wrote "the title and the advertisement" for the Reverend Dr. James Fordyce's *Sermons to Young Women*. He finds a newspaper notice which he concedes might be what Shaw meant by his word "advertisement," [2] but then states that he is "inclined on the whole to ascribe the Preface to Johnson on the authority of Shaw's statement, even though there are sentences in it that hardly sound Johnsonian" (p. 34). Professor Hazen had already said that "advertisement" was "also applied regularly in the eighteenth century to the Preface" as well as "to a newspaper notice in the modern sense." The Preface consists of three paragraphs, the second of which is revised in later editions; this prompts Professor Hazen to note the possibility that the second paragraph "was originally written by Fordyce, and that Johnson's contribution was limited to the first and third paragraphs" (p. 35, n. 2). R. W. Chapman is particularly severe on the style of these paragraphs.[3] I agree with his strictures, and would add that Johnson usually avoided parentheses, of which there is one in the third paragraph, and that he very seldom used "the former" and "the latter," both of which appear in the last two sentences of the first paragraph.[4] The exclamatory "Would to God we often met there with more of the former!" that ends the first paragraph is certainly very rare in Johnson's printed works, his reluctance to invoke God in public

[2] R. W. Chapman, *RES*, XIV (1938), 362, says the style of this notice, reprinted in Hazen (p. 34), is not Johnsonian.

[3] *Ibid.*, 362–63.

[4] But see F. V. Bernard, *N&Q*, CCIV (1959), 280–81, on this matter.

being well known. I would reject the Preface in its entirety as a Johnsonian piece.

A study of the two volumes of Fordyce's *Sermons* confirms this view. The following parallels between some of Fordyce's sermons, as well as the Conclusion to the two volumes, and the Preface will show that the same person wrote them all. Here are the parallels between the Preface and the Conclusion, the latter running to twelve pages. In the Preface we find the writer using the third person singular to refer to himself and, in one place, calling himself "the preacher." The same is true of the Conclusion, with references to the "preacher" occurring on pages 335, 339, and 346. The author of the Preface is fond of upper-case letters, having recourse to such personifications (?) as "Female Sex," closely paralleled by a similar fondness in the writer of the Conclusion, among whose efforts are "Female Excellence." The Preface's "fashionable amongst the Young and the Gay" has its close counterpart in the Conclusion's "the preacher has the Youthful and the Gay for his hearers" (p. 339). A few other parallels include the use of "genteel" in the Preface and "ungenteel" in the Conclusion (p. 341). Johnson very rarely uses the word. The Preface speaks of "an auditory above the vulgar rank"; the Conclusion, of "my dear auditory." The possible argument that Johnson may have written *both* Preface and Conclusion will have to find a way around "my dear auditory," an expression it is hard to believe he would ever use, even in a piece to which he was not to sign his name. One last parallel may be mentioned: the Preface contains a reference to "those who are daily addressed in the language of Flattery," and the Conclusion echoes this with "suffer not . . . Flattery to abuse you" (p. 344).

I have read only the first two sermons, finding in the first a reference to the "preacher" (p. 8) and a sentence, "Flattery you have often heard, and sometimes, I doubt not, listened to" (p. 8), that links the writer of the Sermons with the author of the Preface and the Conclusion. The first sermon also uses "the former" and the "latter" (p. 9); twice uses, as in the Preface, the term "connected" for united by marriage (pp. 12 and 30); and, I was delighted to find, since I had claimed that a similar sentence in the Preface was un-Johnsonian, invokes God in "Would to God you knew how to improve this power to its noblest purposes" (p. 18).

The second sermon reveals, like the first, a real fondness for uppercase letters; there is the presence of "genteely" (p. 58); and the invocation "Would to God it were not too common a case!" The style of the sermons might, in many isolated passages, be mistaken for Johnson's, as there is much and skillful use of doublets and the triadic construction one has come to look for in Johnson's work. But it seems clear that the same hand wrote the Preface, the sermons, and the Conclusion; and that hand was not Johnson's.

III

The ascription to Johnson of the first four paragraphs of John Gwynn's *Thoughts on the Coronation* is based on the appearance of the 8-page pamphlet in volume XIV of the *Works* (1788) and Boswell's later statement that Johnson "lent his friendly assistance to correct and improve it," an echo of "Corrections and Improvements for Mr. Gwyn" in the Chronological Catalogue.[5] However, Bishop Percy attributed "Thoughts on the Coronation of Geo. 3, 1761 folio (The facts by Gwynne an Architect)" to Johnson in a letter to Boswell in 1772.[6] Boswell's note on Percy's attribution is an emphatic "Mr. J. only corrected it." But when, in 1790, Boswell sent a list of Johnson's prose works to Isaac Reed he described the same work as "Corrections and Additions to Thoughts on the Coronation of George III by Gwyn." Whatever else one wishes to deduce from all this, it is clear that Boswell was not quite sure exactly what part Johnson had in the pamphlet beyond "correcting" it, whatever that means and however it is to be distinguished from his "improvements."

[5] Boswell's *Life of Johnson,* ed. G. B. Hill, revised L. F. Powell (Oxford, 1934–50), I, 361, 21.

[6] May 5 and 7, 1772. *The Correspondence and Other Papers of James Boswell Relating to the Making of the Life of Johnson,* ed. Marshall Waingrow (Vol. 2, Research Edition, Yale Editions of the Private Papers of James Boswell, New York, 1970), p. 8.

Percy's statement, unknown to me until after I had reached my own conclusions, tallies very well with my decision on Johnson's share in the pamphlet. This does not add weight to my decision nor does it confer posthumous authority on Percy; the fact that the result of my analysis agrees with Percy's unsupported statement exists merely as coincidence.

The first five paragraphs of the pamphlet were "reprinted in the *London Spy,* 8 August 1761" (Hazen p. 42), arousing the suspicion that they represented an entity of some kind or other. One wishes Hazen had reprinted at least the fifth paragraph, or even a few more, in a footnote, to determine why Johnson's presumed part stopped with the first four paragraphs of the continuing prose of the pamphlet. The pamphlet is rare, and copies of volume XIV of the *Works* are not easily come by. R. W. Chapman contents himself with the statement that "it is not possible to say with precision where Johnson's friendly assistance began or ended," but adds that the third paragraph, which he quotes, was "not written by John Gwynn." [7]

Here is the fifth paragraph of the introductory part of the pamphlet:

All this inconvenience may be easily avoided by choosing a wider and longer course, which may be again enlarged and varied by going one way, and returning another. This is not without a precedent; for, not to enquire into the practice of remoter princes, the procession of Charles the Second's Coronation issued from the Tower, and passed through the whole length of the city to Whitehall.*

The asterisk indicates a footnote, a quotation from the "Life of Lord Clarendon, p. 187"; there is another footnote later in the pamphlet which quotes several pages from "Stow's Annals." These two footnotes, the fact that the fifth paragraph is inextricably linked with the first four, and the additional fact that after this fifth paragraph there follow the actual proposals for nine alternate routes the procession may take, that is, the "technical" part of the

---

[7] With Allen Hazen, "Johnsonian Bibliography, A Supplement to Courtney," in *Oxford Bibliographical Society, Proceedings and Papers,* V (1940), 144.

pamphlet or "the facts," in Percy's words, arouse the suspicion
that it is Johnson's. What is more, it is very probable that Johnson
wrote the whole pamphlet except for what I have termed the
"technical" part (pp. 346–47, largely). Beginning with the first
paragraph after the "technical" part, at the bottom of p. 347,
through to the end, the rest appears to be Johnson's—either his
original composition or a revision of Gwynn so extensive as to
amount to an original composition. A few sentences seemed particularly Johnsonian to me: "The least evil that can be expected is,
that in so close a crowd, some will be trampled upon, and others
smothered; and surely a pomp that costs a single life is too dearly
bought." "Magnificence cannot be cheap, for what is cheap cannot
be magnificent." "Part of my scheme supposes the demolition of
the Gate-house, a building so offensive, that, without any occasional reason, it ought to be put down. . . ." The use of "occasional" in this context is Johnsonian, and the last paragraph,
which also attracted Donald Greene,[8] is, I am convinced, Johnson's:

It would add much to the gratification of the people, if the Horse-
Guards, by which all our processions have been of late encumbered,
and rendered dangerous to the multitude, were to be left behind at the
Coronation; and if, contrary to the desires of the people, the procession must pass in the old track, that the number of foot soldiers be
diminished; since it cannot but offend every *Englishman* to see troops
of soldiers placed between him and his sovereign, as if they were the
most honourable of the people, or the King required guards to secure
his person from his subjects. As their station makes them think themselves important, their insolence is always such as may be expected
from servile authority; and the impatience of the people, under such
immediate oppression, always produces quarrels, tumults, and mis-
chief.

IV

There is no real justification for accepting as Johnson's the
rewriting or revision of the Preface to the third volume of Os-

---

[8] See *The Politics of Samuel Johnson* (New Haven, 1960), p. 267.

borne's *Harleian Catalogue*. It is first assigned to him by virtue of its inclusion in the 1823 *Works,* edited by Chalmers, by itself no inevitable guarantee of its authorship. Professor Hazen admits that "it is assuredly unnecessarily long, for it is chiefly an apology for the methods that Osborne has followed. I dislike to think that Johnson himself would have elaborated such a dull subject to such great length, more particularly since he wrote (forty years later) to Burney, 'A long apology is a hideous thing.' I think, with Mr. Wheatley, that Johnson rewrote or revised Osborne's draught of the Preface" (pp. 44–45). The reference to Wheatley is to an article, "Dr. Johnson as Bibliographer," in *Transactions of the Bibliographical Society of London,* Series 2, viii (1907), 39–61, in which Wheatley writes that the Preface "could scarcely have come from any other pen than that of Dr. Johnson" (p. 47). After this one would expect to find something strongly Johnsonian somewhere or other in the sixteen paragraphs, but I must confess that I do not. There is no reason why the piece could not just as properly be given to William Oldys, Johnson's fellow editor in the *Harleian Miscellany.* Why should Osborne, who had two capable writers working for him on this project, decide that he should write the Preface to the third volume of the *Catalogue?* So far as is known, Osborne took no hand in the preparation of the *Catalogue* or in the *Miscellany* itself. I would arbitrarily assign this Preface to Oldys and would also hope that it would not be reprinted as a Johnsonian piece in the future. How, it may be asked, does one, having only the final version, distinguish what was rewritten or revised from that which was originally written?

v

Johnson provided the dedication for Dr. Robert James's *Medicinal Dictionary,* and, Boswell states, on Johnson's authority, "had written, or assisted in writing, the proposals for this work" (*Life,* I, 159). L. F. Powell found copies of the proposals in the British Museum and the Bodleian and quoted two paragraphs which "prove the assertion" that Johnson helped James to write them (*Life,* III, 473). Professor Hazen (pp. 69–70) reprints four paragraphs of the Proposals, one of the two quoted by Powell and three others, prefacing his remark with the statement that "A study of the text makes it quite clear that Johnson was largely if not wholly the author." The Proposals are described as "four pages in Folio." The question to be raised with this piece is similar to that raised for other pieces: how much of this extended piece of prose should be claimed for Johnson? Two paragraphs? Five paragraphs? The entire four folio pages? I reprint the full text of the proposals at the end of this article so that my own conclusions about the whole piece may be examined against the document itself.

I must confess that I think the Proposals are almost wholly of Johnson's composition. I have read much, although I could not stomach all, of the lengthy Preface (99 folio pages) to the *Medicinal Dictionary*. It is not Johnson's; it must be Dr. James's. Indeed, the manuscript of the Preface in Dr. James's hand was found by his grandson (Hazen, p. 73). The style of the Preface is not the style of the Proposals, except possibly where the latter (most of paragraph 17, for example) could be said to possess no more style than an inventory. One close similarity between the two struck me: paragraph 20 of the Proposals refers to "Aliment, Exercise, Air, and the other Non-naturals"; in the first paragraph of the Preface appear the words "Aliment, Exercise, and all the Non-naturals." There is also the fact that paragraph 32 of the Proposals is devoted to hydrophobia and the "almost infallible" remedy provided by the use of mercury, or at least, the author writes, a multitude of experiments "have lately made it appear" so. Now, it was not until 1760, long after the Proposals had appeared in 1741, that Dr. James published his *Treatise on Canine Madness* in which he recommends mercury for hydrophobia; the only conclusion is that he provided Johnson with this very special bit of information about mercury, or that he inserted that paragraph himself. Some perusal of Dr. James's *Treatise on Canine Madness* revealed no evidence of style that would link him with the author of the Proposals.

The Proposals included a set of "Conditions," also reprinted at the end of this article, which may or may not be of Johnson's composition. Since the principal bookseller concerned was T. Osborne, under whose imprint the volumes appeared, and since in 1742, the year following the publication of the Proposals, Johnson was employed by Osborne and was still working for him in 1743 when the *Medicinal Dictionary* appeared (with a Dedication by Johnson), there is always the slight possibility that he wrote the "Conditions." But it is the Proposals and the extent to which they are Johnson's that is important. There is little doubt in my mind that Johnson wrote the first nineteen paragraphs with the possible though by no means necessary exception of the numbered sections of paragraph 17. In paragraph 20 occurs the parallel with Dr. James's Preface, mentioned above, and the possibility exists that he, rather than Johnson, wrote this one and the next four paragraphs. Paragraphs 25 and 26 are also, I think, by Johnson, simply on the basis of style. Paragraphs 27 through 33 I would assign to Dr. James. Paragraph 34, singled out by Professor Hazen for quotation, is probably by Johnson, and I believe he also wrote the next three paragraphs which conclude the proposals, even though two of them deal with the contents of the presumably yet unwritten Preface. I am painfully aware how arbitrary many, even possibly most, of these decisions must appear. If they have any merit it is owing to their lack of ambiguity—everything is unmistakably labeled—and to their volunteer status as a point of departure for further study. My decisions have had to be solely on the basis of style, and while particular sentences or phrases or usages in various paragraphs could be pointed to as evidence—that is, "Credulity, Obstinacy and Folly, are hourly making Havock in the World," and the elaborate inversion of the fourth paragraph, of which this is a part; the typical openings of paragraphs 5 and 7, "To establish" and "Of these writers"; and the concluding part of paragraph 8, "so that what is not to be found in *this* Dictionary, it will be generally in vain to seek in *any other;* but what is wanting in *others,* may be more successfully inquired for in *this*"—it is largely on a comparison of the Preface with the Proposals that I have made a number of my decisions. I am somewhat emboldened to give some of the writing of the Proposals to Dr. James by Johnson's statement, made years later in 1776, about "Dr. James, whom I helped in writing the proposals for his Dictionary and also a little in the Dictionary itself." [9]

VI

Proof of Johnson's contribution [to Lenglet Du Fresnoy's *Chronological Tables*, 1762] is scanty but certain. In the advertisement of the book in *Lloyd's Evening Post* the booksellers placed at the top "Recommended by Samuel Johnson." This can only refer to the Preface, and the style of the Preface is indubitably Johnson's. Both from the style and the genial thrust at the French, I think that the Dedication may have been revised by Johnson, and I have therefore included the text of the Dedication, but it is hardly a Johnsonian utterance (Hazen, pp. 85–86).

Some of the reasoning here is open to question. It is not at all inevitable that the words "Recommended by Samuel Johnson" should refer "only" to the Preface; indeed, the booksellers would not, one is fairly sure, have been ambiguous if they had a "Preface" by Johnson to use in puffing their publication. That the style is undubitably Johnson's must always be a matter of opinion. I find nothing distinctively Johnsonian about it; R. W. Chapman shared Professor Hazen's belief that it is Johnson's, although he could discover "no reason for thinking that Johnson may have revised the dedication." I would reject both the Preface and the Dedication; Professor Hazen, it is clear, holds no brief for the latter's inclusion in the canon. The only real reason for ascribing the Preface to Johnson is the presence of a few ambiguous words in a bookseller's newspaper advertisement. It might be added, for whatever it is worth, that Johnson in his Preface to Robert Dodsley's *Preceptor* (1748) discusses chronology, naming works by some seven chronologists; Du Fresnoy's work is not mentioned,

---

[9] Donald Greene has suggested to me that Johnson's statement may mean, by taking the first "in" as equivalent to "by," that he wrote *all* the Proposals but only helped a little in the Dictionary itself.

and none of the seven chronologists named in the Preface to *The Preceptor* appears in the Preface to the 1762 translation of Du Fresnoy—although one set of tables, those of Dr. John Blair, *are* referred to in the Du Fresnoy Preface.

It may be well to conclude by quoting a paragraph from R. W. Chapman's review (note 2, above) of Professor Hazen's book.

There is probably no English prose writer to whom the test of style has been applied with greater confidence than it has been applied to Johnson. But Boswell warned us that we must be careful. Johnson's style was freely imitated and some of the imitations were good. I have to confess that I once took the *Adventurer* on a day's outing—being then ignorant of the key furnished by initial signatures—and by the end of the day was at a loss to tell Hawkesworth from Johnson. Often, indeed, a sentence is overwhelmingly affirmative; oftener, I think, a single phrase is damningly negative. But a colourless paragraph may leave a cautious critic unwilling to decide. It is, moreover, necessary to distinguish the marks of Johnson's early, middle, and late styles. The scholastic stiffness of his early bookworm days is very different from the armchair eloquence of the Great Cham.

No one, it is clear, should expect easy acceptance of his intuitive judgment of what is, or is not, Johnson's style unless he can either show striking parallelisms of ideas and stylistic preferences or unless he has enough good external evidence with which to support his opinion.

APPENDIX

CONDITIONS AND PROPOSALS FOR ROBERT JAMES'S
Medicinal Dictionary

CONDITIONS

London, June 24, 1741.

I. That the whole Work will make about Four Hundred Sheets in Two Volumes, *Folio;* to be printed in the same letter as the *General Account of the Work* hereunto annex'd, and on the same Paper with these Proposals.

II. That for the better Accommodation of the Purchasers, Five Sheets will be delivered to the Subscribers every Fortnight, stitch'd in a Cover. Price One Shilling.

It is admitted, that some present Publications give a Sheet more for the same Price; but when it is observed, That the Proprietors of Those have already been reimbursed the Copy-money, and all other Expences, with a considerable Profit, from the Sale of many Editions, it is presumed, a wide Difference will be discerned, and this Article will be thought a very reasonable one; especially when the great Quantity of Matter contained in every Sheet is duly considered.

III. That every Folio Cut shall be reckoned as one Sheet of Print, without any additional Expense to the Subscribers.

IV. The First Number shall be published on the First of *January* next, and the following Numbers regularly every Fourteen Days after, without any Intermission, until the Whole is finished.

That the Publication may not be interrupted by any accidental Difficulty, the Booksellers will take care, that several Numbers shall be printed before the Appearance of the first.

The Printing of this Useful and Laborious Performance being undertaken by the Society of Booksellers for promoting Learning, &c. The better to enable them to ascertain the Number to be printed, such Gentlemen as are inclined to encourage it, are desired to subscribe their Names (or to send Orders so to do) in a Book kept for that Purpose by James Crokatt, at the said Society's Office, near *St. Bride's* Church in *Fleetstreet;* or to T. Osborn, Bookseller, in *Gray's-Inn, Holborn;* and the Numbers shall be sent them regularly; no Money being required but on the Receipt of each Number, as printed.

A GENERAL ACCOUNT OF THE WORK

1. As those to whom the foregoing Proposals shall be offered, may justly require an Account of the Design which they are requested to encourage, it seems necessary to subjoin a distinct View of our Undertaking, by which its Extent may be comprehended, and its Usefulness estimated.

2. It is doubtless of Importance to the Happiness of Mankind, that whatever is generally useful should be generally known; and he therefore that *diffuses* Science, may with Justice claim, among the Benefactors to the Public, the next Rank to him that *improves* it.

3. Physic is an Art which every Man practices, in some degree, either upon himself or others. Many Indispositions appear too trivial to demand the Attendance of a Physician, and many Occasions require immediate Assistance; Men are, in the first Case, tempted by the Prospect of Success, and, in the second, obliged by Necessity, to depend upon their own Skill; and it is therefore their Interest to be so far instructed in Physic, as not to exasperate slight Disorders by an absurd Regimen, and Medicines misapplied, nor suffer themselves, or others, to perish by sudden Illness, or accidental Disasters.

4. That almost every Family is furnished with general Axioms of Physic, to which every Case proves an Exception; and with universal Remedies, by which no Distemper was ever cured; that Superstition, Prejudice, Ignorance and Mistake, have assigned to every Plant, and every Medicine, Qualities widely different from those which Nature has allotted them; and that Credulity, Obstinacy and Folly, are hourly making Havock in the World; is obvious to the slightest Observation.

5. To establish juster Notions in the Bulk of Mankind, and introduce more useful Medicines into Families, has been charitably attempted ·sometimes by familiar and easy Reasonings, and sometimes by Collections of approved and well-proportioned Prescripts; but as the Endeavours of the scientific Writers have hitherto failed, for want of being sufficiently extensive; and as *good* Medicines are neither less liable than *bad* to be misapplied, nor less pernicious in unskilful Hands; we have endeavoured to supply all the Defects of those that have gone before us, and at once to familiarize the Knowledge, and reform the Practice, of Physic, by publishing A Medicinal Dictionary.

6. Many Medicinal Dictionaries have been already written, some by ·men whose only Praise was Assiduity and Labour; others, by such as added Learning to their Industry; and some, perhaps, by those, to whom an impartial Critic would have allowed neither the Wages of Labour, nor the Laurels of Science, who have transcribed Truth and Error without Distinction, have been too ignorant to lop off the Superfluities of their Predecessors, and too lazy to supply their Defects.

7. Of these Writers, the best, equally with the worst, have proceeded upon a Scheme which our Design resembles in nothing but in persuing, like them, the Order of the Alphabet. They endeavor to explain the *Terms* only; we, together with the Terms, the *Science* of Physic. They enable their Readers to *name* Distempers, which we instruct them to *cure.* Their Attempts were indeed useful, and are therefore to be mentioned with Gratitude: The Knowledge of Words must necessarily precede the Study of Science; this Knowledge they undertook to facilitate, and have succeeded so well, that often nothing can be added to the Accuracy of their Explications; and such Passages we have carefully translated without the weak Ambition of concealing the Benefit by unnecessary Variations.

8. The Diligence with which we have consulted and compared them, will probably make them less necessary to future Students, as we have not only transfused all their Collections into our Work, but added many Terms hitherto omitted; so that what is not to be found in *this* Dictionary, it will be generally in vain to seek in *any other;* but what is wanting in *others,* may be more successfully inquired for in *this.*

9. After an exact Explication of the technical Words of Physic, we have laid out our Endeavours upon an accurate Description of the Human Body. In which not only the general Distribution of the Parts and Œconomy of the animal Functions will be shown; but the Texture, Form, Situation, Articulation, and Uses of the Bones, the Origin, Insertion and Uses, of every particular Muscle, the Situation, Texture and Uses of all the Glands, and the Humours separated by them from the Mass of Blood, together with the Texture, Situation, and Functions of all the Viscera, and the Course of the Nerves, Arteries and Veins, will be explained. And under the Article Anatomy, a Catalogue of the Anatomical articles will be given, that the Reader, by turning to them, may have a separate Treatise of Anatomy, in which nothing shall be willingly omitted, that has been transmitted by the Antients, or discovered by the Moderns. We shall endeavour to exhibit every Muscle, Bone, Vein, and Vessel, every thing to which a Name has been assigned, all the minute Inquiries of the Microscope, and all the probable Conjectures of those Philosophers who have endeavoured to extend their Knowledge to Parts and Operations which even the Microscope cannot examine.

10. The Art of dissecting, injecting, and preparing Bodies, is an Appendage of Anatomy too important to be neglected; and we have

therefore endeavoured to illustrate it with the Care particularly necessary in treating of Operations not easily understood without ocular Observation.

11. The *Materia Medica* of the Antients lies, at present, in great confusion: Many Plants, and even Animals, were called by different Names by the *Greeks,* in different Ages, and even at the same time in different Parts of *Greece.* This Variety of Names has so much obscured the Authors who have written on the *Materia Medica,* that it has been not unusual for Botanists to lose their Time in searching after a Plant mentioned by some of the Antients, when they have been well acquainted with it by another Name.

12. Nor has only Labour been wasted by this Perplexity, but Life itself often endanger'd; for great Virtues being attributed to some Plants by the Antients, it has frequently happened, that Physicians, deceived by the Name, have used Plants of very different Qualities. No Care has therefore been omitted, that might contribute to disentangle the Confusion of this Part of physical Learning, by collecting the different Names of the same Things, and distinguishing different Things too frequently mentioned by the same Name, as far as proper Authorities could be found to support our Opinion. And, in order to give the Curious an Opportunity of making further Improvements in this Article, the Sum of what *Theophrastus, Dioscorides, Pliny,* the *Rei Rusticae Scriptores,* &c. have said of particular Plants, Minerals, and Animals, will be given, and compared with the Accounts of more modern Authors.

13. But that we may not appear to have been anxiously employed in Inquiries of Curiosity, or barren Learning, we have inserted every Article of the *Materia Medica* now in Use, whether Animal, Vegetable, or Mineral; with its Description, the Manner of counterfeiting it, its Analysis, Virtues, and History.

14. Nor have we confined ourselves to *Simples;* but have extended our Examination to all the *Officinal Compositions* in present Use, and have remarked their Excellencies and Defects, and the Alterations that have been made in them since their first Introduction into Practice.

15. As it is the Interest at least, and perhaps the Duty, of every Author to consider the Advantages of his own Country with a more particular Regard, an Account will be given of all the *British* Plants made use of either in Medicine or Food, in which their particular Qualities

will be specified. This, with an Analysis of Animal Food, will compose a *Treatise of Aliments,* equally useful for the Preservation and Recovery of Health.

16. The Art of *Chymistry* will only fall under our Consideration as a Branch of Pharmacy, for we are writing not a Philosophical, but a *Medicinal Dictionary;* and we shall think our Labour usefully bestowed, if we shall, by a familiar Explanation of its Terms and Processes, clear it from that Obscurity that has been thrown upon it, generally by the Folly of the Ignorant, but perhaps sometimes by the Envy of the Learned.

17. All these Sciences, however *difficult* and *extensive,* are only preparatory to the great *Hippocratic* Art of Curing Diseases, an Art which we shall endeavour to illustrate with a Degree of Attention in some measure proportioned to its Importance; and conceive no Method more proper than that of exhibiting, under every Distemper.

1. Select Cases of those who died of the Distemper treated of, with an Anatomical Description of the Parts affected, as they have appeared upon Dissection; by which the immediate Causes of Diseases, and the concomitant Symptoms, may with most Certainty be discovered.

2. An accurate Description of the Disease, in which the Symptoms that are peculiar to it, and distinguish it from all other Distempers, will be diligently remarked.

3. The Prognostics, being Directions for judging whether the Disease is likely to terminate in Health, Death, or some other Distemper.

4. The Method of Cure, both in regard to Regimen and Medicine, as laid down by the principal Authors; in which the Practice will be regularly deduced, from the Age of *Hippocrates* to the present time.

5. Select Cases in Confirmation of the Doctrine laid down, which will be collected, not only for the Information of the Reader, but with some regard to his Entertainment.

18. By the careful Perusal of this Part, Students will be made early acquainted with the Doctrine of *Hippocrates,* an Author in general much more talk'd of than read, and whose Writings have contributed more to the Advancement of Physic, than those of all the rest of Mankind; and with which, therefore, Physicians ought to begin and end their Studies, instead of mis-spending their most improveable Days in reading Compilers of Theories and Systems.

19. It is not pretended that this Book will make every Reader a complete Physician; but it will be some Recommendation of the Work, if

it shall enable Mankind to detect the Impostures of confident Pretend-
ers to Physic, and escape those frauds which are often practised at the
Expence of Life; and shall instruct those who live remote from Physicians, so to regulate themselves upon the first Attack of any sudden
illness, as not to make Help ineffectual, before it can be procured.

20. It is well known, that the Cure of many Chronical Distempers,
perhaps all of them, depends more on a proper *Regimen* than *Medicines*. This Part of the Work, therefore, will be of some Importance to
the *Diseased* and *Valetudinary,* as it will give them full Directions
how to conduct themselves with regard to their Aliment, Exercise,
Air, and the other Non-naturals.

21. There are no Cases in which more frequent, and more fatal Errors
are committed, than in those *peculiar* to *Women,* because they usually
commit themselves to the Care of such as are equally ignorant of
Medicine with themselves, and whose Skill consists in a few vulgar
Prejudices, which they religiously adhere to. For this Reason, particular Instructions are given for the Cure of those Disorders, to which
Women are exposed in *every Part* of their Lives.

22. As the *Art of Healing* is of too much Importance to be sacrificed
to Vanity, we have been careful to mention every Medicine, of the ef-
ficacy of which we are convinced by Evidence or Experience, tho' we
are not able to explain its Operation. We have therefore endeavoured
to preserve all the *Empirical Remedies* that have fallen within our Observation, and have been particularly exact in the Examination of
those which have obtained any uncommon Degree of Reputation.

23. Surgery and Physic are equally necessary, were antiently practiced
by the same Persons, and are by their own Nature so much allied, that
they contribute to the Illustration of each other. We have therefore inserted in this Work

A BODY OF SURGERY: Containing,

   I. A General History of Surgery.
  II. An Account of Tumours of all Kinds; with their Prognostics,
     and the Methods of curing them.
 III. A Treatise of Ulcers, with their particular Remedies.
 IV. A Treatise of Wounds in general, and of Wounds in particular
     Parts, and made by particular Instruments.
  V. A Treatise of Fractures and Luxations, with the Art of Reducing
     them.

VI. An Account of Chirurgical Operations and Bandages, and a Description of all the instruments used in Surgery.

24. All the Chirurgical Operations will be annexed to the Anatomical Description of the Parts to which they relate, when they are not distinguished by a particular Name.

25. That the Alphabetical Order, by which these Articles will be dispersed in different Parts of the Work, may produce no Perplexity or Confusion of Ideas; under the Article of Surgery, will be given a Catalogue of the subordinate Articles relating to Surgery, that the Reader may, by consulting it, have a distinct View of the whole Science.

26. There was a Time, when those whom Providence had blessed with Leisure, Affluence, and Dignity, did not think it any Diminution of their Characters to attend to the Necessities of the Indigent, and alleviate the Miseries of the Diseased. And how little they have deserved from Mankind, who have laid out their Rhetoric and their Wit, in representing this kind of Charity as ridiculous, useless, and pernicious, is apparent, from the melancholy Condition of Multitudes, who, disabled by Sickness from their daily Employments, languish and perish without Assistance. Had this Charity been better directed, and the *Warmth of Benevolence* assisted by the *Light of Knowledge,* it had perhaps never sunk into Neglect; its *Success* would have defended it from Contempt, and Levity and Inhumanity would have been afraid to attack it. If it should ever revive, it may perhaps, hereafter, exert a more beneficial Influence; and we shall have this great Satisfaction, That our Endeavours have enabled Virtue to assume its natural Dignity, and to set at Defiance the Insolence of the Proud, the Thoughtless, and the Cruel.

27. The Universal Advantage which we propose to promote by this Work, determined us to insert

THE MEDICINE OF ANIMALS:

28. As Cattle, Horses, Dogs &c. which have been hitherto either intirely neglected, or cultivated by Men very little qualified to advance it. Many Hints have been taken from the Medicine of Brutes, and very rationally applied to that of Man; for the Action of Simples must be nearly the same, in both; and the Parts of different Animals have such a Resemblance, that, with proper Cautions, an Experiment made upon one, may be of great Use with regard to the other. It is not

therefore only for the Preservation of those Animals, tho' that alone is a very important Consideration, that this Part of the Work has been compiled. It is chiefly intended as a System of *Comparative Physic,* and its great Use will be, That by improving the Art of curing the Distempers incident to *Horses,* and other *domestic* Animals, it will contribute to the Advancement of *Physic* in *general.* In order therefore to facilitate the Progress of the Art, proper Hints will be given, and rational Experiments will be recommended, under the particular Articles of each Distemper.

29. The Moderns have been extremely prolix in the Pharmaceutic Part of Farriery, and too negligent in describing the Diagnostics, or Symptoms, by which every Distemper is distinguished from all others. To these, the Antients have been more attentive, and have left us valuable Monuments of their Industry and Sagacity, which were collected into a Volume, by the Direction of the Emperor *Constantine Porphyrogenitus,* and are fortunately preserved. They appeared first, in a *Latin* Translation, by *Ruellius,* printed at *Paris* in 1530. And in 1537, *Grynaus* published them in the original *Greek* at *Basil:* Since then, they have been translated into *Italian* and *French.* There is said to be a very old Manuscript of this Book in the Library of *Emanuel-college, Cambridge;* and it is to be wished, that some Man of Learning and Leisure enough for the Undertaking, would oblige the World with a new Edition of it, as the Matter of it is really valuable, and the *Basil* Edition rarely to be met with.

30. The other Observations on this Part of Physic, are collected from the *Geoponica* published by *Needham, Vegetius,* and the *Rei Rusticae Scriptores,* without omitting the best and most rational Methods of Cure recommended by the Moderns.

31. We hear of frequent Barbarities committed on Animals, without any higher Motive than Curiosity or Wantonness; and of very few Experiments, which have been made with a View of curing their Diseases, tho' of much greater Importance to Mankind; because Horses, Dogs, and other Animals, have Distempers attended with the same Symptoms as our own: Thus Dogs are subject to Epileptic Fits, especially Spaniels and Pointers; and 'tis not to be doubted, that if Mankind had been diligent in finding out a Remedy for them, the same might have been applied with Success to those of Men.

32. The *Hydrophobia,* a Madness produced by the Bite of mad Dogs, had, in all past Ages, eluded the Power of Medicine; but a Multitude

of Experiments made upon Dogs, and afterwards upon Men, have lately made it appear, that Mercury is a Remedy which is infallible for that terrible Disease, which has, in all Ages, been complained of as incurable, and which has been therefore so justly dreaded.

33. We therefore recommend it to every Man, to be diligent in taking all Opportunities of making Experiments on the Distempers of Animals, and candid in communicating them to the Public. Nor shall we fail in this Work to assist them, by pointing out the Methods of persuing them with Probability of Success.

34. As an Inquiry after those who have contributed to our Advantage, is not only the Consequence of a natural Curiosity, but of a laudable Gratitude, the *History of Physicians,* being an Account of the Lives, Writings, and Characters of the principal Authors in Physic, will be inserted in the Work, as their Names occur in the Alphabet.

35. The Whole will be introduced with a Preface giving a Sketch of the Origin, Progress, and State of Physic in all Ages; the different Sects that have arisen, and the various Revolutions the Practice of Physic has been subject to, as different Systems of Philosophy have happened to prevail. In this Part it will be shewn, how far the Progress of this important *Art* has been retarded, by adhering too rigidly to *Theories,* however specious or elaborate.

36. As many Distempers, which were accounted incurable in the earliest Ages, are still equally formidable, it must be owned, not only the Art of Healing is still imperfect, but that it has not been promoted in the same Degree with other Sciences. We have therefore diligently noted the Defects and Desiderata of Physic throughout the Work; and in the Preface, which will contain the History of Physic, shall point out the Causes that have retarded its Improvement.

37. As the Compilers of *Dictionaries of Science* have, either from Negligence or Vanity, for the most part, omitted to support their Assertions by Authorities, their Collections have necessarily this Defect, That their Credit can rise no higher than that of the Compiler, and therefore are of little Use in Questions of Importance. Against this Objection, of which the Weight is felt in every Inquiry, we shall secure our Performance by an accurate and regular Quotation of the Authors whose Doctrine we shall adopt; and shall, by this Practice, add to the other Uses of our Work, that of a copious Repertory of Physic; or, A general index to the best authors.

The Drama

WILLIAM W. APPLETON

The Double Gallant in Eighteenth-Century Comedy

WHEN OSCAR WILDE first discussed *The Importance of Being Earnest* he described it as a comedy of double identity in the eighteenth-century manner. Strictly speaking, he had no real occasion to go back a hundred years to find a play that celebrated the pleasures of being Ernest in town and Jack in the country. Dion Boucicault's *London Assurance* (1841) could have provided him with virtually all the necessary ingredients, but Wilde was right in observing that the theme of double identity particularly preoccupied the eighteenth century. *She Stoops to Conquer* and *The Rivals* are the familiar examples of the genre. There are many lesser examples as well, however, such as Colley Cibber's *The Double Gallant* (1707) and Arthur Murphy's *The Way to Keep Him* (1760). Not only do the heroes with two faces keep turning up in eighteenth-century comedy but also those surrogate figures—the rival brothers and contrasting beaux.

Many factors contributed to this. The divided nature of theatrical audiences in London after 1688 has often been noted. Spectators for the comedies of Cibber included gouty Restoration men-about-town and fresh-faced daughters of merchants, members of the Kit-Kat Club and members of the Society for the Reformation of Manners. The social cleavage in the audience had its parallel in the philosophical shift that was taking place, with the cynical realism of Hobbes slowly giving way to the benevolent optimism of Shaftesbury. Manners were also changing. A span of a hundred years separates Etherege and Sheridan, and though their plays share certain surface similarities, the social attitudes which underlie them differ fundamentally. To illustrate the nature of these changes, a small number of scholars have recently begun to examine the relationship of comedy and courtesy literature. The approach can be illuminating.

The most fully developed such study, D. R. M. Wilkinson's *The Comedy of Habit* (1964), focuses specifically on Francis Osborne's *Advice to a Son* (1656) and its impact on the Restoration theatre. As John E. Mason in his standard work on courtesy literature observes: "Osborne's book is an epitome of the worldly thought of the seventeenth century; and as such it deserves to rank as a mirror of its time with Machiavelli in the sixteenth century, and Chesterfield in the eighteenth." [1] Osborne's cynicism and urbanity, as Wilkinson points out, reflect the late Cavalier mood of Etherege and Sedley. Dorimant, the hero of Etherege's *Man of Mode* (1676), typifies the witty, dissembling, misogynistic beau of the Restoration. But while Osborne's advice epitomized the easygoing morality of the court of Charles II, it had little application to other times and other places. Appointed minister to Ratisbon after the death of Charles, Etherege found the provincial capital stifling and his libertine manner a constant source of scandal. Conversely, Sedley, once the terror of the watch, succumbed to the Glorious Revolution by dwindling into a respectable old age.

After 1688 the Restoration gentleman seemed increasingly

---

[1] *Gentlefolk in the Making* (Philadelphia, 1935), p. 69.

anachronistic both on and off-stage. More and more noticeably women were becoming a power in the theatre, and the playwright Thomas Shadwell was becoming the spokesman for "those damned unfashionable qualities called virtue and modesty." [2] In *The Squire of Alsatia* (1688) he sketched the portraits of two brothers: Belfond Senior, "bred after his father's rustic swinish manner, with great rigor and severity," and the more liberally educated Belfond Junior, "an ingenious, well accomplished gentleman, a man of honor." Modeling his play upon Terence's *Adelphi,* Shadwell set out to define a new Man of Mode, deliberately developing a series of parallels between Belfond Junior and Etherege's Dorimant. Both men are examined in relation to three women—a cast-off mistress, a current mistress, and a wife-to-be—but the calculating egotistical hero of Etherege's comedy has been transformed into a generous, good-hearted rake, who anticipates Fielding's Tom Jones. Shadwell was acutely aware of the changing moral climate, and in *Bury Fair* (1689), as in *The Squire of Alsatia,* he reformed the wild gallant through the agency of a good woman. Similar alterations in the character of the Restoration beau are also evident in the plays of Congreve.[3] Mirabell's constancy to Millamant and Valentine's fundamental seriousness would have astonished the light-hearted Dorimant. (Characteristically, Etherege's Dorimant quotes airily from Waller while Congreve's Valentine cites Epictetus.)

Though both Congreve and Shadwell successfully refashioned their comic heroes to conform to the new age, other playwrights during the critical decade from 1698–1708 were less happy.[4] The floundering comedies of Thomas Baker and Charles Burnaby show how difficult it was to restyle Restoration materials for more sober tastes. Colley Cibber, for one, could accommodate himself to these

[2] *The Miser* (London, 1672), Act 1.

[3] Jean Gagen, "Congreve's Mirabell and the Ideal of the Gentleman," *PMLA,* LXXIX (1964), 422–27.

[4] See John Loftis, *Comedy and Society from Congreve to Fielding* (Stanford, 1959), pp. 43–76.

changes, but equivocation was his forte. In place of the robust comic certainties of Etherege's *She Would if She Could* (1667) he substituted the sly ambiguities of *She Would And She Would Not* (1703). His skill in striking a precarious balance between cynical and homiletic comedy is equally evident in *Love's Last Shift* (1696) and *The Careless Husband* (1705). But nowhere is his awareness of the temper of the age more conspicuous than in *The Double Gallant* (1707). Atall, the title character, clearly derives from the Restoration seducer, but he is sensitive to the changing times and the new techniques they call for. As the gay and rakish Colonel Standfast he woos the romantically-inclined Clarinda; as the modest and demure Freeman he courts the more retiring Lydia. "What a happy fellow is this," his friend Clerimont observes, "that owes his success with women to his inconstancy!" Cibber's resourceful hero calls to mind the Protean Colonel Fainwell in the later comedy *A Bold Stroke for a Wife* (1718), but Mrs. Centlivre's hero undertakes his four different wooing roles not through choice but necessity. Cibber's Atall is keenly aware of the advantages of duplicity in a changing social world.

The difficulties playwrights faced in finding a suitable comic hero are nowhere more evident than in the plays of Farquhar. In his first two comedies he experimented with two variations of the Restoration wild gallant—the coarse-fibered Roebuck and the epicene Sir Harry Wildair. In *The Twin Rivals* (1703), a play of high originality, his search continued.[5] The twin rivals are, however, equally intolerable—the one a chocolate-house version of Richard III, the other a sententious prig. Evidently Farquhar found distasteful both the Restoration man of fashion and the newly emergent man of sentiment. *The Recruiting Officer* (1706), his next-to-last play, draws once again upon conventional Restoration types, but by the simple expedient of removing them from the drawing rooms of London to the fresh air of Lichfield, Farquhar gave them a new vitality. In his last play, *The Beaux' Stratagem*

[5] See Eric Rothstein, "Farquhar's *Twin Rivals* and the Reform of Comedy," *PMLA*, LXXIX (1964), 33–41.

(1707) he resolved the problem of finding a hero by providing the audience with not one but two—the self-seeking Archer and the tender-hearted Aimwell, the one in the tradition of Hobbes, the other a follower of Shaftesbury.

The device of the twin heroes also proved useful to the young Richard Steele. The contradictions in the character of "the sentimental debauchee," as Swinburne called him, are clearly evident in his first play, *The Funeral* (1702), with its two contrasting couples, the grave Lord Hardy and Lady Sharlot and the sprightly Campley and Lady Harriot.[6] (The sour reception of Steele's pietistic *Christian Hero* had taught him the value of compromise.) But despite the farcical undertaker scenes, the prevailing mood of the play is serious, and its tone anticipates *The Conscious Lovers* (1723). During the twenty-one years that elapsed between the production of the two plays, Addison and Steele established themselves as arbiters of taste. The didactic impulse in both men was irresistible. Who can forget Addison's death-bed tableau, as carefully staged as that of his hero Cato? In *The Conscious Lovers,* originally entitled *The Fine Gentleman,* Bevil Junior epitomizes the gentlemanly ideals expressed in *The Tatler* and *The Spectator.* Variously described as a sentimental, genteel, and exemplary comedy, *The Conscious Lovers* is, above all, a courtesy play.

Among the sizable number of theatrical essays in *The Tatler* and *The Spectator* two are devoted to a discussion of Dorimant, the *beau ideal* of an age which Steele deplored.[7] Young Bevil is Steele's answer to Etherege. In the manner of a scientist performing a controlled laboratory experiment, the playwright manipulates Young Bevil into a series of situations designed to test him. The famous original occasion of the play, the hero's adroit and honorable avoidance of a duel, dramatizes a favorite topic of the courtesy books. Also linked to such literature are Bevil's sententious dis-

---

[6] Shadwell anticipates both Steele and Farquhar in his use of contrasting couples. See John H. Smith, *The Gay Couple in Restoration Comedy* (Cambridge, Mass., 1948), *passim.*

[7] *The Spectator,* Nos. 65 and 75.

cussions of opera and European travel and his exemplary displays
of conduct in the presence of his father, Indiana, and Signor Car-
bonelli, the music-master.

While Steele's hero did not, of course, find universal acceptance (John Dennis bluntly characterized him as a "sordid hypo-
crite"), he did at least offer a real alternative to the Restoration
man of mode and Steele's audiences were, for the most part, painfully eager to be instructed. It was a century that abounded in
"School" plays—schools for lovers, fathers, greybeards and
guardians—and eighteenth-century booksellers' shelves groaned
under the weight of guides to conduct.

Typical of such works is William Darrell's much-reprinted
The Gentleman Instructed (1704), a pastiche of earlier courtesy
books, supplemented by generous selections from Locke's *Essay
on Education* (1693). Though Darrell was writing for a public that
presumably subscribed to the doctrines of Shaftesbury, his own assumptions were those of Hobbes. "Man is by nature half beast,"
he writes, but he may be "rendered tractable by education and
discipline." [8] To be a gentleman is to go against nature. In discussing the most effective means of disguising one's true instincts,
Darrell quite properly makes use of the metaphors of the stage.
He counsels his readers thus: "You must act two parts; of a gentleman and of a Christian." "To begin with the part of a gentleman, persuade yourself it's your duty and interest to act it well." [9]
The ladies are similarly cautioned to "act the part of a Christian"
that they may be received with "a plaudite." The Gentleman Instructed, by implication, is above all a successful masquerader.

The tone of Darrell's book would doubtless have astonished
Castiglione, but by the eighteenth century times had changed. The
new Cortegiano called himself Beau Nash. At Bath, the new Ur-
bino, he posted the famous set of rules that codified the standards
of behavior for a new order of society based not on "birth, character, or royal patent, but on the capacity to lead in the beau
monde." [10] One suspects that Castiglione's ideal Renaissance cour-

[8] *The Gentleman Instructed* (London, 9th ed., 1727), p. 85.
[9] *Ibid.*, pp. 7–8.   [10] Mason, *Gentlefolk*, p. 285.

tier would not have greatly appealed to him. Nash's overriding concern was with man as a social being, in the salon or the ball-room. In matters of dress and etiquette he was imperious. Woe to the woman who dared to appear in public in a white apron, or to the man who had the audacity to wear boots at a ball! Though he had his more serious aversions as well—he disapproved strongly, for example, of duelling and scandal-mongering—Nash personi-fied the man of fashion in his attention to decorum and ceremony rather than the gentlemanly ideals of earlier courtesy literature.

But in spite of the example set by the King of Bath, a num-ber of playwrights continued to debate the nature of a gentleman. Typical of these is Elizabeth Cooper. In *The Rival Widows, or The Fair Libertine* (1735), she contrasts the liberally educated and rakish Young Modern with the strictly disciplined Young Free-love. Anxious to impress Lady Bellair, Young Modern, in the manner prescribed by Darrell, adopts a pious manner. His good-hearted uncle, outraged by his imposture, rebukes him for his hy-pocrisy. Only too happy to drop the pretense of piety, Young Modern joyfully promises to return to downright sinning, but his uncle flares up once again. "Dost thou think because I hate hypoc risy I love a profligate and abandoned debauchee?" he asks. De-spairing of finding a true gentleman, the uncle opts for a lady in-stead and disowns Young Modern in favor of Lady Bellair, a libertine "in name only." Apparently she has worn the mask of worldliness more effectively than Young Modern the mask of vir-tue.

Among the most interesting minor plays dealing with the dis-integrated gentleman is Arthur Murphy's *The Way to Keep Him* (1760). The central character, Lovemore, clearly derives from Sir Charles Easy in Colley Cibber's *The Careless Husband* (1705). "Subdued by a dose of matrimony," he finds himself irresistibly drawn to an attractive widow of Protean charms—"That quick-ness of transition from one thing to another! that round of variety! and every new attitude does so become her!" Posing as Lord Eth-eridge (the choice of name can hardly have been accidental), Lovemore decides to court this Mayfair Cleopatra. In a scene which foreshadows *The School for Scandal,* Mrs. Lovemore conceals herself while her husband, as Lord Etheridge, makes his addresses to the widow. Interrupted by the entrance of a rival suitor, he finds his true identity revealed and retires in confusion. His imposture is sympathetically treated, however. An infinite variety, Murphy suggests, is not only the spice of life but also the best possible insurance against the creeping monotony of marriage. In such circumstances who can blame a husband for assuming the mask of "the gay, the florid, and the magnifique" Lord Etheridge?

In *She Stoops to Conquer* (1773) Goldsmith not only made use of the theme of double identity but also dramatized the dilemma of the would-be gentleman. Like Farquhar, he rejected both the harsh cynicism of the Restoration *ethos* and the pious hypocrisies of genteel society. Young Marlow, by nature a warmhearted, brisk young man, in the presence of Miss Hardcastle freezes into a shy, inarticulate suitor. Unable to reconcile pleasure and virtue, he seems to have taken to heart William Darrell's advice to avoid wit, high spirits, and the artful snares of women. Understandably, Miss Hardcastle sets out to effect his cure, and assuming the role of barmaid, she tricks him into reverting once more to his normal, engaging self.

Though Goldsmith deplored the hypocrisies of the age— "There are few that do not condemn in public what they practice in private"—the mask and the imposture were increasingly taken for granted. While the eighteenth century prided itself upon its capacity for reason, it was also an age of fraud—of a Cock Lane ghost and a rabbit-woman, a William Ireland and an Ossian. The hero with two faces is the characteristic product of such an age.

Richard Cumberland's *The Choleric Man* (1774), like *She Stoops to Conquer,* is in part a play of double identity, in part a courtesy play. But Cumberland's modest comedy was completely overshadowed by the appearance, during the same year, of Lord Chesterfield's *Letters.* Despite his emphasis on the importance of the graces and the necessity of cultivating an ingratiating social manner, Chesterfield considered himself in the great tradition of courtesy-writers. His somewhat frigid attitude toward Beau Nash perhaps stemmed from the suspicion that he saw in the Bath dictator a parody of his own ideas. But while Chesterfield insisted upon the importance of Christian virtues and professed a concern with the whole man rather than merely social man, he did so in terms of such suave ambiguity that they disturbed many. "Every man of any education would rather be called a rascal, than accused of deficiency in the graces," [11] growled Dr. Johnson, and Boswell piously echoed his sentiments, deploring the "glossy duplicity" of Chesterfield's advice.

Thanks to the Reverend John Trusler's *Principles of Politeness* (1775), his lordship's worldly counsels had reverberations far beyond the fashionable salons. It was not Trusler's purpose to clarify the paradoxes in Chesterfield but to simplify the letters and make them "useful to every class of youth." His book was evidently designed as a companion-piece to his other best-sellers, *How to be Rich and Respectable* and *The Art of Carving*, forerunners of today's self-improvement manuals. From the time of Richardson the size of the reading public had vastly increased, and Trusler's highly successful digest shows how widely appreciated was the practicality of Chesterfield's advice. The public was willing enough to accept the superficial definition of a gentleman.

Sheridan was no exception. Since the dissolution of the Restoration ideal, playwrights had been in search of a gentleman-hero and a new tradition of manners. Sheridan was by nature too lazy to waste much time in such a search. That the times had changed and "deprived [him] of any acceptable ideal of manners and decorum" [12] does not seem to have bothered him. If his was an age of fraud and compromise, no man was better suited to give it dramatic expression.

Drawing upon familiar materials and situations, *The Rivals*

[11] James Boswell, *Life of Johnson* ed. Hill-Powell (Oxford, 1934–50), III, 54.

[12] Marvin Mudrick, "Restoration Comedy and Later," *English Stage Comedy* (English Institute Essays, 1954), p. 125.

(1775) is a pastiche of earlier comedies, among them Steele's *Tender Husband,* Cibber's *The Double Gallant,* and Frances Sheridan's unfinished *Journey to Bath.* One might go still further and describe *The School for Scandal* (1777) as an anthology.[13] In *The Rivals* Young Absolute's masquerade as the penniless Ensign Beverly typifies the hero of the comedy of double identity. In *The School for Scandal* Sheridan gives us the most complex of such comedies by contrasting Joseph Surface, the hypocritical "man of sentiment," with his brash, good-natured brother, Charles. They epitomize the dichotomy of the age.

A writer in *The London Magazine* commented, "Every man under thirty is, indeed, in some measure, a Joseph or a Charles." [14] A good many, like Sheridan himself, were both. It has become commonplace nowadays to interpret the mid-eighteenth century as an age of paradox and contradiction. Even the robustly cynical Samuel Foote has been unmasked as a "sentimental satirist," [15] and the sentimentalists themselves reappraised as highly ambiguous figures, compounded of benevolence and self-interest, humility and pride.[16] It would not have occurred to Sheridan that there was anything unnatural in these seeming contradictions. He obviously did not share Mrs. Malaprop's sense of outrage when Captain Absolute's imposture as the penniless Ensign Beverly is revealed: "There's no more *trick* is there? You are not like Cerberus three gentlemen at once, are you?" It was an essential part of Sheridan's talent as a politician, playwright, and patentee that he could indeed play three gentlemen at once.

The attacks on Sheridan's plays as mere pastiches, brilliantly devised, but artificial in effect because they are not informed by

[13] Sheridan's debts to Wycherley and Congreve are obvious. See also *Plays and Poems of R. B. Sheridan,* ed. R. Crompton Rhodes (New York, 1929), II, 10–13.

[14] Quoted in Rhodes, II, 12.

[15] Robert V. Wharton, "The Divided Sensibility of Samuel Foote," *Educational Theatre Journal,* XVII (1965), 31–37.

[16] Paul E. Parnell, "The Sentimental Mask," *PMLA,* LXXVIII (1963), 529–35.

any clear set of values, are familiar enough. But if the values in his comedies are muddled and superficial, it is not necessarily the playwright who is at fault, for to a very real extent he dramatizes for us the world of Nash and Chesterfield.

The Slanderers, one of Sheridan's preliminary sketches for *The School for Scandal,* has as its setting the Pump Room in Bath.[17] It centers on the efforts of Lady Sneerwell to break up a match between her ward, Maria, and Clerimont, the young hero. Enlisted in her campaign are Mrs. Candour and Sir Benjamin Backbite, fellow-members of the College of Scandal. In its light-hearted way Sheridan's sketchy two acts might be called a modest *drame à thèse* on Beau Nash's life-long attempt to discourage gossip and vilification. The theme is, of course, carried over into *The School for Scandal,* and the conclusion of the play, with the ignominious dismissal of Lady Sneerwell and Joseph Surface, would have had the unqualified approval of the King of Bath, who concluded his famous code with the hope that: "All whisperers of lies and scandal be taken for their authors. That all repeaters of such lies and scandal be shunned by all the company—except such as have been guilty of the same crime." [18]

Joseph Surface is judged not only by the standards of Beau Nash but also by those of Chesterfield. Quite clearly, he is a gentleman *manqué.* Although he has evidently taken to heart Chesterfield's observations on the utility of acquiring a reputation for virtue, he has never really mastered the art of dissembling, and his oily hypocrisies deceive no one except the gullible Sir Peter. However perfunctory Chesterfield may have seemed in paying lip service to Christianity, he stressed that the compliance so necessary to social success related to manners, not morals.[19] He was careful also to draw a fine distinction between simulation and dissimulation [20]—a distinction which, one suspects, escaped Jo-

[17] See Rhodes, II, 126–38.
[18] Oliver Goldsmith, *Life of Richard Nash* (London, 1762), p. 33.
[19] See Chesterfield's letter to his son dated October 19, 1748.
[20] See Chesterfield's letter to his son dated January 8, 1750.

seph Surface. In short, Chesterfield would have indicted Joseph on more than one count for his failure as a gentleman.

It is a commonplace of criticism to see Joseph as the Blifil of Sheridan's comedy and Charles as its Tom Jones. To a very real extent they do, of course, represent two polarities. But to reject Joseph is not necessarily to accept Charles. For all his good humor and generosity, Charles is conspicuously lacking in the *je ne sais quoi*. His drinking bouts, his extravagance, and even his casual disposal of the family portraits relate him to the cautionary examples in the courtesy books.

Sheridan in *The Rivals* had compelled his hero to play two parts. In *The School for Scandal* he divided him. As his own father observed, "He had but to dip in his own heart and find there the characters of Joseph and Charles." [21] As a businessman and parliamentarian Sheridan schemed and manipulated with a skill that would have dazzled Joseph. In his private life he outdid Charles in his extravagance, charm, and recklessness. It did not occur to him that the two brothers represented irreconcilable alternatives. Like so many men in his period, he accepted both.

Sheridan, like Cibber, has paid a heavy penalty for his nonchalant refusal to impose upon his work a unified point of view, though such notable earlier plays as *The Plain Dealer* are equally subject to this charge. It was more than a mere matter of chance that both he and Goldsmith instinctively turned for inspiration to the playwrights of the last decade of the seventeenth century. Both the 1690s and the 1770s were marked by the same sense of social confusion, and the playwrights of both periods resorted to the same devices to express that confusion—double identity and the double-hero. In the course of a century society had undergone conspicuous changes. In Sheridan's time it had become a society in which servants not only assumed the names of their masters but affected their manners as well. It was increasingly difficult, in fact, to tell exactly who or what anybody was. As Sir George Airy comments in Mrs. Cowley's *The Belle's Stratagem* (1782):

[21] Quoted in Rhodes, II, 12.

And what is the society of which you boast?—a mere chaos, in which all distinction of rank is lost in a ridiculous affectation of ease, and every different order of beings huddled together as they were before the creation. In the same *select party* you will often find the wife of a Bishop and a sharper, of an Earl and a fiddler. In short, 'tis one universal masquerade, all disguised in the same habits and manners (II. i).

In such a society the concept of a gentleman had become hopelessly blurred. Congreve was perhaps the last to make effective use of the conventions codified in Francis Osborne, but even he modified his heroes to conform to a changed climate of opinion, and later comic dramatists, with the exception of Steele, found great difficulty in recognizing the true gentleman among the masqueraders. Sheridan's confusion becomes even more understandable when one recalls that a century later dramatists such as Robertson were still asking the question: "What is a gentleman?"

MORRIS FREEDMAN

Milton and Dryden on Tragedy

I

OF THE SEVERAL POINTS of relationship between Milton and Dryden, none reveals their characteristic differences more sharply than their writing of tragedy and their theorizing about it. While Dryden in his criticism was often tentative, exploratory, hypothesizing, wide ranging, prolific, occasionally apologetic, Milton was certain, definitive, traditional, peremptory, unqualified, sharply committed, almost cursory, certainly brief. "Dryden wrote his criticism experimentally and skeptically," Samuel Holt Monk wrote, "and he was never ashamed of changing his mind." [1] W. P. Ker said of Dryden: "He is sceptical, tentative, disengaged, where most of his contemporaries, and most of his successors for a hundred years, are pledged to certain dogmas and principles." [2] Dryden's criticism is voluminous. Very nearly all of Milton's critical comment may be found in the prefaces to *Paradise Lost* and *Samson Agonistes*. In these, he leaves the impression of an unchanging single-mindedness. In his writing of tragedy, Dryden worked in virtually all the modes and tried every

[1] "Dryden Studies: A Survey," *ELH*, XIV (1947), 63.
[2] *Essays of John Dryden* (Oxford, 1900), I, xv.

technique popular during his lifetime. Milton published only one tragedy, on the classical model, although he put down notes for a number of tragedies. Originally, of course, he had thought of *Paradise Lost* as a drama and retained features in it of classical tragedy even in the final, epic form.

Each writer pursued critical ends independently of the other, and each had different purposes in the writing of tragedy, but we may read their works in and on tragedy as a dialogue, each of them representing separate but obviously related traditions. In the decade between 1668 and 1678 appeared their major contributions in tragedy: Dryden's *Essay of Dramatic Poesy* (1668) with its satellite works, both before and after; his *Secret Love* (1668), which, written in the same period as the *Essay,* may be read as a practical illustration of its principles; [3] Milton's *Samson Agonistes* (1671) with its preface, the title of which evokes that of Dryden's *Essay:* "Of That Sort of Dramatic Poem Which Is Called Tragedy"; *The State of Innocence* (1677), Dryden's attempt, after eliciting Milton's consent, to adapt *Paradise Lost* as a rhymed tragedy; and, finally, Dryden's *All for Love* (1678), with its preface, the only other drama of the time to be written so nearly in the manner of *Samson Agonistes.*

II

The Essay of Dramatic Poesy is one of the great critical discussions by a writer about some of the practical and theoretical problems he had to consider and to resolve. Like such later declarations by "an artificer in his own art," [4] those by Coleridge,

[3] "Probably he wrote it before *Annus Mirabilis* and after the first draft of *An Essay of Dramatick Poesie:* most likely in the winter and spring of 1665–66," writes John Loftis. "He thus wrote it at approximately the time he was taken up with the speculations recorded in the essay, a circumstance that helps to explain the obvious relevance of the theories examined there to the dramatic practice embodied in the play." *The Works of John Dryden,* ed. Loftis and Vinton A. Dearing (Berkeley and Los Angeles, 1966), IX, 333.

[4] Preface to *All for Love* in *Of Dramatic Poesy and Other Critical Essays,* ed. George Watson (London, 1962), I, 225.

Wordsworth, Arnold, and Eliot, for example, it must have influenced taste in Dryden's own time and, by establishing certain expectations, affected standards of judgment. Milton's own great works of that period, an epic in blank verse and a tragedy in the ancient manner, specifically violated the rules proclaimed as proper regarding rime and tragedy by the prominent dramatist and critic shortly to be named Poet Laureate. Since Dryden's *Essay* might prejudice readers against *Paradise Lost* and *Samson Agonistes,* Milton had to speak critically in his own defense. George Saintsbury early noted that "the insertion of the paragraph [on rime preceding *Paradise Lost*] was an afterthought; and that Milton was not in the best of tempers at having to write it is pretty evident." [5] Milton's preface to *Paradise Lost* may also be read as his curt contribution to the general controversy on rhyme versus blank verse then going on as well as his defiant defense of the verse of the epic. [6] It would be surprising, however, if Milton, after going through the *Essay,* had been moved to take exception only to the arguments supporting rhyme, which were not so important as the more inclusive and more expansively discussed questions about tragedy. Milton's views on tragedy were less ambivalent than those on rhyme, stronger, and of longer standing [7] (after all, we do find rhyme in his works before and after *Paradise Lost,* and even in the epic, although unsystematically and spottily there).

Several scholars have disagreed about the date of composition of *Samson Agonistes.* [8] The arguments for an early dating of

[5] *A History of English Prosody* (London, 1908), II, 236. See also my "Milton and Dryden on Rhyme," *HLQ,* XXIV (1961), 337–44.

[6] David Masson described Milton's paragraph as "nothing else than Milton's contribution to the controversy in his own interest." *The Life of John Milton . . .* (London, 1880), VI, 634.

[7] Ida Langdon, *Milton's Theory of Poetry and Fine Art* (New Haven, 1924; New York, 1965), *passim.*

[8] A summary of their arguments may be found in *Complete Poems and Major Prose,* ed. Merritt Y. Hughes (New York, 1957), pp. 531–32. Allan H. Gilbert has argued for an earlier date than 1671 for the preface itself: "Is *Samson Agonistes* Unfinished?" *Philological Quarterly,* XXVIII (1949), 98–106. Ernest Sirluck in *JEGP,* LX (1961), 773–81, vigorously rejected

the play, however, do not apply with equal force to the dating of
the preface, which only one scholar has wished to date earlier than
1671. This element of uncertainty somewhat inhibits a consideration of the preface as a direct "response" to Dryden's *Essay*. Nevertheless, it may still be argued that, regardless of when Milton
began or finished the play, he could have written the preface itself
shortly before publication, after the appearance of the several critical exchanges between Dryden and Sir Robert Howard about
the nature of tragedy. Perhaps of greater importance is the fact
simply that the play and its preface were presented to a public
already addressed at length by Dryden, both in criticism and in the
theatre. That is, *Samson* and its preface would have been read in
their time in the context of the prevailing discussion about tragedy,
and it is how we may read them too.

  Milton's theory of tragedy, expressed at length in only one
place and embodied in only one play, seems simple, possibly even
simplistic, compared with Dryden's complex, sometimes complicated, certainly changing and more elaborated positions, from the
time of the *Essay of Dramatic Poesy* (1668) to "The Grounds of
Criticism in Tragedy" (the preface to *Troilus and Cressida*, 1679).
Dryden, obviously, kept modifying his theory and his practice, in
response to experience, observation, and argument. His shifts and
modulations reflected a pragmatic, empirical, working involvement
with the critical issues.[9] In striking contrast, Milton's preface has
the quality of an idealized distillation, summary and magisterial, a
pronouncement *ex cathedra:* it carries both authority and history.
Samson itself stands as a monument to the traditional, crystallizing
a form, perhaps the only example: a Christian tragedy with a
Greek structure and tone.[10] Like his other major poems, Milton's

---

"the two main arguments for dating the composition of *S.A.* in the period
from the early 1640s to the early 1650s," that of Gilbert and that of William Riley Parker.

  [9] See Arthur C. Kirsch, *Dryden's Heroic Drama* (Princeton, 1965), pp.
3–33, esp. pp. 3–8, "Some provisos for reading Dryden's criticism."

  [10] George Steiner acutely points to the dilemma of definition: *"Samson
Agonistes* is difficult to get into focus, exactly because it comes so near to

drama constituted an original, highly individual work on a solid, tried foundation. Dryden's examinations of tragedy are nearly conversational, an attentively searching dialogue with himself and others, the musings aloud of a literary man on his craft. His tragedies make up an anthology of the range of tragic forms of the time.

The provenance of Milton's theories was Aristotle and Horace as filtered mainly through the Italian critics, but possibly also through Heinsius.[11] For Dryden, the immediate sources, as they emerge in his several essays of the decade, were Boileau, Bossu, Corneille, Racine, and Rapin,[12] even though he regularly defended English against French drama. Milton's preface to *Samson Agonistes* emerged from the stream of tragic theory that flowed into England by way of Italy; Dryden's commentaries helped introduce into England the predominantly French stream. Eric Rothstein has summed up Dryden's critical importance: "The general position held by Rapin received the support, in England, of Dryden's extraordinary authority: slightly modified, that position dominated English speculation on tragedy for at least the next fifty years." [13] Earl R. Wasserman, in describing the division in the views about the pleasures of tragedy that occurred during the middle of the seventeenth century, allies Milton's with the earlier, predominantly

---

making good its presumptions. . . . Like all Christian tragedy, a notion in itself paradoxical, *Samson Agonistes* is in part a *commedia*" (*The Death of Tragedy* [New York, 1963], p. 31).

[11] Joel E. Spingarn, *A History of Literary Criticism in the Renaissance* (New York, 1898), pp. 80–81; Langdon, *passim;* Marvin Theodore Herrick, *The Poetics of Aristotle in England* (New Haven, 1930), pp. 35–79. Allan H. Gilbert, *Literary Criticism: Plato to Dryden* (New York, 1940), p. 517, nn. 15, 17; Paul R. Sellin, "Sources of Milton's Catharsis: A Reconsideration," *JEGP*, LX (1961), 712–30.

[12] Ker, I, xiii–lxxi; John M. Aden, "Dryden and Boileau: The Question of Critical Influence," *SP*, L (1953), 491–509; Aden, "Dryden, Corneille, and the *Essay of Dramatic Poesy*," *RES*, n.s., VI (1955), 147–56; Watson, I, v–xvii.

[13] "English Tragic Theory in the Late Seventeenth Century," *ELH*, XXIX (1962), 314.

Italian theories (he quotes a portion of Milton's preface to *Samson Agonistes* as an instance of these); of the later theories, one was predominantly French, Descartes by way of Rapin and Dennis, two writers whose criticism was intimately related to Dryden's.[14]

Milton's participation in the seventeenth-century symposium on tragedy, however, was not so much in his offering specific new theories as in his enlarging the territory, shifting the emphasis, elevating the tone; actually, his stands on the mixing of the serious and the comic and on the unities were defended vigorously enough by other participants, although no one talked about catharsis in quite the same terms as he did. The focus of the Dryden-Howard debate was, finally, on recent and contemporary examples, Corneille, Shakespeare, Beaumont and Fletcher, Jonson; the ancients were cited respectfully enough, but somewhat tangentially. The emphasis was practical and immediate. All but one of the individual essays by Dryden and Howard that cluster around the *Essay of Dramatic Poesy* were issued as prefaces to published versions of produced plays.[15] Milton's concerns by contrast were not narrow, "practical," or immediate. He unequivocally favored the ancients over the moderns, reversing the balance in Dryden. He explicitly rejected a stage presentation of *Samson Agonistes*. It was a strictly literary work, to be read not to be acted. Modern theatrical needs had reduced tragedy to a "small esteem, or rather infamy." [16] He cited writers of tragedy and critics remote in time and place from Corneille or Jonson, who, it happened, did respect forms of the classical rules but were "modern" writers, concerned with gratifying audiences. In his preface Milton was determined to provide a

---

[14] "The Pleasures of Tragedy," *ELH,* XIV (1947), 287. See also H. G. Paul, *John Dennis* (New York, 1911), p. 172.

[15] Sir Robert Howard's *Four New Plays* (1665) and *The Great Favourite* (1668); Dryden's *Rival Ladies* (1664) and *The Indian Emperor* (1668). The exception was the preface to *Annus Mirabilis* (1667).

[16] From Milton's preface to *Samson Agonistes,* "Of That Sort of Dramatic Poem Which Is Called Tragedy," in *The Complete Poetical Works of John Milton,* ed. Douglas Bush (Boston, 1965), p. 517. All subsequent quotations from the preface are from this source, pp. 517–18.

traditional, an ancient, a universal, a pre-Christian and Christian, an authoritatively settled sanction for the writing of tragedy.

Tragedy for Milton was as distinguished a medium for prophetic statement as epic. Milton, writer of epic, sometime spokesman for the English people, was no less a man "in highest dignity" than the great nonprofessional writers of tragedy whose names he called as witnesses in support of his own role. Thus, he particularly separated himself from such writers for the stage as Dryden. Milton asked to be judged in the company of Aeschylus, Sophocles, and Euripides, "unequaled yet by any," and not in that of the recent French and English writers, *even* Jonson and Shakespeare, of whom in his youth he had said a good word. Milton's reminder was brusque: that tragedy belongs to an ancient, decorous order of noble discourse, and that its governance is subject to graver determinants than the corrupt gratification of an unfit audience in the company of "other common interludes." Milton thought the rules well established, needing only to be well observed. Dryden, of course, was pioneering in the reconsideration of the old rules and the search for new ones.[17]

III

Samson Agonistes and its preface added up to a formidable contribution to the contemporary discussion of the proper forms tragedy should take. Masson called Samson "Milton's third appearance in behalf of blank verse in the controversy then raging," and he noted about the preface that "the points discussed are exactly such as might have been discussed in a critical essay by Dryden or Boileau." [18] Ker felt it necessary to remind us that "*Samson Agonistes* was not written merely as an experiment in Greek poetic form." [19] Dryden's involvement with Milton's work after 1671 may be understood as his critical and creative responses to the challenges offered by both *Paradise Lost* and *Samson Agon-*

[17] See Hoyt Trowbridge, "The Place of Rules in Dryden's Criticism," *MP,* XLIV (1946), 84–89.
[18] *Life,* VI, 666 and 670.   [19] *The Art of Poetry* (Oxford, 1923), p. 57.

istes with their accompanying critical appendages. The reasoned searching after proper forms and "probable rules," to use Trowbridge's phrase, which marked the *Essay of Dramatic Poesy* continued to be a defining quality of Dryden's career through the 1670s.[20]

Sometime after *Samson Agonistes* appeared, Dryden visited Milton to ask permission to turn *Paradise Lost* into a "Drama in Rhyme." [21] All the references we have to Dryden's "memorable visit" to Milton, as Masson called it,[22] however, were recorded after Dryden's adaptation was done and may have taken into account the accomplished task as well as the initial intention. It is possible that Dryden wanted to see the epic merely in rhyme and not necessarily in play form also. As Scott put it, Dryden hoped to supply the "essential deficiency" in *Paradise Lost* of the "want of the dignity of rhyme." [23] But between Dryden's first reading of the epic, possibly in 1669, and his adapting it, probably sometime late in 1673 or early in 1674, *Samson Agonistes* appeared, a drama largely in blank verse, and Dryden may have modified his original plans in order to test the question of rhyme in epic and in drama simultaneously.

Whatever Dryden's original intention, the finished work, on which he spent only a month, suggests that he was subdued by the Miltonic materials. He disclaimed any attempt to rival the original, virtually apologizing for having to publish his version.

To satisfy the curiosity of those who will give themselves the trouble of reading the ensuing poem, I think myself obliged to render them a reason why I publish an opera which was never acted. . . . I was . . . induced to it in my own defence; many hundred copies of it being dispersed abroad without my knowledge or consent: so that every one gathering new faults, it became at length a libel against me; and I saw,

[20] "Place of Rules in Dryden's Criticism," p. 96; also Watson, *passim*.
[21] See my "Dryden's 'Memorable Visit' to Milton," *HLQ*, XVIII (1955), 99–108. See also John Aubrey, "Minutes of the Life of Mr. John Milton," in *The Early Lives of Milton*, ed. Helen Darbishire (London, 1932), p. 7.
[22] *Life*, VI, 708. ·
[23] Walter Scott, *Memoirs of John Dryden* (Paris, 1826), I, 158–60.

with some disdain, more nonsense than either I, or as bad a poet, could have crammed into it at a month's warning; in which time 'twas wholly written, and not since revised. After this, I cannot, without injury to the deceased author of *Paradise Lost*, but acknowledge that this poem received its entire foundation, part of the design, and many of the ornaments, from him. What I have borrowed will be so easily discerned from my mean productions, that I shall not need to point the reader to the places: and truly I should be sorry, for my own sake, that any one should take the pains to compare them together; the original being undoubtedly one of the greatest, most noble, and most sublime poems which either this age or nation has produced.[24]

Although *The State of Innocence* was one of Dryden's most popular published plays,[25] its main importance for us is its testimony that Dryden was working closely with Milton's text in the mid-seventies.

IV

In 1678, a year after *The State of Innocence* was published, prefaced by its extravagant declaration of debt to Milton, *All for Love* appeared. By this time, Dryden appears to have known *Samson* especially well. A number of verbal echoes from Milton's play have been found in Dryden's other plays of that time; more to the point, such echoes have been found in *All for Love* itself.[26] In writing a blank verse drama modeled on what were then more or less thought of as the classical rules, Dryden the artist was taking up a form whose worth Dryden the critic was implicitly acknowledging. Milton's play was part of the preparation Dryden brought

[24] Watson, I, 195–96.

[25] Hugh MacDonald, *John Dryden: A Bibliography* . . . (Oxford, 1939), pp. 115 ff.

[26] Samuel Langbaine in 1691 found an "Instance . . . of his borrowing from Mr. Milton's *Sampson Agonistes*" in *Aureng-Zebe* (1675); see *Critical Essays of the Seventeenth Century* (Oxford, 1909), ed. Joel Spingarn, III, 131. Mark Van Doren suggested (*John Dryden,* New York, 1946, p. 104) that the opening lines of *Samson* affected at least one scene in Dryden and Lee's *Oedipus* (1679). See my note *"All for Love* and *Samson Agonistes," N&Q,* CCI (1956), 514–17; also, Edward S. Le Comte, *"Samson Agonistes* and *Aureng-Zebe," Études Anglaises,* XI (1958), 18–22.

to the writing of *All for Love*. Whatever other works may have also influenced Dryden's handling of the Shakespearean Antony-Cleopatra raw material, none was so substantial as *Samson*.[27]

Perhaps the most significant dramaturgic contribution of *Samson Agonistes* to *All for Love* was in its providing a compressed framework into which the sprawling Shakespearean matter might fit. The tone and texture, if not the details of plot, derive from Milton rather than from Shakespeare. Like Samson, Antony goes through a series of self-revealing confrontations. "Dryden's play begins with Antony in utter despair, shut off from the world in the temple of Isis," [28] like Samson in Milton's play, eyeless in Gaza. Both men have insulated themselves from their worldly failures. The Olympian Shakespearean hero who makes his own worlds, seemingly self-conceived and self-determined, recognizably mortal, is diminished, domesticated, in both Milton and Dryden to a figure shaped by patriotic and familial sentiments. Dryden's Antony resembles Samson in his filial character particularly; his pieties are Puritanical rather than Roman. Ventidius incorporates in his role some of the functions of Manoa and the chorus of *Samson*. The structural rhythm of *All for Love* resembles that of *Samson* in its waiting, in its succession of set scenes, in its accretive movement toward a climactically defining act. In both works, as R. J. Kaufmann said about *All for Love,* the "identity crisis" comes at the end of a career.[29] It is the seeking after and finding of *his*

---

[27] See Kirsch, p. 134 ff.; also H. Neville Davies, "Dryden's *All for Love* and Thomas May's *The Tragedie of Cleopatra Queen of Egypt*," *N&Q*, CCX (1965), 139–44, and "Dryden's *All for Love* and Sedley's *Antony and Cleopatra*," *N&Q*, CCXII (1967), 221–27. An interesting possibility is that Dryden caught hints in Milton's *Samson* of Shakespeare's *Antony and Cleopatra:* see Alwin Thaler, *Shakespeare's Silences* (Cambridge, Mass., 1929), pp. 167–68, which notes some thin verbal echoes from Shakespeare's play in Milton's.

[28] Moody E. Prior, "Tragedy and the Heroic Play," in *Dryden: A Collection of Critical Essays,* ed. Bernard N. Schilling (Englewood Cliffs, N.J., 1963), p. 96.

[29] R. J. Kaufmann, "On the Poetics of Terminal Tragedy: Dryden's *All for Love,*" in Schilling, p. 92.

final "true self" that frees Samson from his suicidal despair and commits him to a triumphant death that becomes other than self-annihilation, that makes a life, a world, well lost. So also does Antony progress to a triumph of self over self. In their chosen deaths, Samson and Antony defined their lives.

The critical links between *All for Love* and *Samson* suggest how Dryden was modifying some of his suppositions about tragedy as he was writing in the genre. In the preface to *All for Love* Dryden announced that he wished "to be tried by the laws of my own country; for it seems unjust to me that the French should prescribe here till they have conquered." [30] This disclaimer of French influence is especially striking since the play has such clear French neoclassical antecedents. Dryden singled out the artist-critic as the master to follow in matters of creation: "Poets themselves are the most proper, though I conclude not the only critics. But till some genius as universal as Aristotle shall arise, one who can penetrate into all the arts and sciences without the practice of them, I shall think it reasonable that the judgment of an artificer in his own art should be preferable to the opinion of another man. . . ." [31] Aside from Dryden himself, Milton was the only writer of stature of the time who met the criterion for criticism that Dryden formulated here. Milton was a practising artist, and his *Samson,* in stated intention and fulfillment, offered an English model, the preface to which was "the judgment of an artificer in his own art."

The preface to *All for Love* was a curious piece of criticism in several respects. "The cavalier dismissal of rhyme towards the end of the preface," Watson points out, "strikes a new note in [Dryden's] criticism, and one to be heard often in his later career: a confident indifference to public favour, except as it may affect his pocket, and a readiness to indulge his own current interests in his prefaces without much regard for relevance." [32]

At least some of these "current interests" may well have had to do with Milton, and they therefore suggest a greater relevance in the preface than at first appears. The rejection of rhyme, for ex-

[30] Watson, I, 225.   [31] *Ibid.*   [32] *Ibid.,* I, 221.

ample, may be Dryden's momentary concession to Milton's argument against it; it follows hard upon the nearly humble, gracious acknowledgment to Milton in the introductory remarks to *The State of Innocence.* We may hear a number of piquant echoes here from Milton's preface to *Samson Agonistes.* The opening of the *All for Love* preface repeats some of the formulations of the *Samson* preface.

> The fabric of the play is regular enough, as to the inferior parts of it; and the unities of time, place, and action more exactly observed than, perhaps, the English theatre requires. Particularly, the action is so much one that it is the only of the kind without episode, or under-plot; every scene in the tragedy conducing to the main design, and every act concluding with a turn of it.[33]

Later, Dryden cites Dionysius and Seneca as Milton does, and, finally, toward the conclusion, virtually paraphrases Milton although alluding to Rymer. "It remains that I acquaint the reader that I have endeavoured in this play to follow the practice of the Ancients, who, as Mr. Rymer has judiciously observed, are and ought to be our masters." [34] Dryden was soon to address himself extensively to Rymer, in 1679, in "The Grounds of Criticism in Tragedy," but even there one passage in particular parallels Milton in sound and sense:

> . . . two different independent actions distract the attention and concernment of the audience, and consequently destroy the intention of the poet: if his business be to move terror and pity, and one of his actions be comical, the other tragical, the former will divert the people, and utterly make void his greater purpose. Therefore, as in perspective, so in tragedy, there must be a point of sight in which all the lines terminate; otherwise the eye wanders, and the work is false. This was the practice of the Grecian stage.[35]

Milton:

> . . . the poet's error of intermixing comic stuff with tragic sadness and gravity, or introducing trivial and vulgar persons, which by all judicious hath been counted absurd, and brought in without discretion, corruptly to gratify the people.

[33] *Ibid.,* I, 222.   [34] *Ibid.,* I, 230.   [35] *Ibid.,* I, 244.

A few lines later Milton speaks of "the Greek manner." George
R. Noyes believes that Dryden's passage was influenced by Boileau, Rapin, Bossu, and Rymer.[36] In view of Dryden's rejection
earlier in the preface both of French critics and of critics who
were not also artists, Milton as an English poet-critic has at least
an equal claim with them to inspiring Dryden on these points.

Although we may regard Milton's and Dryden's contributions
to tragedy in terms of a dialogue, Milton nowhere refers directly
to Dryden, and Dryden's direct references to Milton—most of
them to *Paradise Lost*—may be enumerated quickly. Yet even this
empty space has meaning. The paucity of direct links reveals how
differently each addressed himself to the problems.

Milton's focus was on the work of art, on the statement it
made in form and in content. His comment on the verse of *Paradise Lost* was elicited by the publisher in an effort to "satisfy"
readers who might be expecting rhyme as a consequence of the
new fashion. The preface to *Samson Agonistes* prepares readers
expecting a different form of tragedy. In both the epic and the
tragedy, the prefaces scarcely hoped to accomplish the critical
ends that the works themselves would. Although Milton maintained varying degrees and kinds of intimacy with Andrew Mar-
vell and Sir Robert Howard, among others in the literary world,
he was quite isolated from the current literary scene after the Restoration. While we may comfortably assume that he talked with
friends and visitors about theoretical questions, he did so from the
sidelines, not as an active participant. He did not engage in any
direct critical exchange with members of the literary establish-
ment, for example, much less seek their approval, although he
may well have welcomed Dryden's recognition and respect.

By contrast, Dryden was exceptionally, perhaps excessively,
conscious of his image as a literary figure.[37] Although he displayed courage in praising *Paradise Lost* so soon after Milton's
death, his normal response to Milton was more naturally reticent

---

[36] *The Poetical Works of Dryden,* ed. Noyes (Boston, 1950), xxxiv.
[37] See Kirsch, pp. 5–6.

and qualified, implicit rather than explicit. Dryden openly confronted contemporary writers, mean or exalted, only when they
might too readily change public taste and judgment in directions
he deemed inappropriate by the eminence of their persons, the
force of their arguments, or the popularity of their works. For example, Dryden felt, "lest his own critical respectability should
suffer," [38] as Watson puts it, that he had to take most soberly Rymer's contorted strictures on tragedy, which have largely amused,
annoyed, and baffled later readers. "His deference to Rymer,"
Kirsch writes, "amounted almost to fear." [39] He had already delivered some of his most important and extensive critical comments
in exchanges with Sir Robert Howard, his brother-in-law, whose
literary status depended largely on his family connection. But
Rymer and Howard were figures whose critical pronouncements,
for whatever reason, carried more weight than those of a poet in
obscurity and disgrace. Dryden might read Milton and might as-
similate his arguments, but it was hardly necessary to make a
point gratuitously, so to speak, of answering them specifically and
publicly at any length. Dryden absorbed and applied Milton crea-
tively and critically, the highest acknowledgment by one professional literary man of another.

[38] Watson, I, 238.   [39] Kirsch, p. 6.

MALCOLM GOLDSTEIN

Pathos and Personality in the Tragedies of Nicholas Rowe

"HE? WHY, HE WOULD LAUGH all day long! He would do nothing else but laugh!" [1] In this pleasant fashion Alexander Pope once spoke of his friend Nicholas Rowe. Such a comment reminds us that the temperament of an author does not always affect the tone and style of his work in the most obvious or predictable manner, for Rowe wrote seven tragedies and only one comedy: *The Biter,* a dull, confused work. Of the tragedies, three were, moreover, popular for generations; during the eighteenth century *Tamerlane, The Tragedy of Jane Shore,* and *The Fair Penitent* were so frequently staged that virtually every great performer from Thomas Betterton to the Kembles appeared in them.[2]

[1] Joseph Spence, *Observations, Anecdotes, and Characters of Books and Men,* ed. James M. Osborn (Oxford, 1966), I, 109.

[2] Emmett L. Avery, "The Popularity of *The Mourning Bride* in the London Theaters in the Eighteenth Century," *Research Studies of the State College of Washington,* IX (1941), 115–16, shows that after Shakespeare

All seven are crowded with emotional scenes designed to wring the hearts of viewers. Yet, sad though they may be, they are not profound plays, but plays of the sort that a light-hearted man would be likely to write. In their exaggerated emotional passages Rowe's disposition reveals itself, if only obliquely. It is evident also in the shaping of the plots, many of which are rich and lively, but in some instances at the expense of consistency in character development. Pathos, not tragedy on the grand scale of the drama of antiquity or the English Renaissance, was the level of his aspiration. On occasion he wrote passages of direct, vigorous verse, but frequently his dialogue is so overwrought as to seem lacking in serious purpose.

With good reason, Rowe is recalled today as, above all else, a creator of tragic roles for women. His most interesting works are *The Fair Penitent* and *Jane Shore,* two of his three "she-tragedies." The term "she-tragedies" itself is presumably Rowe's own invention, for its first recorded use occurs in the epilogue to *Jane Shore*. He was not, of course, the first dramatist of his age to write ample feminine roles; Lee, Dryden, Otway, and Banks, to name only four writers, offered memorable tragic parts to Restoration actresses. But with the exception of Banks, no other playwright so frequently turned to the feminine view for tragic themes as did Rowe. All his tragedies, not the "she-tragedies" alone, contain substantial parts for women, and most are concerned chiefly with the attitudes of the female characters toward love, marital fidelity, and the double sexual standard—that is, toward matters pertaining to private rather than to public concerns, such as state, religion, and politics, although to a degree these also figure in the plays. Devoted, hostile, meek, stormy, open-handed, selfish, worldly, and naive, women continually take the center of Rowe's stage, pushing aside even such formidable figures as Tamerlane and Ulysses. To examine representative female roles in his plays

the three plays were, as listed above, the second, third, and sixth most frequently performed tragedies between 1702 and 1776.

is to note what is most characteristic of his style in its best and worst aspects alike and to learn something of the expectations of his audiences, as well as something of the expectations of his actresses.

Writing a quarter of a century after the first production of *The Ambitious Stepmother* (1700), Rowe's first play, John Dennis somewhat cryptically asserted that Rowe had originally taken the work to Drury Lane, where it was refused.[3] If this is true, the rejection was most fortunate, for the company that produced the play at Lincoln's Inn Fields—at the time, the only other company —was especially strong. Along with Betterton, John Verbruggen, and George Powell, it included two of the greatest actresses of the late Restoration stage: Elizabeth Barry and Anne Bracegirdle. Barry, who had made her first appearance in the theater at least as early as 1675, "created" the leading women's roles in many admired plays, including Otway's *The Orphan* and *Venice Preserved*. Bracegirdle, whose earliest recorded performance took place in 1688, was probably younger than Barry, but by 1700 her equal in fame. In their frequent appearances together, it was usual for Bracegirdle to play a character of unquestionable respectability, whether a matron or a still unmarried young woman, and for Barry to play a different—in many ways quite different—type: domineering, immoral, or simply older or more forceful than the character played by Bracegirdle.[4] For example, in Congreve's *The Way of the World,* produced less than a year before *The Ambitious Stepmother,* Barry played Marwood to Bracegirdle's Millamant. Through the company's many changes of personnel and management and its moves to the Haymarket in 1705 and to

[3] Dennis, "The Causes of the Decay and Defects of Dramatick Poetry . . . ," in *The Critical Works of John Dennis,* ed. Edwin Niles Hooker, II (Baltimore, 1943), 278.

[4] On the lives of Barry and Bracegirdle, see John Harold Wilson, *All the King's Ladies* (Chicago, 1958), pp. 110–17, 122–27. On the type-casting of the actresses, see Eric Rothstein, *Restoration Tragedy* (Madison, Wisconsin, 1967), pp. 141–44. Rothstein notes two plays, Charles Hopkins's *Boadicea* and *Friendship Improved,* in which Barry played Bracegirdle's mother.

Drury Lane in 1710, Rowe wrote plays for it. Barry and Brace-girdle appeared together in his first five plays. In the sixth, pro-duced after Bracegirdle's retirement, Barry appeared with Anne Oldfield, and in the seventh and eighth Oldfield acted with Mary Porter. Thus a continuity was maintained. It was fitting that in the last appearance together of Bracegirdle and Barry, the lines should be Rowe's. The occasion was a benefit performance for Betterton in 1709 of Congreve's *Love for Love,* for which Rowe composed a new epilogue. When the play was over, the actresses came on stage with the aging Betterton, and Barry spoke. The epilogue pays homage to the actor with an epic simile that summarizes the contents of plays written for him and his colleagues by Rowe and others:

> As Some Brave *Knight,* who once with Spear and Shield
> Had sought Renown in many a well-fought Field,
> But now no more with Sacred Fame inspir'd,
> Was to a peaceful Hermitage retir'd;
> There, if by Chance disast'rous Tales he hears,
> Of Matrons Wrongs, and captive Virgins Tears,
> He feels soft Pity urge his Gen'rous Breast,
> And vows once more, to succour the Distress'd.
> Buckl'd in *Mail* he sallies on the Plain,
> And turns him to the Feats of Arms again.[5]

Matrons' wrongs, virgins' tears, soft pity: such were the ma-terials of which Rowe composed his tragedies. Perhaps he put the phrases into the epilogue with conscious irony, knowing how far he had gone in the use of these familiar devices to appeal to the public's taste for pathos. Nor was he a writer to introduce new forms of construction. His widest departures from Augustan con-cepts of dramaturgy appear in *Jane Shore,* where he allows a break in time between the fourth and fifth acts, and in a remark in the preface to his edition of Shakespeare, published in 1709.

If one undertook, [he wrote] to examine the greatest part of these [*Macbeth* and *Hamlet*] by those Rules which are establish'd by *Aristo-*

---

[5] Rowe, *Poems on Several Occasions* (London, 1714), pp. 32–33.

tle, and taken from the Model of the *Grecian* Stage, it would be no very hard Task to find a great many Faults: But as *Shakespear* liv'd under a kind of mere Light of Nature, and had never been made acquainted with the Regularity of those written Precepts, so it would be hard to judge him by a Law he knew nothing of.[6]

The Biter aside, Rowe's plays divide almost equally between the two varieties of "regular" tragedy familiar to the Augustan audience, heroic and pathetic. *The Ambitious Stepmother, Tamerlane, Ulysses,* and *The Royal Convert* are heroic plays. That is, they are works whose major characters are viewed not only as individuals moved by personal interests but also as public figures; in the palace intrigues that constitute the main lines of action, opposing factions outfight or outscheme one another repeatedly through the five acts, until, finally, order and morality are established. By 1700 this type of plot was old-fashioned, and Rowe was hard put to revitalize it. The agitated affairs of state in his heroic plays serve chiefly to provide situations within which the actresses can cry out in pain or desperation. Pathos is as essential to their design as to that of the "she-tragedies." But the major difference between the two types of tragedy is more striking than this point of agreement. In Rowe's heroic plays, the personages named or referred to in the titles—men in all but one—do not die; like many other plays that Restoration writers called tragedies, these works are grave in language but not wholly doom-ridden at the final exeunt. The protagonists of the "she-tragedies," however, do not escape death.

Of the leading feminine characters in the heroic plays, one —that was given by custom to Barry—is always a woman of great intensity and perseverance. Weaker roles, allowing for tears and anguish, are also present; in the first three of the heroic plays these were taken by Bracegirdle, and in *The Royal Convert* by Oldfield. The three pathetic tragedies also include secondary women's roles, but only in *The Fair Penitent,* written while Bracegirdle

[6] In *Eighteenth Century Essays on Shakespeare,* ed. D. Nicol Smith, 2nd (rev.) ed. (Oxford, 1963), p. 15.

was still a member of the company, is the role soft, sweet, and un-
worldly. Because the design of these plays highlights the distresses
of the tragic protagonists and their families and sympathizers, the
protagonists are necessarily strong figures, despite the fact that
their plights are calculated to move the audience to pity. Barry
took the lead in the first pathetic tragedy, Oldfield in the second
and third.[7]

Rowe demonstrated his liking for the passionate gesture and
the affective phrase with his first play. In a small way *The Ambitious Stepmother* is experimental, for in it Rowe allows a pair of
innocent young lovers, Artaxerxes and Amestris, to die, although
this was contrary to the expectations of his audience. With this
turn of the action he may have gone against the doctrine of poetic
justice, but, as was his intention, he deepened the pathetic tonal-
ity. He set down some afterthoughts on the play in a dedicatory
letter to the Earl of Jersey, defending his development of the plot;
the general opinions expressed in the dedication were to remain
with him through the fifteen years of his career as a playwright.
One possible ending for the tragedy, he noted, was to allow the
good characters to live on, and to live happily; thus he might have
drawn a moral. "But," he observed,

since Terror and Pity are laid down for the Ends of Tragedy, by the
great Master and Father of Criticism, I was always inclin'd to fancy,
that the last and remaining Impressions, which ought to be left on the
minds of an Audience, should proceed from one of these two. They
should be struck with Terror in several parts of the Play, but always
Conclude and go away with Pity, a sort of regret proceeding from
good nature, which tho an uneasiness, is not always disagreeable, to
the person who feels it. It was this passion that the famous Mr. *Otway*
succeeded so well in touching, and must and will at all times affect

---

[7] *Lady Jane Gray,* the last of the three "she-tragedies" and one of
Rowe's least satisfactory plays, does not quite fit the pattern, for the second
feminine role, taken by Mary Porter, is of little consequence. Lady Jane
herself is too obviously the victim of circumstance to become an effective
tragic protagonist. *The Ambitious Stepmother* is the only one of the tragedies with three sizable women's roles.

people, who have any tenderness or humanity. . . . As for that part of
the Objection, which says, that Innocent persons ought not to be
shewn unfortunate; The success and general approbation, which many
of the best Tragedies that have been writ, and which were built on
that foundation, have met with, will be a sufficient answer for me.[8]

In the prologue also Rowe stressed the idea of pathos and called
in Otway to his defense:

> If Dying Lovers yet deserve a Tear,
> If a sad Story of a Maids Despair,
> Yet move Compassion in the pitying Fair,
> This Day the Poet does his Art employ,
> The soft Accesses of your Souls to try. . . .
> Nor let the men, the weeping fair accuse
> Those kind Protectors of the Tragick Muse,
> Whose Tears did moving Otway's labours crown,
> And made the poor Monimia's Grief their own . . .

With Barry, the original Monimia, a member of his own cast,
Rowe doubtless felt himself to be in a line of descent from Otway.
Artemisa, Barry's part in *The Ambitious Stepmother,* does not,
however, resemble Monimia. The character is a domineering
queen of Persia who is determined that her son Artaban shall
have the throne, although her stepson Artaxerxes is the rightful
heir. Whether originally written for Barry or not, the part unquestionably lay within her range. Amestris, the tragic princess, is the
soft role played by Bracegirdle. Retaining the pathetic pattern,
Rowe alternates scenes of political intrigue, in which Artemisa is
permitted to assert her strength of personality, with scenes of troubled romantic love in which Amestris takes the stage in a swirl of
pathetic images. The public issue of the succession and the personal matter of the future of Artaxerxes and Amestris are stressed
alternately as the women's roles interweave.

In this first play Rowe established the styles of diction, the
bitter against the sweet, that he was always to employ in composing lines for his actresses. Artemisa in her first appearance (I) so-
liloquizes:

---

[8] All quotations from Rowe's plays are taken from the first editions.

> Be fixt, my Soul, fixt on thy own firm basis!
> Be constant to thy self; nor know the weakness,
> The poor Irresolution of my Sex:
> Disdain those shews of danger, that would bar
> My way to glory.

Amestris, addressing her lover, provides a contrast soon afterward (I):

> Can you blame me?
> If from retirement drawn and pleasing solitude,
> I fear to tempt this Stormy Sea the World,
> Whose every Beach is strew'd with wrecks of wretches
> That daily perish in it. Curst Ambition!
> Why dost thou come to trouble my repose,
> Who have even from my Infancy disclaim'd thee?

Barry continues to declaim aggressively, and Bracegirdle to suffer in low tones. Amestris is assaulted by Mirza, the First Minister of State, stabs him in self-defense, and is stabbed in return. More than a hundred lines of dialogue come between Mirza's delivery of the fatal blow and the girl's death. Artemisa's scenes are less sensational, and in the last acts it becomes obvious that Rowe has found the part difficult to develop. "For know (Young King!) that I am Fate in Persia, / And Life and Death depend upon my Pleasure," she tells her son Artaban in her next-to-last appearance (IV), but in her imperiled court the words are mere sound.

The problem of balancing the two women's roles continued to be troublesome to Rowe. In *The Fair Penitent,* the first of the "she-tragedies," the difficulty was created, not by the role to be played by Barry, but by the pathetic role for Bracegirdle. The tragedy, as Rowe described it in the prologue, is a "private tale," not a play of court intrigue, and its cast is small—much smaller than the cast of Philip Massinger and Nathan Field's *The Fatal Dowry,* on which it is based. Although comments on affairs of state form part of the exposition, the plot remains a taut and pointed arrangement of recriminations and admissions of guilt, with only the secondary feminine role to weaken its structure. Calista, the strong-willed protagonist who resents the double sexual standard, was obviously designed for Barry and is the longest and most arresting of her parts in Rowe's plays. Her vigorous, terse speech on the status of women (III), written to illustrate an important theme of the play as well as to speak for the most forward-looking women in the audience, is one of Rowe's finest:

> How hard is the Condition of our Sex,
> Thro' ev'ry State of Life the Slaves of Man?
> In all the dear, delightful Days of Youth,
> A rigid Father dictates to our Wills,
> And deals out Pleasure with a scanty Hand;
> To his, the Tyrant Husband's Reign succeeds
> Proud with Opinion of superior Reason,
> He holds Domestick Bus'ness and Devotion
> All we are capable to know, and shuts us,
> Like Cloyster'd Ideots, from the World's Acquaintance,
> And all the Joys of Freedom; wherefore are we
> Born with high souls, but to assert our selves,
> Shake off this vile Obedience they exact,
> And claim an equal Empire o'er the World?

Lavinia, the part designed for Bracegirdle, is the sister of Calista's husband. She has no equivalent in the source and makes no important contribution to the plot; as Francis Gentleman noted, she "is a mere make-shift to eke out the piece." [9] Tearful and yielding, living only for her husband and brother, she provides a contrast to Calista, but so pathetic and halting is her language that each of her three appearances impedes the progress of the play. On two occasions her language seems designed to reveal her as vulnerable as a child, despite her years and her position as a matron. Her "little Heart" is the subject of one of the speeches (I), her "little Wealth" of the other (III). In the first of these, in which she expresses her amazement on hearing that not all partners in marriage are true to their spouses, Rowe's tendency toward excess is especially evident:

[9] Gentleman, *The Dramatic Censor: or, Critical Companion* (London, 1770), I, 276.

> Can there be such? And have they peace of Mind?
> Have they in all the Series of their changing
> One happy Hour? If Women are such things,
> How was I form'd so different from my Sex?
> My little Heart is satisfy'd with you,
> You take up all her room; as in a Cottage
> Which harbours some Benighted Princely Stranger,
> Where the good Man, proud of his Hospitality,
> Yields all his homely Dwelling to his Guest,
> And hardly keeps a Corner for himself.

Bracegirdle's role in *Ulysses* created similar problems for Rowe. The play, a vehicle for the aging Betterton, is a heroic tragedy based on the conclusion of the *Odyssey,* in which the great warrior returns to Ithaca to find his wife Penelope besieged by suitors. A woman old enough to have raised a son to adulthood, Penelope was a suitable part for Barry. To balance it with a role for Bracegirdle, Rowe invented the character of Semanthe, a young Samian princess who is the bride of Telemachus. Faced with the difficulty of creating pathetic scenes for her, Rowe shows her to be torn between love of Telemachus and duty toward the goddess Cynthia, whom she has served as a votaress. An awkwardly contrived turn of the plot provides a solution to her dilemma. On his wedding night, the night of his father's return to Ithaca, Telemachus fatally wounds Eurymachus, Semanthe's father, as the older man attempts to enter Penelope's bedroom. So disturbed is Semanthe to find her husband the slayer of her father that she decides to return to Samos. In view of the guilty intention of Eurymachus, her decision is not reasonable, and Rowe is unable to defend it successfully. She faints, revives, and renounces love, only to realize that the event has not after all destroyed her feeling for Telemachus. Nevertheless she leaves, departing for her island home with a speech that could well serve as a parody of all pathetic farewells (V):

> For ever I cou'd listen—But the Gods,
> The cruel Gods forbid, and thus they part us.
> Remember—oh remember me, *Telemachus!*

Perhaps thou wilt forget me; but no matter,
I will be true to thee, preserve thee ever,
The sad Companion of this faithful Breast,
While Life and Thought remain, and when at last
I feel the Icy Hand of Death prevail,
My Heart-strings break, and all my Senses fail,
I'll fix thy Image in my closing Eye,
Sigh thy dear Name, then lay me down and die.

Because the reunion of Ulysses and Penelope is the happy sort of
event that heralds the end of a comic rather than a tragic plot,
Rowe would seem to have brought about the separation of his
younger couple in order to leave the audience with the sense that
it had witnessed a tragedy after all. The situation does not ring
true. At the close, Telemachus announces to his father that only
he in Ithaca is unhappy: "Joy like the chearful Morning dawns on
all, / And none but your unhappy Son shall mourn."

For *The Royal Convert,* his next play, Rowe invented an especially elaborate plot with, as before, display roles for two actresses. When the tragedy was first produced, in November 1707,
Barry was still active, but Bracegirdle had been in retirement for
ten months, and the part of the pathetic Ethelinda was taken by
Anne Oldfield. Ethelinda is a young woman with whom both King
Hengist of Kent and his brother Aribert are in love. The domineering, disagreeable feminine character, her enemy, is Rodogune,
a Saxon princess engaged to Hengist but in love with Aribert. The
plot turns on the love of the brothers for the Christian girl. Hengist, not knowing that Aribert has become a Christian and has married Ethelinda, asks him to marry Rodogune, so that he himself
will be free to pursue Ethelinda. Aribert must of course deny his
brother's wish and is right to do so. Ruses and military maneuvers
ensue. The Christian pair become the prisoners of Rodogune, who
has planned to take the life of her rival in a pagan ceremony.
"The SCENE draws," runs Rowe's description of the setting (V),
"and discovers the inner Part of the Temple. A Fire is prepar'd
on one of the Altars, near it are plac'd a Rack, Knives, Axes, and

other Instruments of Torture; several Priests attending as for a Sacrifice." The situation is suspenseful. It ends, as we might hope, with the arrival of the wounded, dying Hengist accompanied by his troops, the release of the Christians, and the withdrawal of Rodogune.

Because of its complex plot and its spectacular and melodramatic scenes, the play frequently flashes with excitement. Ultimately, however, it is disappointing, as a result of Rowe's treatment of Rodogune. Harsh and rigid in her determination to take the upper hand in all dealings with men, she is not believable as a woman in love. The part was played by Barry at the age of forty-nine—no great age, to be sure, but a time when the glow of youth is no longer easy to revive, a time when, that is, an actress can look and speak the part of a stern, unfeminine type more convincingly than the part of an innocent girl. The masculine note of command is present in all of Rodogune's speeches, from her scoffing rejection of Hengist on through the play. Presumably it was Rowe's intention that she be formidably unyielding, since she must provide a foil to Ethelinda. But the role is a failure, for, although Rodogune's harsh personality does contrast with that of the sympathetic British girl, it is drawn with no touch of modesty or reticence to redeem it. Typical is her thundering final statement (V), when, having failed in all her plans, she leaves the scene:

> Yes, I will go; fly, far as the Earth can bear me,
> From thee, and from the Face of Man for ever.
> Curst be your Sex, the Cause of all our Sorrows;
> Curst be your Looks, your Tongues, and all your false Arts,
> That cheat our Eyes, and wound our easy Hearts;
> Curst may you be for all the Pains you give,
> And for the scanty Pleasures we receive;
> Curst be your brutal Pow'r, your tyrant Sway.
> By which you bend, and force us to obey.
> Oh Nature! partial Goddess, let thy Hand
> Be just for once, and equal the Command;
> Let Woman once be Mistress in her turn,

184 MALCOLM GOLDSTEIN

> Subdue Mankind beneath her haughty Scorn,
> And smile to see the proud Oppressor mourn.

Compared to Calista's measured comment on the male sex, the speech is glaringly unfeminine.

It would, of course, be both incorrect and ungallant to suggest that Rowe's plays should be viewed only as infelicitous designs of contrasting roles for the great ladies of the Augustan stage. With their suspenseful plots, rapidly moving stage business, and spectacular settings, they are obviously more than that. But, to take away with the left hand what one gives with the right, it is necessary to note that Rowe's tendency toward excess was not confined to his treatment of the female roles. His diction, if it may be considered apart from character development, is the most unsatisfactory element in his work. Repeatedly, no matter the sex or temperament of the character speaking, ornamental phrases dampen the lines. The language is flowery in a literal sense, for roses abound in speeches on death and dying. Caves open and tempests rise.[10] To point up moments of sadness, exclamatory ohs and ahs disrupt the flow of sentences. One scene from the last act of *Tamerlane* will serve to recall the peaks of agitation to which Rowe's characters are driven by ill fortune. It is a moment when Arpasia, much overcome, appeals to Moneses, whom she loves, to think of "something soft, / Tender, and kind, of something wondrous sad" and then commands him to speak to her—while four mutes employed by Bajazet attempt to strangle him with a bowstring. After the mutes have finished their work, she cries out,

[10] For example: ". . . an ashy Pale/ Grows o'er the Roses, the red Lips have lost/ Their flagrant Hew" (*Tamerlane,* V); "There let the Mirtle and the Rose be strow'd,/ For 'tis my second better Bridal Day" (*The Royal Convert,* IV); "Oh shield me; shield me from that ugly Fantome/ The Cave of Death! how dark and deep it is!" (*The Ambitious Stepmother,* V); "Madness! Confusion! let the Storm come on,/ Let the tumultuous Roar drive all upon me,/ Dash my devoted Bark; ye Surges, break it;/ 'Tis for my ruin that the Tempest rises" (*The Fair Penitent,* IV); "Hide me ye Rocks, within your secret Caverns,/ Cast thy black Veil upon my Shame, O Night!" (*Jane Shore,* V). Yet it should be noted that Samuel Johnson praised Rowe's diction for its elegance; see *Lives of the Poets,* ed. George Birkbeck Hill (Oxford, 1905), II, 76.

Oh! dismal! 'tis not to be borne. Ye Moralists,
Ye Talkers, what are all your Precepts now?
Patience? Distraction? blast the Tyrant, blast him,
Avenging Lightnings; snatch him hence, ye Fiends!
Love! Death! *Moneses!* Nature can no more,
Ruin is on her, and she sinks at once.   [*She sinks down.*]

No doubt Barry, who had been the first to play Belvidera in *Venice Preserved,* could deliver this speech in fine fashion, but it is not easy for a modern reader to imagine her doing so.

Yet without such aid as the imagination can give, we would find it difficult to sense the theatrical impact of Rowe's plays at all, for almost never do we have the opportunity to see them. Today even the best of them have disappeared from the professional repertory, along with all other English tragedies written between John Ford's *'Tis Pity She's a Whore* and Bernard Shaw's *Saint Joan.* Nor is it likely that they will ever regain their popularity, for over the last century and a half the English-speaking public has all but completely lost its taste for the neoclassical manner on the stage. But Rowe, despite his lack of high seriousness of purpose, has a claim to our attention still, if only by virtue of his great past fame. And if we read his work with good will, perhaps we can sense something of the pleasure audiences took in it when it was new.

The Novel

ALICE GREEN FREDMAN

The Picaresque in Decline:
Smollett's First Novel

Roderick Random IS AN INSTANCE of an author's setting out to create a deliberate picaresque; the twenty-six-year-old Smollett decided on the mode, and on the model: Le Sage. I am not sure that he altogether succeeded. What he created was a kind of "modified" picaresque, for want of a better term. And the result of this is, I think, the picaresque in decline.

To take the model first: *Gil Blas* unquestionably utilizes the tendency toward satire inherent in the picaresque. But it is a generalized, universalized satire—detached, cheerful, ironic. Le Sage's impulse is largely that of a good-humored cynic and skeptic; he has no reformist zeal and no illusions about humanity. Smollett expresses his attitude toward his source very clearly in his preface to *Roderick Random:*

The disgraces of Gil Blas are, for the most part, such as *rather excite mirth than compassion:* he himself laughs at them; and his transitions from distress to happiness, or at least ease, are so sudden, that *neither the reader has time to pity him, nor himself to be acquainted with affliction.* This conduct, in my opinion, not only deviates from probability, but *prevents that generous indignation which ought to animate the reader against the sordid and vicious disposition of the world* (my italics).

He raises objections to precisely those features which make Gil Blas so gaily irreverent and irrepressible and sophisticated: man is a laughing animal. Smollett's tone in the preface is severe and censorious, and this is carried over into the attitude that informs *his* picaresque fiction. One cannot help suspecting that he missed the point, and much of the fun of Le Sage's novel, if he criticizes Gil Blas for laughing at his own disgraces and Le Sage for neglecting to evoke the reader's sympathy.

For after all, that *is* part of the fun: the biter bit, and the shrewd picaro resiliently bouncing back after misfortune; presuming himself wiser, though not necessarily sadder; and then cheerfully trotting off to outmaneuver himself again, while the reader anticipates with amusement the next installment in a series of setbacks. Surely this is one of the attitudes that differentiates Gil Blas from Roderick Random: that Gil Blas *is* a laughing animal ("I lost all my gaiety; I became gloomy and thoughtful. In a word, a stupid animal"), and is attractive precisely because of this. And this is one of our problems with Roderick Random: that he is really not particularly attractive, in part because he lacks those irrepressible high spirits of Gil Blas and tends to be rather sulky and small-natured. As many people have pointed out, it is somewhat hard to be confronted by any hero of a long narrative who is an unmitigated cad or scoundrel.

I am not suggesting that Roderick Random is quite that bad, but when one compares him to such assorted subsequent picaros as Gulley Jimson, Giles Goatboy, Henry Burlingame, or Ebenezer Cooke, he surely does not have much charm. Nor does it seem to me that Smollett conceived him with anything like the imperturbable, amused detachment that we find in his model, Le Sage. But perhaps that is the point: Smollett was a young man when he wrote his first novel, but he was an Angry Young Man. "Generous indignation," more likely a generous helping of indignation, animates his vision. And it is an indignation that often turns excessively savage, lacking as it does the mediating action of irony which provided even so savagely indignant a man as Swift a mechanism for control.

For when Smollett refers to the "sordid and vicious disposition of the world" he is not being either ironic or pontifical; he is totally convinced of it. Smollett is impelled by satire, the ferocious, lashing satire in the tradition of Juvenal.[1] There is nothing Olympian about his stance, nothing urbanely Horatian about his mode of satire, as his preface to a later novel, *Ferdinand Count Fathom,* so clearly declares: "to instruct the ignorant, and entertain the vacant . . . to subject folly to ridicule, and vice to indignation." [2]

But there is something else operating here, too, which Smollett explains in the paragraph of his preface to *Roderick Random* following his reference to Le Sage:

I have attempted to represent modest merit struggling with every difficulty to which a friendless orphan is exposed, from his own want of experience, as well as from the selfishness, envy, malice, and base indifference of mankind. To secure a favourable prepossession, I have allowed him the advantages of birth and education, which, in the series of his misfortunes, will, I hope, engage the ingenuous more warmly in his behalf.

He wants to evoke compassion for his hero, and his description of this friendless orphan suggests another peculiarity of his "modified" picaresque: Smollett actually believes that Roderick Random is a hero, not an anti-hero or a picaro. And Smollett does not al-

---

[1] See Ronald Paulson, "Satire in the Early Novels of Smollett," *JEGP* (July, 1960), 391 ff.; Alan Dugald McKillop, *The Early Masters of English Fiction* (Kansas, 1962; 1st ed., 1956), p. 151; Lewis Mansfield Knapp, *Tobias Smollett, Doctor of Men and Manners* (Princeton, 1949), p. 71; Donald Bruce, *Radical Doctor Smollett* (London, 1964), pp. 159–62.

[2] See Eugene Joliat, *Smollett et La France* (Paris, 1935), p. 12: "La satire est donc chez lui une sorte de seconde nature."

together detach himself from this lad of modest merit; he does not achieve that "spectator" quality of classic comedy so succinctly described by Fontenelle.[3] Instead, he tends to identify with his hero.[4] Everybody knows that at several points in Roderick Random's history there are marked parallels to young Smollett's struggles in the world—or more likely, with the world. Smollett himself apparently did not realize the extent of these, for he subsequently deplored what he regarded as a misreading of his novel.[5] The result of his identification, whatever his intentions may have been, is the introduction of an attitude that is really quite alien to the picaresque: Smollett tends to sentimentalize his hero, or perhaps his apprehension of his hero.

It is not a very successful undertaking, but it is significant as symptomatic not only of young Smollett's attitude but perhaps also of the temper of the times. A young fellow writing a picaresque novel in the late 1740s may well have absorbed some of the currents of the rising tides of sensibility.[6] But the contribution of the

[3] "Nature, through comedy, has given us a marvelous faculty to prevent us from becoming the dupes of ourselves. How many times has it happened that while one part of us does something with ardor and earnestness, another part mocks it? And if there were need for it, one could find a third part which could mock the other two." *Dialogues des morts modernes: Dialogue II, Paracelse, Moliere.* My translation.

[4] I am not in complete agreement with Paulson, p. 391, in what seems to me to be a somewhat heavier emphasis on minimizing Smollett's self-projection than the novel warrants.

[5] "Some Persons to whom I have been extremely obliged, being weak enough to take Umbrage at many passages of the work, on the Supposition that I myself am the Hero of the Book, and they, of consequence, concerned in the History." *The Letters of Tobias Smollett,* edited by Lewis M. Knapp (Oxford, 1970), p. 7, letter 5, June 7, 1748.

[6] M. A. Goldberg, *Smollett and the Scottish School* (Albuquerque, 1959), believes that *Roderick Random* is semi-picaresque, semi-*bildungsroman.* He contends that its first section (chapters I–LXIII) deals with Roderick Random in adversity and at the mercy of his passions; its second section (chapters LXIV–LXIX) deals with "the triumph of reason which, coupled with the passions, now enables him to control his own destiny and to achieve those goals which he has set for himself" (p. 39). Goldberg stresses that "this conflict between reason and passion, *internal* to Roderick, and central to the development of the novel, is certainly one of the major problems with which eighteenth-century England was absorbed" (p. 24; my italics).

school of sensibility is negative in its effect on the novel; although Roderick is supposed to be a focus of sympathy, I doubt if one much cares. Smollett undeniably does go to some lengths to modify the picaresque to suit his requirements for his hero; and this is an important straw in the wind, for it moves Roderick Random in a different direction from his predecessors.

One of the major features that sets Roderick Random apart from Lazarillo and Simplicissimus and Gil Blas is implicit in Smollett's prefatory statement: "To secure a favourable prepossession, I have allowed him the advantages of birth and education." Roderick Random is not a typical picaro. He has, and he knows he has, a place and position and status and, theoretically, expectations. But he has been unfairly deprived of them, and I think we ought to emphasize unfairly because Smollett and Roderick certainly do. This young sprig blunders through a multiplicity of adventures with a chip on his shoulder and a grudge against mankind: everyone else is more to blame than Roderick Random. And there is nothing to indicate that Smollett does not agree with him.[7] Indeed, Smollett admits he has gone to considerable pains to make us agree with him, to evoke pity for this creature of "modest merit."

Of course, so far as the form of the picaresque is concerned, Smollett cannot be faulted. His hero's name is the clue, and it is appropriate: Random. He is introduced auspiciously for the protagonist of a picaresque: his pregnant mother's dream of prognostication, which is also in the mock-heroic tradition of prophesying something unusual for the hero. Smollett himself apparently subscribed to the "tennis ball of fortune" metaphor, for as late as

[7] See, for example, *Letters* 12, pp. 17–18; *Letters* 21: ". . . [England, a land where] Felicity is held to consist in stupifying Port and overgrown Buttocks of Beef, where Genius is lost, Learning undervalued, and Taste altogether extinguished" (p. 33); *Letters* 56: ". . . I will venture to say that nothing base or dishonourable can be justly charged upon my Character. Yet, I am daily persecuted by the most malicious slanders meerly because I have written with some Success" (p. 73); *Letters* 12: "I am an unfortunate Dog whose Pride Providence thinks proper to punish with the Tortures of incessant Mortification; & I resent my Lot accordingly" (p. 18).

1761 he wrote to Garrick: "I am old enough to have seen and observed that we are all playthings of fortune, and that it depends upon something as insignificant and precarious as the tossing up of a halfpenny whether a man rises to affluence and honours, or continues to his dying day struggling with the difficulties and disgraces of life." [8]

As John Barth writes in the Afterword to the Signet edition of *Roderick Random,* there is something typical of the Age of Reason's attitude in Mrs. Random's dream: it is not mysterious or even very metaphorical; it means exactly what it says—her son is to be the tennis ball of fortune. I would suggest, in line with the reference to fortune, that despite all the bouncing about which Roderick Random is subjected to, fortune emerges as being securely in Smollett's hands. In accordance with a rationalistic concept of the universe (though I am not sure this is so consciously or confidently operative in Smollett as it is in Fielding) or with a wish-fulfillment, he so contrives things that everything works out very neatly for the deprived orphan of his fancy. Roderick Random meets his father, who is rich; Roderick Random gets his girl, and can barely restrain himself from getting at her; Roderick Random returns in triumph to his family seat, warmly welcomed by all the loyal villagers, and has the exquisitely vindictive satisfaction of seeing the once-favored heir disendowed, a nasty cousin turned off by his father, and another nasty cousin married well beneath herself to an indigent coachman.

As for the movement and vitality associated with the picaresque, the novel is crammed with it, along with much else.[9] It begins in the country, with the young man from the provinces; it

[8] *Letters* 77, p. 98.

[9] See James L. Clifford's introduction to *Peregrine Pickle* (London, 1964), pp. xxv–xxvi: "What gives Smollett his own particular flavour is the mingling in his novels of so many diverse traditions—the picaresque, classical formal satire, comedy, melodrama, the new sensibility, and at times stark realism. Yet his fertility is so great, his vigour of presentation so appealing, that the reader simply does not care. The story drags him headlong through every slough and side road."

includes adventures along the road; adventures in the city; the sea episodes; a brief return, a love interest, and more adventure; travel on the continent and a fling at military service; return to England and London, with London wits and fortune-hunting at Bath; and after debtors' prison, a trip to South America and the discovery of Roderick's father, reunion with the love interest and Roderick's restoration to his rightful place in the country. This is about as packed as any picaresque could be, charged through with the dynamism of Smollett's fierce invention and his exhaustless proliferation of single units of adventure. That so many of his humorous figures do manage to stick in one's memory is largely a tribute to Smollett's energetic caricature, for he seems to have had little talent for, or interest in, subtleties.

Yet this very matter of caricature leads us to something else that is a modification of the picaresque. When one thinks of preceding picaresque fictions, one does not recall either much extensive use of caricature or much intensive exploitation of this type of portrait. But Smollett excels at the exaggeration and distortion of prominent features to make a person appear ludicrous. Of course, caricature can be used for the purpose of broad comedy or superb wit, but I think Smollett's use of it reflects something else: he is always rendering people contemptible by it; or making them into animals or insects. There is a strain of cruelty in Smollett's caricatures, even of those figures whom he likes, and his method creates the effect of the ludicrous by its action to dehumanize.

This is inspired by Smollett's vision which, it seems to me, is not really a picaresque vision at all, even allowing for the vast flexibility inherent in the picaresque itself. I have already mentioned some of the differences between *Roderick Random* and *Gil Blas* and other picaresques: Roderick Random has a place, but he is cast out of it; he has status, but he is denied it; he has a position, but he is unfairly deprived of it. All this engenders a prevailing attitude: the world is in a malign conspiracy against him.[10] Uncle

[10] See *Letters* 67, Dec. 10, 1759, p. 85, written ten years after *Roderick Random,* wherein Smollett complains that he has "been baited like a bear

Tom shows up to help and then disappears; school friends fade
out or turn into cads; strangers offer aid and then dupe him—one
could multiply this indefinitely but there is no need to, since Smollett does. My point is that, starting with the persecutions in his
boyhood, Roderick Random is presented as the victim of a sadis-
tic cosmic conspiracy. Merely a glance at the heading for Chapter
2 will set the tone sufficiently for what follows: "I grow up—am
hated by my relations—sent to school—neglected by my
grandfather—maltreated by my master—seasoned to adversity—I
form cabals against the pedant—am debarred access to my
grandfather—hunted by his heir—I demolish the teeth of his
tutor." He really is the butt, the scapegoat of a relentless and cruel
combination of chance and mankind. Gil Blas, by contrast, gets
gulled or knocked down by fortune; picks himself up; ruefully
shakes his head, then, grinning at his setbacks, sallies forth to be
bounced again. More often than not, he is his own dupe and he is
amused by it. Roderick Random is shoved out to encounter experience; he gets slapped down and then stomped; he picks himself
up only to be flattened and kicked some more. It is no wonder that
he begins to develop a surly attitude and carry a grudge.

The vision that emerges from this is of a cruel, persecuting
concatenation of energetically malicious forces, springing on him
without respite. The recurrent pattern of his adventures is: a
promising start, if he is lucky enough to get that, followed by a
tantalizing taste of what seems to be success; then a cruel deflation or disabusing of his ingenuous hope or clumsy schemes. If he
is the biter bit, which often happens, the disclosure has no amusement or humor; more often than not, it is a loathsome, dirty joke.
A representative instance occurs when, scorned by Melinda, Roderick plots to avenge himself on her. Billy Chatter promises to aid
him by introducing him to a lady reputed to be worth thirty-thou-
sand pounds. Roderick disguises himself as a marquis and attends

---

by all the hounds of Grub-street. . . . I have been abused, reviled, and ca-
lumniated, for satires I never saw; I have been censured for absurdities of
which I could not possibly be guilty."

the ball, which attracts all society, as dancing partner to Miss Biddy Gripewell, the heiress. He succeeds in arousing both Melinda's envy and the affections of an unknown lady who encourages his suit, induces him to believe she is beautiful, and assures him that her independent income of twelve-thousand pounds is at his disposal. Transported with joy at his anticipated victory, and totally forgetting his love for "the gentle Narcissa, . . . my thoughts were wholly employed in planning triumphs over the malice and contempt of the world," Roderick rushes off to an assignation with Miss Sparkle:

My heart took the alarm and beat quick; my cheeks glowed, my nerves thrilled, and my knees shook with ecstasy! I perceived the door opening, saw a gold brocade petticoat advance, and sprung forward to embrace my charmer! Heaven and earth!—how shall I paint my situation when I found Miss Sparkle converted into a wrinkled hag, turned of seventy! I was struck dumb with amazement and petrified with horror!

Predictably, she turns out to be not Miss Sparkle but a governess to Sir John Sparkle's daughter.

Now this sort of thing can have a detrimental effect, even on "modest merit struggling with every difficulty to which a poor friendless orphan is exposed"—and Smollett exposes Roderick to a multiplicity of difficulties. In consequence, Roderick Random is largely motivated by something quite alien to the picaresque vision: what keeps him going is revenge or, to use his own words, "planning triumphs over the malice and contempt of the world." [11] The result is a singularly consistent strain of sheer vindictiveness, a feature to be encountered in none of the picaresques preceding *Roderick Random* to such an extensive and sustained degree. In point of fact, there is nothing insouciant about Roderick Random; instead, he is truculent and often quite gratuitously ungrateful and selfish (take, for example, his relationship with Strap, whose generosity to the thankless Roderick Random is exceeded only by his

[11] See Paulson, p. 389: *revenge* is "one of the most frequently repeated words in the novel."

own stupidity in persisting to be so generous). And Roderick Random's personal unpleasantness casts a rather oppressive atmosphere over the entire novel, constituting as it does so large a part of the vision. It is not that one expects anything really morally edifying: most heroes of the picaresque are no better than they should be. But they are no worse, either; and the unfortunate comparison with Le Sage which Smollett invites certainly puts Smollett at a disadvantage. There is something rather offensive about Roderick Random and his case against society, albeit society, too, is offensive in Smollett's vision. Roderick Random has the dubious distinction of being a downright unpleasant young hero.

Of course, this is an unintentional by-product of Smollett's vision, for Smollett certainly does not regard Roderick Random as being unpleasant. And the by-product is the result of something suggested by the contrast between Smollett and Le Sage which I mentioned earlier: Smollett is an indignant satirist. That is one of the reasons he turns so readily to caricature and invective. Perhaps to compensate for lacking protective irony as a mode of defense and mediation from experience, Smollett introduces an attitude of ferocity as part of his vision. This attitude can take various forms in his novel, and certainly one of the most frequent is vindictiveness. When people get their teeth knocked out or their heads broken or get beaten up, it is not just rough-and-tumble physical horseplay and boisterous high spirits of the oh-what-a-lovely-brawl variety. It is usually because Roderick wants to get back at them, to avenge some insult or slight. This all functions to release, through physical violence, some of that pent-up anger that not just Roderick Random but also, one suspects, his creator is carrying around with the chip on the shoulder.[12] There seems to

[12] See *Letters* 15, February 23, 1753, pp. 21–26, for a splendidly vitriolic "release." A little more than a decade later, Smollett wrote his *Travels Through France and Italy,* which abound in vigorous and occasionally even paranoid explosions against foreign roads, foods, landlords, conveyances, manners, customs, climates, and other multiple offenders. While it is true that he departed from England in no charitable mood, scourging his country in his first letter "as a scene of illiberal dispute, and incredible in-

be a kind of vicarious revenge element in all this, which is why, as I stressed before, we find a motivation for Roderick Random which sets him apart from other heroes of the picaresque: he wants to get even. Resentment sustains him, until he is able to follow it up with revenge. (Again, see the titles of the chapters: "I demolish the teeth of his tutor"; "Gawky's treachery—my revenge"; "Concert a scheme of revenge, and put it in execution"; "I get on shore, challenge the captain to single combat"; "Narcissa . . . is rescued by me, who revenge myself on my rival"; "I long to be revenged on Melinda," etc.) And he takes particular relish in his revenge, a relish that Smollett presumably shares because he is constantly enabling Roderick Random to score off his resentments—from the time he hit the tutor in the mouth with a stone to the duel where he not only runs Quiverwit through, but also knocks out his teeth with his sword hilt. It is a cruel world that Roderick Random inhabits; and the most satisfactory way of dealing with it seems to be to return blow for blow, and work off personal grudge by physical violence.

And this is quite consonant with Smollett's vision: when he describes the world as being sordid and vicious, he understands *vicious* to mean not only addicted to vice, but also savage or fierce.[13] Three years after *Roderick Random,* Smollett has a character in *Peregrine Pickle* say: "I have travelled over the greatest part of Europe. . . . I have learned that the characters of mankind are everywhere the same; that common sense and honesty bear an infinitely small proportion to folly and vice; and that life

---

fatuation," a place inflamed by "a few worthless incendiaries" where Smollett himself had been "traduced by malice, persecuted by faction, abandoned by false patrons"; all this is as nothing compared to the veritably enthusiastic denunciations of the continent and the continentals. Indeed, one could do an illuminating word study of the recurrence of Smollett's favorite terms of opprobrium throughout the *Travels.*

[13] The relationship between *Roderick Random,* Smollett's first satire in fiction, and his two earlier verse satires, "Advice" and "Reproof," has been commented on by Paulson, Bruce, McKillop, and Knapp in the studies cited above.

is at best a paltry province." The vision is un-picaresque, for the typical picaro sees life as something to be explored and exploited: the world is his oyster. That is one of the reasons why the typical picaro keeps bounding back; and perhaps it is why Smollett, that much put-upon but resilient man, was attracted to the picaresque form—the prevailing mode of his fictions. But Smollett, even at twenty-six, was seeing the world through a glass, darkly. The rather sullen, pessimistic vision he expresses is a deviation from the attitude informing the typical picaresque, for what informs Smollett's modified picaresque, in part, is the attitude of the fierce moral satirist.[14]

This is my concluding point about Smollett and the picaresque in decline: as I have been constantly stressing, he is a satirist; and his satire, as well as his unpicaresque vision, derive from his position as an affronted idealist.[15] Naturally, this puts him at a considerable distance from Le Sage, whose imperturbable remoteness and detachment seem spawned by an attitude that life *is* that way, and there is nothing one can do about it except laugh. But Smollett, with his resentment and irritation and misanthropy, can-

[14] I suspect that Smollett finds in the very flexibility of the picaresque form a latitude and focus he can modify for the purpose of satire. Consider his definition, in the preface to *Ferdinand Count Fathom:* "A novel is a large, diffused picture, comprehending the characters of life, disposed in different groups, and exhibited in various attitudes, for the purposes of an uniform plan, and general occurrence, to which every individual figure is subservient. But this plan cannot be executed with propriety, probability, or success, without a principal personage to attract the attention, unite the incidents, unwind the clue of the labyrinth, and at last close the scene, by virtue of his importance." It is in this same preface, cited above, p. 191, that Smollett states his intention to "subject folly to ridicule, and vice to indignation."

[15] See Goldberg: "Passionate, ebullient, a prey to his own untutored feelings as much as to the guile of a calloused world which artfully turns these feelings to its own advantage, Roderick must learn that only feelings controlled by reason, emotions reined by the understanding can be productive of the happiness and success he seeks," p. 22; Knapp speaks of ". . . Smollett's essential idealism and humanitarian desire to amend society. Amendment necessitated attack, and attack utilized the weapon of satire, which, in turn, involved libel, even personal libel," p. 63.

not really disguise the fact that he belongs to the Sensibility School,[16] including that class of it that believed in the perfectibility of human nature. He turns to abuse and invective and satire partly because he is outraged at how far man has fallen from the ideal; and partly because he subscribes to the classic notion, so often reflected by the eighteenth-century neoclassics, of the regenerative power of satire.[17] Sometimes this results in incongruous conversations which actually tend to blunt the edge of his satirical force, for Smollett occasionally turns his heroes into mouthpieces and has them deliver vigorous and sensible and well-reasoned lectures of the "I could not help thinking" or "This brought to my mind" variety. Usually there is nothing in the least wrong with the substance of the lectures, but the speakers are frequently inappropriate or just simply disconnected from the statements Smollett uses them to make. In any case, the lectures suggest a mind given over to reflection, whereas picaros are not notorious for any sustained reflective powers: life is too lively and changes too abruptly to allow them to indulge in long attention spans.

But this is minor evidence of Smollett's moralistic stance, and not very characteristic in his early novels. His affronted idealism and satiric indignation find much more characteristic vent in the ferocity and vindictiveness I mentioned earlier: "Drown the world!" as Swift once raged, and Smollett shares some of this impulse to scourge offending life. Of course, the picaresque itself traditionally uses hard-hitting and rough, crude physical slap-stick. This may be another reason for Smollett's being attracted to the genre.[18] Yet even granting the picaresque its proclivity for head-

[16] See George M. Kahrl, *Tobias Smollett, Traveler-Novelist* (Chicago, 1945), p. 96n.: "And, after all, there are serious reasons for believing that Smollett was not unlike Mrs. Gummidge of *David Copperfield:* 'Yes, yes. I feel more than other people do, and I show it more. It's my misfortun'.' "

[17] See Paulson, "Satire in the Early Novels of Smollett"; see also Robert Alter, *Rogue's Progress* (Cambridge, Mass., 1964), pp. 63–64. I admire Mr. Alter's study, and doubtless owe much to him that I have not documented, largely because I have assimilated so many of his insights.

[18] At least one critic has suggested that "he seems to have chosen the picaresque, with the familiar gallery of odd characters, usually criminal

smashing, bone-crunching—to say nothing of its enthusiasm for what current-day child psychologists refer to as bathroom jokes—Smollett's tendency is to deal in excesses. His satiric thrusts are constantly invaded by that predominant current of cruel violence in *Roderick Random,* as though it obsesses him. One finds it in Smollett's subsequent writings, too: whenever he is confronted by the craftiness and cruelty of man to man, he launches into furious fulminations which can be expressed only by graphic descriptions of brutality. It is not simply that young Smollett was proud and hot-headed, like young Roderick Random. He seems so offended by the evidence of the sordid and vicious tendency of the world that the only way his sensibilities can cope with it is by violence. It is a kind of calculated toughness, not to soften but to withstand the traumatic shocks of life. And somewhere along the line, whatever notions Smollett may have had for sustained satiric purpose in a fictional form got jettisoned. The violence is just too harsh for satiric control; it gets away from Smollett, as it were, and we are periodically confronted with lurid sadism and cruelty practised with a sort of inventive delight in having ingeniously contrived some engine of torment. I am thinking particularly of the schoolmaster's device for preventing Roderick Random from writing; and that whole sequence of nightmares on board the *Thunder:* Smollett just keeps piling it on. This is a very different order of violence from the "more normal" and everyday variety in the cosmos of *Roderick Random* where, as one critic observes, "a repartee consists of a punch in the jaw, an argument of a butt in the stomach." [19]

This whole complex of brutality tends to become offensive after a while. What with the unpleasant hero, the entire affair

---

types, strung together in a series of episodes, because he had a grudge against society." Laurence Brander, *Tobias Smollett* in *British Writers and Their Work,* no. 6 (Lincoln, Nebraska, 1965), p. 122; see also F. C. Green, *Minuet* (New York, 1935), p. 350.

[19] A. R. Humphreys, "Fielding and Smollett," in *From Dryden to Johnson* (Baltimore, Md., 1963), p. 327.

rather affronts one's normal sense; one's emotional responses just do not work; and Smollett's hopes of securing sustained "humane passions" for his hero cannot be actualized. An interesting feature of this excessive cruelty in Smollett's vision is its unquestionably genuine physical realism. The moral and physical sordidness represents an aspect of eighteenth-century life which was certainly apparent to all beholders, as even a cursory study of Hogarth shows. And if the noise and stench and filth and squalor—the grotesque disease that so much lower class life was—are only rarely reflected in literature, this does not mean that they were only rarely perceptible. Of all the eighteenth-century writers, Smollett is the one who most fully captures that sense of violent and brutal existence, that "edge to life" which J. H. Plumb so brilliantly describes. In line with this, Smollett includes a graphically anti-heroic depiction of the stupidities and hell of military service and warfare.

But he has to match violence with violence in order to behold it; and the affronting grotesquerie that life is forces him to make a crueler grotesque of it by sort of "juicing up" the brutality and ferocity. One of the most striking effects of this attitude is in that caricaturing impulse I mentioned earlier, which exhibits a cruel streak. It is not simply what is picturesque or odd or fantastic; the constant and exclusive exaggeration of physical traits suggests something almost ill-natured. One can apprehend it more clearly if one thinks of Jonsonian satirical caricature: Jonson also portrays his characters as stereotyped manifestations of a ruling passion, but he conceives of the ruling passion in terms of temperament. Smollett largely ignores this more sophisticated conception, limiting his caricature to the physical (possibly he assumes that such an emphasis can also speak for the temperament and moral context). Even people he likes, such as Uncle Tom and, later, Hawser Trunnion and Lismahago, get harsh treatment from Smollett's crude and vigorous caricature.

I do not know how ill-natured Smollett was, if at all. He did get into many acrimonious fights with an assortment of people—

and he did have some very hard words to say about things which deserved criticism. He was an angry man, notorious for a hot temper in an era when tempers ran hot, and he was exposed to many conflicts and frustrations. In his early verse and fiction, he displays ruthless personal satire and invective—undoubtedly the product of his temper. And one suspects that literature, including frequent outbursts in his letters and reviews, was a major channel for venting his rages. Which is all well and good, but it is incompatible with the picaresque vision. It occurs to me that one of the requirements for a genuine picaro was the ability not to "lose his cool," as some modern picaros would phrase it. Smollett and Roderick Random were always losing theirs. However, Smollett could never have written anything other than modified picaresque, because he cared too much, responded too strongly; because he was, in short, not only a sentimentalist but also an idealist whose toughness was only skin deep. As he says of himself in that fine self-portrait, Matthew Bramble, "he is as tender as a man without a skin, who cannot bear the slightest touch without flinching." [20] A further insight comes from another passage in Smollett's last novel: "He affects misanthropy, in order to conceal the sensibility of a heart which is tender even to a degree of weakness." [21]

I think this hits it precisely: Smollett may have tried to indoctrinate himself with Augustan Age rationalism, but underneath it all where the passions and emotions lie he was a Man of Sensibility.[22] It made him do curious things with the picaresque, and

[20] See also his dedication in *Ferdinand Count Fathom*, a perceptive self-portrait; and A. D. McKillop's comment that Goldsmith's Man in Black in *Citizen of the World*, Letter XXVI, is the "mellow" Smollett, p. 176.

[21] For an illuminating study of the mature Smollett's success in combining the "satire with a scourge" with the "Man of Feeling," see Thomas R. Preston, "Smollett and the Benevolent Misanthrope," *PMLA*, LXXIX (March, 1964), 51–57.

[22] See *Letters* 2, mourning the death of a friend in language that almost sounds like a set-piece of sensibility with his "imagination brood[ing] o'er [his] melancholy," his throbbing heart, and his "weeping muse [which] would fain pay a tribute to his *Manes*," and so on. (p. 2). Edward S. Noyes calls attention to the remarkable similarity between these sentiments and

with the basic assumption of the picaresque vision that while life is hard, it is also pretty good and experience is worth seeking. One cannot be too sure of this assumption in the world of *Roderick Random*. I suppose essentially there is not a great difference between Gil Blas's being buffeted about by chance and mischance, and Roderick Random's being the tennis ball of fortune. But there certainly is a difference in attitude: Gil Blas, in his energetic and blithe masquerading, thinks he is the master of his destiny and demonstrates a genius for adaptability. Roderick Random, as he is tossed about, seems more moved by a stoic resolution to hang on until he can get revenge; about the best that happens to him is that he survives from one bout with adversity to the next—a real scapegrace, a ne'er-do-well who escapes grace, as Robert Alter points out.

And the paradigm of the vision of Roderick Random's world is in the midst of those grisly sea-going chapters, particularly chapter XXX, where Roderick Random is falsely accused of espionage because the malicious idiots who persecute him insist the Greek characters he writes in his diary are a code. Although hostile witnesses lie in claiming to know Greek and speak Gaelic to prove their knowledge, nobody will believe the innocent Roderick Random. *He* knows the truth, his words *are* the truth, but on this ship of malign fools—a microcosm of the universe [23]—everyone is against him and no one believes him. It is a stunning example of the vision, and a horrifying vision, too; it could drive a man mad. Nothing could be further from the picaresque vision than this.

A final comment about Smollett's picaresque in decline: the last part of Roderick Random's adventures has nothing to do with

---

diction and Renaldo's lament for Monimia several years later in *Ferdinand Count Fathom*, chapter 62 (*Letters,* Cambridge, Mass., 1926, p. 115).

[23] See Claude E. Jones, *Smollett Studies* (Berkeley, 1942), pp. 31–32: "Each ship had to carry men to fight her and repair her, men to set the course and men to steer it, surgeons to tend the sick and cooks to feed the healthy; she was a microcosm complete in almost every detail."

the picaresque at all, as many people have noticed. These final chapters deal with his love for Narcissa, and they are ludicrous and badly written. Romance has no place in the picaresque; it is part of the sentimental literature and vision which run counter to the picaresque. For the picaro is made for action, not for savored and treasured feeling and reaction. Moreover, romance requires a different orientation—slower, more inward, with the characters possessing an inner life that this type of fiction explores. Roderick Random's protestations of love are silly and unconvincing; his actions as a man transported by love are even sillier; and his descriptions of the object of his love are silliest of all—and Smollett is not writing intentional parody. He appears to be attempting, most unsuccessfully, to fuse two incompatible modes.

But the failure is significant. By 1748 the Sensibility Movement was assuming increasing dominance, both in France and in England, and it contributed to the decline of the picaresque. For in its attitude; in its inward, emotional focus; in its techniques of presentation, there is no place for the energy of invention and improvisation, for the world of physical action, and for the multiplicity of quick, transitory surface relationships that make up the world of the picaresque. Paulson finds in Smollett an instructive instance:

The early novels, then, show us an instructive progression in technique by a writer who could (or would) no longer write in the forms of Pope and Swift. We have seen some of the problems the novel form offers a writer who wishes to write satire; and Smollett's example may tell us something of why satire, in the age of the novel, died.[24]

I think Smollett's picaresque in decline offers an instructive example, too; but I suspect satire did not die because of the novel's inability to encompass features of formal, traditional verse satire. I think it died because so committed a man of feeling as Smollett could not contain his emotions sufficiently to produce "good" satire. And I think it died because the Sensibility School, prone to

[24] p. 402.

weep over "who killed Cock Robin," drowned the cocky picaresque in a plethora of emotionalism. Smollett's *Roderick Random,* first modifying the picaresque in an attempt to absorb the
outraged feelings of the moral satirist, then awkwardly introducing
an inappropriate love interest, shows us something of how it happened.

HAROLD E. PAGLIARO

Structural Patterns of Control
in *Rasselas*

I

THOSE WHO HAVE WRITTEN about *Rasselas* have sel-
dom regarded the work seriously as a piece of fiction, except to
refer it to the tradition of the oriental tale, for the most part to
show that it draws upon and yet deviates from that genre.[1]
Usually they have treated it as a moral tract; and having discovered that Imlac may often be thought of as Johnson's spokesman,
they have understood the "meaning" of the work to inhere in its
explicit statements, particularly in Imlac's. Occasionally a critic
has pointed to Johnson's irony, but he has done so primarily to
clarify the moral level of the work, not to help explore its tech-

[1] Gwin J. Kolb, "The Structure of *Rasselas*," *PMLA,* LXVI (1951),
698–717, by reason of his emphasis, provides an exception; though, like
most other critics, Kolb reasonably assumes that *Rasselas* has a moral aim,
he characterizes the novel's structure, in detail, in order to indicate something about the fictional means by which the book accomplishes its moral
purpose and to demonstrate that it is not an Eastern tale, except for its setting.

niques as fiction. Similarly, treatments of time in *Rasselas* have tried to show that its temporal references contribute to the novel's religious rather than to its fictional powers.[2] Although there can be no serious doubt that the book is capable of bearing an enormous moral burden, it seems reasonable to try to consider the work as fiction, and to try to see whether it has "meaning" in the interplay of certain of its rhetorical elements, rather than in Johnson's "intention" or in Imlac's observations. Its form invites such an appraisal. In addition, the memory it has left in the minds of many—the memory of a complicated world of people, which the reader has visited and left behind and to which he contemplates his return with pleasure, in the knowledge that he will find it as he left it—suggests its fictional as distinct from its probably related moral impact.

Throughout the novel Johnson's narrator presents a point of view (or a principle), and at almost the same time another point of view (or principle) that somehow opposes the first. Implied or stated explicitly by a single character, or developed by means of the dialogue, or delivered by the narrator himself, these opposed elements cover a wide range. They may in effect say that art requires a knowledge of general nature and a knowledge of particulars, that human activity is vain repetition and profitable endeavor, that age brings wisdom and tranquility, and it brings doubt and restlessness; they may also require one's simultaneous regard of youth and age, wisdom and folly, joy and sorrow, motion and stability, faith and skepticism, fullness and emptiness. The important point is that the narrator of *Rasselas* does not permit such paired elements (which are in fact very often related to each other in

[2] Agostino Lombardo, "The Importance of Imlac," *Bicentenary Essays on Rasselas* (Cairo, 1959), 31–49, in a way typical of criticism about *Rasselas*, begins by demonstrating that Imlac is Johnson's spokesman. Later on, however, his essay explores the novel for the fictional as well as the moral consequences of Johnson's irony. Geoffrey Tillotson, "Time in *Rasselas*," *Bicentenary Essays*, 97–103, considers the moral and religious effects of Johnson's uses of time, and in the process pays some attention to the work as fiction.

human experience) to reveal themselves in what might be regarded as natural ways. Instead, he seems to yoke them together, a technique that may leave the reader pulled to one or the other of the two elements, or undecided between them, or (a delayed reaction, perhaps) willing to accommodate himself to whatever new and unusual principle or experience their enforced connection with each other may move him to discover. In fact, it may be that readers experience two, or all three, of these responses, given enough time.

Before I take up a few examples of these yoked pairs—like Imlac-Rasselas, detail-generalization, quest-withdrawal, time-eternity—in an attempt to indicate that they are artfully rather than naturally joined, and further to suggest that in some ways this pattern defines the fictional world of the work, I should like to clarify an important point. It will become apparent that, logically speaking, the elements in these various pairs may be related to each other in one (or more) of many ways. For example, the second may contradict the first or it may synthesize particulars provided in the first; or the two confronting elements may be parallel statements of similar (or of contrasting) actions; they may be two characters who share remarkably similar or remarkably different histories or attitudes, or remarkably similar as well as remarkably different histories or attitudes. Despite the variety of logical relationship between the two elements, the elements in pairs of whatever class have in common a single factor; that is, their enforced proximity points up differences as well as similarities between them, such that for a time, at least, neither one alone seems to have a usual meaning. In one sense, while they are rhetorically joined, the elements modify each other's meanings to produce a third or mediated significance. Obviously such an effect from Johnson's use of yoked pairs—long since observed by his critics, incidentally [3]—cannot be uniform; at least it seems unlikely that it

[3] Many critics have observed that Johnson writes (probably thinks) in pairs of various kinds; they have also pointed out that it is very hard to say what the relationship between the two elements in these pairs may be;

should be so. In fact, apart from the general psychological force I have claimed to be common to all of them, each one doubtless behaves in its own peculiar way. But instead of attempting as a preliminary step to classify all of the kinds of relationships between paired elements in the novel, I hope to make critical use of them immediately, giving attention to the individual ways in which a pair may work rhetorically, but not necessarily trying to point out all of its formal characteristics.

Without at all violating one's sense for the changing world of men, the world of *Rasselas* is made to seem eternal. Johnson creates and sustains this illusion by repeating until it is ubiquitous a single binary pattern—in the form of yoked pairs—in countless variations. For the moment, the pattern may be simply, though rather cryptically, expressed as (a) the quest for data (or the occurrence of data) in the physical world and (b) the integration of that data into such apparently stable forms as works of art, fixed and protected locations, ways of life, or finished histories. As I have already suggested, the point is not merely that in *Rasselas* one may observe both these sets of data and the stable forms into which they are gathered—one might justly point out such a relationship in many literary works—but that Johnson juxtaposes the one and the other so consistently that the world of the work is defined primarily by the technique. It governs not only the characters and their relationships with each other, their attitude toward experience, and the specific problems they encounter; it also controls the features of narrative episode, the value assigned to space and locations, and the idea of time.

The novel's most nearly ubiquitous pair is Imlac-Rasselas.

---

further, they have thought the relationship between the elements in pairs to be important. Among these critics are W. K. Wimsatt, *The Prose Style of Samuel Johnson* (New Haven, 1941), pp. 36, 52, 61–62; Jean Hagstrum, *Samuel Johnson's Literary Criticism* (Minneapolis, 1952), p. 6; Walter Jackson Bate, *The Achievement of Samuel Johnson* (New York, 1955), p. 68; Robert Voitle, *Samuel Johnson the Moralist* (Cambridge, Mass., 1961), pp. 20–21; Paul Kent Alkon, *Samuel Johnson and Moral Discipline* (Evanston, Ill., 1967), pp. 5–6.

Despite the early chapters in which Rasselas appears alone, the two men are essentially characterized by means of distinct contrasts, comparisons, and interpenetrations of their characters. That is, after their identities are nominally established, their characters are made out to be adversatively different from each other, the same as each other, and composites of each other. Rasselas is young, Imlac is old; the one is a prince, the other a commoner; Imlac has completed a futile quest, after which he has retired, whereas Rasselas, imprisoned in the Happy Valley, longs to begin a search for the good life. Imlac, in part an emblem of full and completed things, generalizes his experience into art—the story of his own life; Rasselas, the empty vessel, ". . . asked a thousand questions about things . . . [and] commanded Imlac to relate his history. . . ." [4] Imlac characterizes the present in the terms of the past; Rasselas finds the present disconcerting and insufficient, except insofar as it promises a future. It is chiefly by the means of these contrasts that the two men are symmetrically opposed to each other.

Like the differences, the similarities between them are also symmetrical—in some ways too symmetrical to be usual in occurrence. As soon as it has been established that Rasselas is a young man living in an incredibly secure environment, which he regards as deadly and from which he longs to escape to explore the world, because he suffers from restlessness, perhaps caused (but not calmed) by his considerable intelligence, the reader sees him confronted by an intelligent old man, who was in his youth much like Rasselas—sensitive, idealistic, naive. The son of a wealthy merchant, young Imlac, too, longed to leave his secure home because he was restless; and prompted by largely undefined aspirations (like Rasselas, seeking the good life), he wandered for years, forsaking his patrimony. The two are made to be like each other by implied as well as by stated similarities; indeed, one would have

[4] Samuel Johnson, *History of Rasselas,* ed. George Birkbeck Hill (Oxford, 1887); impression of 1954, p. 54. Hereafter, quotations from Birkbeck Hill's edition will be located by page references in the body of my essay.

to struggle to discover a real difference in their intellects and temperaments. Neither is more moral, more intelligent, more charitable, more passionate, more sensitive than the other.

In order to explain such a lack of differentiation, one might say that like all characters in Eastern tales, Johnson's are flat. Certainly some of the techniques employed in *Rasselas* are conventions of a genre, and in some ways it is true that here Johnson follows the tradition. On the other hand, he also adds to, reshaping thereby, the genre's conventional method of characterization, so that it seems reasonable to suggest for the moment what I hope will emerge clearly later—that a new dimension results from the fact that Imlac and Rasselas are not just different from each other —their differences are adversative; they are not just similar to each other—their similarities are duplicating.

The first paragraph of the novel foreshadows these features of difference and sameness in the two characters.

> Ye who listen with credulity to the whispers of fancy, and pursue with eagerness the phantoms of hope, who expect that age will perform the promises of youth, and that the deficiencies of the present day will be supplied by the morrow,—attend to the history of Rasselas, prince of Abyssinia. (p. 37)

In this opening sentence, generalized youth and age, like Rasselas and Imlac throughout the earlier parts of the novel, are separated by their different expectations for the future. Implicit in this statement of difference, however, is the promise of ultimate sameness, to be brought about by the art of the novel *Rasselas*. In a similar way, Imlac's history, which begins with a youth in Rasselas's predicament, anticipates that the old storyteller and the young listener, about to begin his own adventures, will be united finally. Both these early prophecies are fulfilled, of course. Throughout the duration of the work Rasselas (the nominal Rasselas) moves toward the thing that Imlac (the nominal Imlac) has already become. By the time of the concluding chapter, though still distinguishable by age and rank, the two are almost the same; each has achieved a point of view he temperately maintains—the view being that one may lead a useful life but that to quest for the good life is futile.

Johnson employs another technique to characterize a different level of the relationship between Imlac and Rasselas. Unlike the devices that stress adversative or duplicating qualities in the two, and unlike the devices that forecast their ultimate identity, while asserting their difference in the present, this one accomplishes their interpenetration. In effect, even while the technique makes emphatic the nominal identification of one of the men, it gives him qualities peculiar to the nominal identification of the other. For example, Imlac, though experience is in many ways behind him, shows a quick willingness to join the prince, soon to be on the move, in part because the old man, despite his knowledge of the world, has grown weary of the Happy Valley; and Rasselas, who is restless for want of the opportunity to explore the outside world, desires to discover a settled way of life and to adhere to it. Another dimension of this connection becomes available if one observes first that all three young people (Rasselas, Nekayah, Pekuah) have a more or less single view of Imlac and of the quest, just as Imlac regards them more or less collectively as representing youth; and if one recalls next that Imlac, though he knows the futility of an absolute quest like the one Rasselas embarks upon, nevertheless responsibly and unobtrusively guides his charges (he more than casually associates himself with them); the questing young people, who reject the second-hand experience with which Imlac could provide them, nevertheless respect him profoundly (they associate themselves with him). As a result of the interpenetration of the characters, the reader who responds to this device identifies himself neither with the tale's completed elder (who is not merely set in his ways) nor with the peripatetic young people (who after all long for a regulated life), but with their joint worlds. In a way, Imlac is Rasselas grown wise; and Rasselas is the Imlac who leaves his father's home. It seems worth the comment that evidence for regarding the young man as mature (for example, he is generally "responsible"; he has force enough—can it be only his rank?—to stop Imlac's "enthusiastic fit" in Chapter XI) and the old man as adventurous is available early in the novel; that is, Johnson's mediation between their roles occurs throughout major sections of the work and so contributes to the illusion that Imlac-Rasselas exists eternally, independent of the world of circumstance, though the component men are of course not free of it.

Johnson's other, previously cited, methods of characterization, which force upon the reader's attention the differences and similarities between Imlac and Rasselas, also contribute to the merger of their characters. It might seem as if Johnson began with adversative differences between them too bold to be overcome. The two men are divided enormously by age and therefore by experience; it might appear impossible that they should be united. But in fact their differences are of little consequence except in time, whose inexorable passage guarantees their union, because they are in many ways duplicates of each other, separated only by a generation or so. Fulfillment of the prophecy of the opening paragraph and of Imlac's history is aided, as time moves in the novel, by the fated congruity of their basic characters. Slight idiosyncratic differences between them survive to the end of the work, but they have been bound to each other at a much deeper level of significance.

II

The novel's repeated pattern of the quest for data (personified by Rasselas) and the integration of data into stable forms (personified by Imlac) is given an even more obvious form in Chapter X than it is in the other parts of the narrative. The chapter is generally remembered for its passage about the streaks of the tulip, which is included in Imlac's opinion that "the business of a poet . . . is to examine, not the individual, but the species; to remark general properties and large appearances. He does not number the streaks of the tulip . . ." (p. 62). Immediately preceding this well-known speech about the generalizing nature of art, there occurs a brief exchange between Imlac and Rasselas. In the first part of this dialogue the older man explains that he prepared himself to write poetry by examining nature in great detail; in the second part Rasselas questions what his teacher says; after he is questioned Imlac delivers his famous words about the poet's need to remark general properties:

"Being now resolved to be a poet, I saw everything with a new purpose; my sphere of attention was suddenly magnified; no kind of knowledge was to be overlooked. I ranged mountains and deserts for images and resemblances, and pictured upon my mind every tree of the forest and flower of the valley. I observed with equal care the crags of the rock and the pinnacles of the palace. Sometimes I wandered along the mazes of the rivulet, and sometimes watched the changes of the summer. clouds. To a poet nothing can be useless. Whatever is beautiful, and whatever is dreadful, must be familiar to his imagination: he must be conversant with all that is awfully vast or elegantly little. The plants of the garden, the animals of the wood, the minerals of the earth, and meteors of the sky, must all concur to store his mind with inexhaustible variety: for every idea is useful for the enforcement or decoration of moral or religious truth; and he who knows most, will have most power of diversifying his scenes, and of gratifying his reader with remote allusions and unexpected instruction.

"All the appearances of nature I was therefore careful to study; and every country which I have surveyed has contributed something to my poetical powers."

"In so wide a survey," said the prince, "you must surely have left much unobserved. I have lived, till now, within the circuit of these mountains, and yet cannot walk abroad without the sight of something which I had never beheld before, or never heeded."

"The business of a poet," said Imlac, "is to examine, not the individual, but the species; to remark general properties and large appearances. He does not number the streaks of the tulip, or describe the different shades in the verdure of the forest: he is to exhibit in his portraits of nature such prominent and striking features, as recal [sic] the original to every mind; and must neglect the minuter discriminations, which one may have remarked, and another have neglected, for those characteristics which are alike obvious to vigilance and carelessness." (pp. 62–63)

This sequence of speeches, apparently easy to understand, has in fact inspired at least three general responses. Probably most casual readers remember the words "streaks of the tulip," which they associate with the idea that art ought to generalize experience, in part by avoiding the presentation of details. Another group, taking into account both Imlac's first statement about the necessity for gathering detail, and his second, about remarking general properties, regard the two as the steps that characterize induction—gathering data and forming conclusions from the evidence—the first describing the poet as observer, the second the poet as writer. A third group points out that the streaks-of-the-tulip passage encourages too much abstraction in art; this group is divided between those who believe Johnson elsewhere compensates for this critical bias and those who argue that he does not.[5] That the dialogue has provoked a wide range of response indicates both its difficulty and its fascination.

One may observe that in the general-properties or streaks-of-the-tulip section of the discourse, Imlac uses certain terms—one term in particular—that have two meanings, one of which obtains when the term applies to the search for detail, and the other, when it applies to the process of forming generalizations. A glance at the quoted text above will reveal that after he delivers the fairly long speech about the poet's need "to store his mind with inexhaustible variety . . ." so that among other things he may gratify ". . . his reader with remote allusions and unexpected instruction"; and after he hears from Rasselas the view that one could never complete such an ambitious undertaking, Imlac begins the general-properties speech by saying, "The business of the poet . . . is to examine, not the individual, but the species. . . ." In the *Dictionary*, Johnson defines "examine" so that it may signify either the observation of detail or the testing of general principles

[5] René Wellek (*A History of Modern Criticism: 1750–1950*, I, New Haven, 1955, 85–87) hardly qualifies his opinion that Johnson overstresses the need in art for general and transcendental truths. On the other hand, M. H. Abrams (*The Mirror and the Lamp*, New York, 1953, p. 40) says, "Imlac's admonition to the poet to describe the general properties and familiar appearances of nature must be taken in conjunction with Johnson's acclaim of Shakespeare as 'an exact surveyor of the inanimate world' whose 'descriptions have always some peculiarities. . .' ".

arrived at after the close study of a subject. That he should do so is reasonable, not at all surprising. But Imlac's use of the term in the context of Chapter X raises at least two questions. First, why should the old man, who just moments before had urged the young poet's scrutiny of detail, suddenly deny—unequivocally deny—its place in the poetical process? "The business of the poet . . . is to examine, *not the individual*,[6] but the species. . . ." The contradiction suggests either that Imlac (abruptly checked by Rasselas) feels socially uncomfortable about the very high value he has placed on the search for data, or that he is attempting to correct a misapprehension, in the prince's mind, about the value of detail, a misapprehension for which he feels himself responsible. Whatever Imlac's reason, the effect of his argumentative shift is to mar the otherwise neat relationship, inferred by many readers, between the poet's early observation of data and his later "remark [ing] general properties. . . ." Second, how can one examine a species? Where does a species exist that it may be scrutinized? One may abstract the idea of a species from one's knowledge of individuals, but as Locke (whom Johnson quotes in defining "examine") points out in Book III, "Of Words," in *An Essay Concerning Human Understanding,* ". . . general and universal belong not to the real existence of things; but are the inventions of the creatures of understanding, made by it, for its own use, and concern only signs. . . ." Obviously, the species has no dwelling place; it is available only to the mind's eye, and therefore can be examined only as an idea, through the agency of imagination. To secure the conclusion inferred (and as I believe erroneously inferred) by many readers —that the passage simply means the poet should examine particulars first and make generalizations afterwards—Johnson might have had Imlac respond to Rasselas's objection that the examination of particulars could never be completed, with words like these: "Of course you are right; no poet can complete his investigation of particulars; nor did I say he could, nor for that matter,

---

[6] The italics are mine.

that he should; but after he has studied particulars diligently for some time, he may safely draw upon his knowledge of the individual to formulate generalizations about the species." The formulation Imlac uses, however, seems rather to say something like this: "When the poet examines the world of particulars, it is not his business to examine particulars for their own sake, nor for his necessarily later reference to them, but to provide himself with as many opportunities as possible to imagine the general idea they suggest, stimulated (at the moment, or later on through his memory) by the physical world of examples; in one sense, the business of the poet is to examine not the individual, but the species which the world's many individuals may suggest to his mind's eye."

To be sure, Imlac's two-part delivery is indeed a presentation of the two steps in the inductive process, but the manner of the delivery stresses the mediation between the process of gathering data and the process of generalization. For Imlac the relationship between the two steps is not precisely temporal—it is not the crucial matter, nor, indeed, need it be true, that *after* one examines particulars, one formulates generalizations; nor is the relationship between them precisely causal— it is not the crucial matter, nor need it be true, that *because* one examines particulars, one formulates generalizations. The operation, Imlac's words suggest, may be better regarded as having two levels, such that to perceive particulars may be simultaneously to conceive generalizations. Even if one performs the induction after he has left the laboratory containing the data, he may be said "to examine" in memory both that data and the species he "sees" in them, at one and the same time; and his art, as M. H. Abrams suggests, may partake of both elements.[7]

The ironic treatment of Imlac in Chapter X, and the beginning of Chapter XI, both by Rasselas and by the narrator, raises the question of whether what the old man says in this section of the novel may be seriously regarded. According to the narrator,

[7] Abrams, p. 40.

Imlac is at one point ridiculous because he is seized by an "enthusiastic fit"; and Rasselas, who elsewhere respects his guide's views,
twice takes exception to Imlac's opinions in these two chapters.
The first time, it will be recalled, he expresses doubt that the poet
can ever complete his preparation for composition; the second
time, he puts a stop to Imlac's ludicrous extravagance—the "enthusiastic fit." It seems important that Rasselas does not object to
the streaks-of-the-tulip passage, a fact, incidentally, that may help
to account for its detachability from context and its isolated sur-
vival in almost every reader's memory. Indeed, it is only when
Imlac aggrandizes his profession by stressing the poet's acquisition
of detailed information that he is satirized; otherwise, he is at
least neutrally regarded. In one way, this selective irony helps to
alter what might otherwise be the workaday relationship between
the processes of gathering data and of generalization. When the
first process, gathering data, becomes the basis of Imlac's aggran-
dizement of the poet's profession—and therefore an end in itself
—it is reduced satirically; but when Imlac, probably startled and
embarrassed by Rasselas's charge that the poet can never complete
his preparation, asserts the interpenetration of the two processes,
as he has been shown to do, his view seems to be accepted.

III

        The general pattern of the quest for data and the integration
of data into stable forms is also expressed in the novel's uses of
space. Throughout *Rasselas,* places are usually either fixed locations for meditation, recuperation, or retreat from the dangerous
world of action, or they are areas through which one journeys in
quest of diversity. It is important to recognize that other novels
which make use of this same polarity modify its operation by
using space in other than these two ways; but in *Rasselas,* alternative possibilities occur rarely. For example, space is only once (the
time of Pekuah's abduction) ground to be coursed over in a limited time; only twice does it separate people from each other (Pekuah from Nekayah; and Imlac, briefly, toward the end of his first

long journey from family and friends); with few exceptions no interest is shown in topography as topography; and, of course, land is unimportant as personal property. Besides, it may be observed even of these few exceptions, that their importance is invariably reduced by one or the other of Johnson's two customary uses of space.

The Happy Valley is the principal emblem of a place that is circumscribed and defined (its data integrated); it is, moreover, a place in one way or another associated with security, secrecy, stability, permanence, privacy, and remoteness from erratic action, so that its definition as a fixed place is in a sense guaranteed. In the same category of locus are young Imlac's father's household, the pyramids, the "obscure [island] residence" of Pekuah's Arab captor (as well as his " . . . tower set apart for celestial observations"), the hermit's cave, the astronomer's observatory, the catacombs, monasteries in the abstract, and (with important qualifications) Cairo, the starting point and terminus of many excursions. Throughout the novel the spiritual condition of characters is largely defined by their remaining in or their moving toward, or away from, such established places—occasionally, by their thwarted desire to do so. Generally, when they are in secure retirement, they long for the opportunity to replenish themselves with explorations; and as they explore, they hope for stability and rest; for " . . . some desire is necessary to keep life in motion; and he whose real wants are supplied, must admit those of fancy" (p. 56).

Johnson intensifies the reader's sense for the juxtaposition of fixed place and exploration ("life in motion") in several ways. His chief device is to introduce characters who through choice or circumstance are about to leave a place (closely associated with their defined way of life) for some less clearly defined locale. Imlac (both as youth and elder), Rasselas, Nekayah, Pekuah, the hermit, and (after some delay) the astronomer are all caught up in the action of this pattern. Even the philosopher, though he leaves no specific location, is metaphorically returned to the unstable world of random data, transformed into " . . . a lonely being disunited from society" (p. 84), whereas only hours before, he had ostensibly lived according to reason, a faculty like " . . . the [stable] sun, of which the light is constant, uniform, and lasting" (p. 82). Wherever in the novel the reader finds himself, characters and actions are in part defined, figuratively or literally, in spatial terms referring to stable and confined places or to erratic and questing motion.

Often Johnson uses dialogue rather than the direct movement of characters to juxtapose the bold static-kinetic alternatives in the world of space. For example, the Arab chief, who has returned with Pekuah to his ". . . strong and spacious house built with stone in an island of the Nile," characterizes his own full life in the terms of swift spatial alternation (enjoyed by him alone of all the characters in the world of the work); and he implies at the very time that he assures her of her safety, that she will be missing half of life while she remains confined in his protection.

"Lady . . . , you shall rest after your journey a few weeks in this place, where you are to consider yourself as sovereign. My occupation is war: I have therefore chosen this obscure residence from which *I can issue unexpected,* and to which *I can retire unpursued.* You may now repose in security; here there are *few pleasures,* but here is *no danger"* [Italics added]. (p. 129)

In a speech similarly sympathetic to the human longing for the peace one may find in retirement, Imlac weighs the value of the monastic life, which his words "weak," "timorous," "weary," and "penitent" very heavily qualify.

"In monasteries, the weak and timorous may be happily sheltered, the weary may repose, and the penitent may meditate. Those retreats of prayer and contemplation have something so congenial to the mind of men, that, perhaps, there is scarcely one that does not purpose to close his life in pious abstraction, with a few associates serious as himself." (p. 152)

One infers that the full life, the closest thing in this world to the good life, requires a special combination of exploration and withdrawal.

It is in the complicated pyramid-abduction episode that Johnson most dramatically treats this theme, through his controlled uses of space. To put the matter simply, one might say that the pyramid they visited, of ". . . such stability as defeated all the common attacks of the elements, and could scarcely be overthrown by earthquakes themselves . . ." (p. 111), is the unrivalled example of fixed and defined location; its appropriate counterpoise in Johnson's persistently symmetrical world of the novel would be some frantic motion, which Pekuah's kidnapping, the only violent action of the entire work, clearly provides. But in addition to this dramatic culmination in the use of a technique controlling much of the novel, the episode presents very strong clues as to the nature of mediation between static and kinetic worlds; it is here that "meaning" emerges from the author's uses of space.

After the abduction, Nekayah's identification with the static world of the pyramid (in a sense she is part of the realm she urged the reluctant Pekuah to enter) is verbally reaffirmed by her announcements of tenacious (static) mourning, by means of which she clings to the image of the lost Pekuah; at the same time Imlac and Rasselas try, at first with only momentary success, to move her (spatially) away from the fixed idea: ". . . [Nekayah's] mind, though forced into short excursions, always recurred to the image of her friend" (p. 119). Then, as if rebuking herself for the "short excursions" away from the lost companion, she ". . . resolved to retire from the world with all its flatteries and deceits, and . . . hide . . . in solitude . . ." (p. 119). Her intensified desire for fixed and stable things, which through the loss of her friend she feels to be both invaluable and unattainable, is gradually reduced; and unwillingly she takes Imlac's advice, offered, it seems inevitably, in the terms of movement and inaction:

"Do not suffer life to stagnate; it will grow muddy for want of motion; commit yourself again to the current of the world; Pekuah will vanish by degrees: you will meet on your way some other favourite, or learn to diffuse yourself in general conversation." (p. 121)

Pekuah, on the other hand, having refused the static pyramid, is made to endure a strenuous excursion, after which she slowly and

reluctantly accommodates herself to confinement by the Arab
chief, who is himself a uniquely composite figure—made up of the
still and the moving—his occupation being war, for which he "issue[s] unexpected," and his avocation, astronomy, for which he
repairs to "a tower set apart" (p. 129). The reader who is made to
observe Nekayah and Pekuah in their forlorn conditions comes to
see their inadequacy until they are changed by time and circumstance; as a result of this change, they are momentarily a combination of their former selves, seen from one point of view. But it is
the Arab who most dramatically mediates between their attitudes.
Quite literally, he has covered the distance that separates the two
young women, and later he is shown to represent both their original points of view. In addition to representing, by means of his
way of life, the themes both of movement and retreat, he anticipates (in a distorted form) Imlac's definition of the place that is no
place—the heavenly city where the Nekayah-Pekuah problem cannot exist. "You may now repose in security," the Arab tells Pekuah, having delivered her to his hideaway; "here . . . are few
pleasures, but here is no danger." And thereafter Imlac, referring
to that order of eternity which does not require poetry to combine
the idea of permanence and man's restless will, alters and yet
echoes the Arab's words: "In the state of future perfection, to
which we all aspire, there will be *pleasure* without *danger,* and *security* without *restraint*" [Italics added] (p. 152).

Speaking figuratively, one might say that throughout the
novel Johnson's treatment of Imlac-Rasselas blurs the clear sense
for time by forecasting and accomplishing the merger of youth and
age; for in a variety of ways Johnson lets the reader know that
Imlac was/is/will be Rasselas, and that Rasselas is/will be
Imlac, though each man is of course his nominal self as well.
Similarly, he blurs the distinction between the two steps of induction, so that data-questing ("youth") and generalizing ("age")
are also one. Moreover, the novel works to merge one's ideas of
place and motion, the ostensibly known here and unknown there;
and in the process illustrates the futility of trying to live the full

life either in perpetual quest or in complete retirement. Finally, it seems clear, no combination of quest and withdrawal can produce the good life. It is in this connection that Imlac's skewed repetition of the Arab's words is tantalizing, because that repetition implicitly rejects the best the Arab can do with his own life. That is, even though the warrior-astronomer (the Arab) is capable of mediating between static and kinetic forces, between Pekuah and Nekayah, between here and there, he himself merely alternates between the one and the other, at best a mechanical accomplishment. He knows how to live the full life, and he may even momentarily induce in others a sense for the good life, but he is as far from its attainment as anyone else.

It is, of course, Imlac (offering a conventional religious prediction) who characterizes the good life, using the Arab's terms to suggest not opposition, nor alternation, between motion and retirement, but their interpenetration: "In the state of future perfection . . . , there will be pleasure [whose source for mortals is diversity through quest, which is unstable hence dangerous] without danger, and security [whose source for mortals is retirement, a restricting condition] without restraint." In such a condition one has the blessings of both elements at once, and the pains of neither.

IV

The narrator's numerous references to time (particularly time in relation to space) add yet another dimension to the art-wrought eternity of mediated alternatives in *Rasselas*. Indeed, from the novel's first sentence—addressed to those who ". . . pursue with eagerness the phantoms of hope . . . [expecting] . . . that the deficiencies of the present day will be supplied by the morrow . . ."—to its last—in which the characters ". . . resolved, when the inundation should cease, to return to Abyssinia"—time and movement are closely connected. Again, it is important to observe that the two elements are neither casually nor infrequently joined, but combined in significant ways. For example, in attempting to console Nekayah, Imlac graphically relates time to space-motion:

"Distance has the same effect on the mind as on the eye, and while
we glide along the stream of time, whatever we leave behind us is always lessening, and that which we approach increasing, in magnitude."
(p. 121)

Similarly, Johnson's narrator thereafter associates time's passage
with Nekayah's giving up the idea of a retreat from active life:
"Imlac had, indeed, no great hope of regaining Pekuah; but he
supposed, that if he could secure the interval of a year, the princess would be then in no danger of a cloister" (p. 121). Very
often, time is joined not only to static-kinetic elements, but also to
the closely related pairs, uniform-diverse experiences (Rasselas in
the Happy Valley and on the move), and to the characters' sense
that life is stale-profitable (the hermit in his cave and among
men). Rasselas complains, for example, of lectures that ". . .
pleased only while they were new, and to become new again must
be forgotten" (p. 43). At the same time, he knows that his longing
for variety (again expressed temporally) is not reasonable—
". . . possessing all that I can want, I find one day and one hour
exactly like another . . ." (p. 44). Clearly, time needs a lot of fill-
ing: "But pleasures never can be so multiplied or continued, as
not to leave much of life unemployed . . ." (p. 45). And if one
should fill it steadily, he either commits himself to the insanity of
a fixed idea, like the astronomer, who ". . . spent forty years in
unwearied attention to the motions and appearances of the celestial bodies . . ." (p. 133) or to a discipline not his own, like the
monks, for whom ". . . one duty succeeds another, so that they
are not left open to the distraction of unguided choice, nor lost in
the shades of listless inactivity" (p. 151). But all men find time a
difficult power to contend with rationally. Rasselas, having ". . .
been before terrified at the length of life which nature promised
him . . ." (p. 45), so completely changes in feeling when he deter-
mines to leave the Happy Valley ". . . that he forgot his real solitude, and, amidst hourly preparations for the various incidents of
human affairs, neglected to consider by what means he should
mingle with mankind" (p. 46). Imlac is similarly irrational when
the desire to return to his father's house overtakes him—". . . I

considered every moment as wasted which did not bring me nearer to Abyssinia" (p. 68)—but despite himself, he delays his home-coming. Such delusions as these of Rasselas and Imlac, that plea-sure awaits some new use of time, occur over and over in the work. "I hope that time and variety will dissipate the gloom that has so long surrounded me, and the latter part of my days will be spent in peace" (p. 150), says the astronomer; but the truth is spo-ken by Nekayah, as the weight of evidence throughout the novel makes clear: ". . . none are happy but by the anticipation of change: the change itself is nothing; when we have made it, the next wish is to change again" (pp. 150–51).

At one level of its meaning in the novel, man's inability to use time constructively is common to several other thematic ele-ments. Among these are the aspiring poet's search for data; the life of movement through the world outside the Happy Valley and outside other fixed places as well; Rasselas, actively dissatisfied, anticipating a life of exploration; Imlac's quick willingness to join the prince in his quest; the philosopher's, hermit's, and astrono-mer's fortuitously timed reintroductions (of various kinds) into the unstable world; Pekuah's abduction into a world apparently without order; and her Arab captor's occupation of war by incur-sion. I have tried with varying degrees of thoroughness to indicate the nature of the mediation between each of these elements and its psychologically ordered alternative in the novel. It seems reason-able to ask whether Johnson's hundreds of references to time are not opposed by alternatives of their own, and if so, to speculate as to the nature of the ultimate relationship between these pairs.

Geoffrey Tillotson suggests that eternity, more or less reli-giously defined, is the element that opposes man's futile use of time in the novel.[8] No doubt can reasonably exist, of course, that beginning with Rasselas's strong feeling that he cannot return to childhood, the state in which his perception is fresh and full (p. 44), there is an almost steady march through experience to man's anticipation of defeat by time—death—and his subsequent long-

[8] Tillotson, p. 102.

ing (confined to a single chapter of the novel) for resurrection. One ostensible exception interrupts this progress of mortality. The visit to the stable pyramid, an apparently immutable symbol of a powerful man's life, sets off a flurry of activity, one of whose results (Pekuah's knowledge of astronomy) is part of the reason for the astronomer's return to health in the following episode. But his salvation from a fixed idea leaves him no better off than other men—as Nekayah and the reader well know (pp. 150–51). Pekuah has been freed from confinement, only to return to the futility of a questing life; she, in turn, helps save the astronomer from insanity, to just the same end. Indeed, the inane quality of man's hope that tomorrow will provide a fulfillment of today's expectation is reinforced, not eliminated, by these closely connected episodes. And so the march continues to the catacombs, where, the company speculates, the underground commemoration of every man's death may explain what life has failed to make clear. It is this last journey that stimulates a chapter on the soul's immortality, at the end of which Nekayah, in one sense, speaks for everyone when she observes, "To me . . . the choice of life is become less important; I hope hereafter to think only on the choice of eternity" (p. 157). But the chapter is more a confined presentation of man's desire for an afterlife than the aesthetic counterweight to the time-wasting vanity of human wishes that one might expect in Johnson's work. Except for a few references in the preceding chapter, its content is touched upon directly nowhere else. This restricted declaration of the human desire for life everlasting—man's will to survive death—is probably the novel's chief device of mediation between time and eternity, but it is not that eternity itself. It seems, rather, one of those infrequent pauses that all men experience, when they are clear-sighted enough to see the futility of reaching for personal happiness and begin to console themselves with abstract speculation, to conclude that because an ". . . ideal form has no extension . . . ," it is impossible for time to cause such a form to ". . . suffer laceration" (p. 156). In this unique chapter, the finally ". . . silent and collected . . ." assembly of characters has been discoursing, ostensibly, on the immutability of the human soul; but their arguments (as distinct from their religious aspirations) apply at least as well to the permanence of the world of ideas as to the permanence of the individual life of the spirit. Aesthetically the effect of this chapter about the nature of the soul is to dramatize, through the agency of the assembled characters, the relation between man's natural fondness for the mutable world on the one hand, and his hope for some order of salvation on the other. In a sense, at this point in the novel all the characters together yearn intensely in both directions, much as each of them has yearned privately between less dramatic alternatives before.

Although the reader may sympathize with such yearning, he need not (like the characters) turn heavenward for resolution of the tension in this episode; instead he may (unlike the characters) turn to the novel itself. The thing one can count on in *Rasselas*— the eternity that for the reader (as reader) withstands frittering time—is the collection of all the novel's mediated pairs of forces —both their antagonism and their interpenetration, in perpetuity Rasselas and Imlac, each of whom is both himself and the other, are both always aspiring to enter and to leave both the Happy Valley and the world outside. The mind's eye collects, "examines," and knows as one, a dozen or more such complex relationships, which together are the eternal world of the work. True, it is a world in which individual men waste time and choose futilely between alternatives; but it is also a world in which all alternatives are mediated, so that in one sense all things always are the same. One need not know the meanings of the word "conclude" given in the *Dictionary* to realize that "The conclusion in which Nothing is Concluded" is not only the last chapter, in which nothing is decided; it is also the last chapter, in which nothing is ended. The characters return /do not return to the Happy Valley; and their continuing ambivalent engagements make for a world without end.

Criticism and Language

MAURICE JOHNSON

Swift's Poetry Reconsidered

I

EXISTING AUTOGRAPHS of Jonathan Swift's poems show three different styles of handwriting. There is a formal, impersonal script like that engraved in metal for frontispieces to eighteenth-century books, with precise, elegant capitals and uniform *d*'s, each with an overhead flourish. There is Swift's easier script, more relaxed and less rigorously employed. And there is his cruder and somewhat hesitating script, the so-called disguised hand, though it might perhaps be called a "private" hand. For it is in the painfully formed letters of this third style that one finds, on the final page of the Morgan Library autograph of "The Discovery" (1699), the poet's vexed rejection of his pen: *"this i i is impossible to mend this is/so sog goo/for nothing/ . . . . this must not/not not one once upon a/time isi iis impossible."* [1] The manuscripts, whether they appear as works of calligraphic art or as impatient outcries, are valuable because they contain the texts of Swift's poems in his own hand. But they are significant as well

[1] The Fountaine MS. of "The Discovery," 3 pp., now in the Pierpont Morgan Library, New York. Courtesy of the Pierpont Morgan Library.

because of what they reveal to us about Swift's methods and attitudes—for what they suggest about Swift biographically.

Like the manuscripts, the poems themselves have a biographical interest. Some, indeed, meant as off-the-cuff jokes, doodles, jingles, and private mutterings, have little interest of any other kind. Many of the deservedly famous poems are self-dramatizations of personality, depicting Jonathan Swift not only in the ways he looked to himself but as he imagined he appeared to other eyes. Some of the more formal, impersonal poems, though they seem detached from Swift's career and the historical background of his time, can perhaps achieve deeper interest and meaning when read in a biographical context.

For almost fifty years critics have warned against the tendency to infer events of a poet's life from his poem. They have also warned against the temptation to project into a poem the "true" events and experiences of the poet's life as we know or imagine them to be. A proper reader, many of us have been convinced, does not imagine his relationship with the poet to be that between one man and another. A poem is to be read not as self-expression but as a rendering of certain principles of rhetoric: not as illumination on aspects of the author's identity but as a "verbal contraption" (the term is W. H. Auden's).

There was certainly a real need to rescue Swift's works, both in prose and verse, from the prejudicially biographical "Swift"—neurotic and malevolent—invented by nineteenth-century commentators who were exquisitely fascinated by his negative qualities. Even T. S. Eliot, who, perhaps more than any other single critic in the twentieth century pressed the discrediting of the biographical approach to literature, saw behind Swift's writings an "amazing madman," a master of disgust whose *Gulliver* manifests "the progressive cynicism of the mature and disappointed man of the world." [2] Eliot read Swift under the influence of nineteenth-century commentators. Those commentators or their ghosts are

[2] T. S. Eliot, "Charles Whibley" and "Cyril Tourneur," in *Selected Essays 1917–1932* (New York, 1932), pp. 404, 166–67.

still with us, though they nowadays especially praise a "Swift" who was fashionably mad with sex and excrement obsessions.

Considering Swift's poetry more or less from the "verbal contraption" point of view, and rejecting the nineteenth-century idea of a "mad" Swift, recent studies have some new things to say about conscious craftsmanship in the poems. Not that such studies are frequent. In the past twenty years there have been only my own general book on the subject; an appreciation in the Oxford History of English Literature; and four or five independently published critical explications of any length that deal with individual poems.[3] Quite properly a recent assessment of unexplored areas for future study in Restoration and eighteenth-century literature opens by noting that interpretation of "many of Swift's poems has scarcely begun." [4]

II

In modern studies it has been demonstrated that Swift's versification is expert and his phonetic effects and meter are skilfully adjusted to enforce his meaning. To suit his theme and mood he effectively employs devices like alliteration: sometimes he diffuses alliteration throughout a passage, sometimes he concentrates it in a single line. Experimenting with a variety of styles, he works most characteristically in the octosyllabic couplet, which he can attune to Hudibrastic high (or low) jinks, or to the tender delicacy

[3] Maurice Johnson, *The Sin of Wit: Jonathan Swift as a Poet* (Syracuse, 1950; reprinted with corrections, New York, 1966); Bonamy Dobrée, *English Literature in the Early Eighteenth Century: 1700–1740* (Oxford, 1959); notably Brendan O Hehir, "Meaning in Swift's 'Description of a City Shower'," *ELH*, XXVII (1960), 194–207; Charles Peake, "Swift's 'Satirical Elegy on a Late Famous General'," *Review of English Literature*, III (1962), 80–89; Barry Slepian, "The Ironic Intention of Swift's Verses on His Own Death," *Review of English Studies*, XIV (1963), 249–56; John M. Aden, "Corinna and the Sterner Muse of Swift," *English Language Notes*, IV (1966), 23–31. All take their text from *The Poems of Jonathan Swift*, ed. Harold Williams (Oxford, 1937, 2nd ed. 1958), 3 vols.

[4] David M. Vieth, "Introductory Note," *Papers on Language and Literature*, special issue, II (1966), 291.

of seventeenth-century lyrics, or—unusual in the work of any poet
—to an intersecting and blending of these two disparate modes.
Such a blending is most readily recognized in the poems addressed
to Stella, which join loving-kindness and laughter. After relin-
quishing his early experiments with the Pindaric form, Swift sur-
prises the ear with audacious rhymes and parodies, deliberately
avoiding the pretentious and would-be sublime. He employs almost no ornamental imagery seriously intended. Instead, he con-
fers unexpected interpretations upon conventional metaphors,
which suddenly are shown to be canting or empty. He borrows elevated images only to twist, shrink, shred, or dissolve them, altering clichés into puns by treating them as though they were not verbal abstractions but palpable things to be sat on, cooked and
eaten, made love to, mailed in a letter, slammed down like a window, or watched flying away through the sky. His diction and syntax are colloquial and often elliptical, especially when they imitate
the rhythms and language of garrulous monologuists, town gossips,
and persons trapped in the false etiquette of social intercourse.

There is no question, either, about the formal complexity of
structure in Swift's best poems, often at tension with the racy colloquial diction and familiar style. An able strategist in his verse as
well as in his more famous prose, Swift proceeds in a manner
shaped by an energetic and conscious art. Three general patterns
or schemes control the structure in those poems that seem of permanent interest.

One pattern is that of mutually exclusive opposites, often in a
satiric confrontation of opposed exaggerations. In certain poems a
middle ground of common sense is made explicit, as in Swift's de-
lineation of contrasting events on a wedding night. The bride-
groom's exaggerated embarrassment at being bedded with a "cold
and snowy" goddess "unsusceptible of Stain" is contrasted with
his sudden change to an exaggerated state of reciprocated bedroom animality in which "They soon from all Constraint are
freed." But more than a third of the poem goes on to outline a les-
son of mutual respect and common sense: "Let Prudence with

Good Nature strive,/ To keep Esteem and Love alive." [5] Other poems, more characteristic of Swift, leave the middle ground of intention to be inferred. In "Verses on the Death of Dr. Swift," for instance, the pretended weaknesses of character Swift imputes to himself, as well as the pretended account of general indifference to the news of his death, are balanced by the shamelessly exaggerated praise for the "dead" Dean with which the poem concludes. Elsewhere in his prose and verse Swift similarly dramatizes a need for moderation when he poses an impossible choice between Fool and Knave or between Yahoo and Houyhnhnm. Such a confrontation must be resolved in the mind of the reader. In poems of this first pattern, that of locking irreconcilable extremes in opposition, the thematic or structural device is ultimately moral in its implications.[6]

Another structural pattern is exemplified by his verses on the death of the Duke of Marlborough, which in only thirty-two lines stun the reader by offering an elegiac ode of conventional patriotic piety and then debasing it, item by item. As we read, we descend from the exclamatory announcement "His Grace! impossible! what dead!" to his Grace's unmourned funeral, and thence to his Grace's ignominious interment: "From all his *ill-got* honours flung,/ Turn'd to that *dirt* from whence he sprung" [italics mine].[7] The device is that of deflation, unmasking, and stripping bare. One of the high points of wisdom for Swift, it is well known, lies in the art of exposing weak sides and publishing infirmities. As in the metaphorical prose of *A Tale of a Tub* the carcass of a beau is stripped of its clothes, its brain laid open, and its heart and spleen dissected to discover more defects, in a number of poems the stripping bare is literally achieved. The prosthetic whore in "A Beautiful Young Nymph Going to Bed" is dreadfully allowed

[5] "Strephon and Chloe," ll. 205, 309–10.
[6] I have noticed this pattern elsewhere (*Notes and Queries*, CXCIX [1954], 473–74, rephrased here).
[7] "A Satirical Elegy on the Death of a Late Famous General," ll. 1, 31–32.

to take herself apart. She is not, after all, a beautiful young nymph. Sometimes, especially in the shorter poems like "The Day of Judgement," exposure is accomplished by a sudden twist in the concluding couplet, altering all that has preceded. A curtain is flicked up to reveal things as they are. Exposure by reversal, undercutting, or moral unmasking is intensified in its effect by an abruptly altered tone, plummeting from the elevated to diction that is rudely colloquial, earthy, and real.

A third pattern in Swift's poetry has been termed that of "a comedy of continuity." [8] For example, in "Verses wrote in a Lady's Ivory Table-Book" and "The Furniture of a Woman's Mind," with their amusingly incongruous parallels to insinuate a confusion of values, the method is often that of a seemingly undiscriminating continuum of items. Incongruous catalogues, inventories, connections, and correspondences accumulate with a total effect of strong force. "I am not in the least provoked [Lemuel Gulliver writes when his travels are ended] at the sight of a Lawyer, a Pick-pocket, a Colonel, a Fool, a Lord, a Gamester, a Politician, a Whoremunger, a Physician, an Evidence, a Suborner, an Attorney, a Traytor, or the like." [9] The reader is confounded to imagine what "the like" would be in order to fit into such an outrageous list. The point of course is that Pick-pocket, Colonel, Fool, and the rest are truly indistinguishable as fallen creatures "smitten with *Pride*." Such an incongruous catalogue can provide the entire structural outline for a poem like "The Beasts Confession to the Priest," where distinctions between one man and another, as well as between man and animal, are blurred. Or, concentrated in an eighteen-line paragraph, there is the better-known tour de force in which the Dean's "female Friends" interruptedly

[8] Ricardo Quintana, *"The Rape of the Lock* as a Comedy of Continuity," *REL,* VII (1966), 9–19. Quintana earlier characterized Swift's "The Lady's Dressing-Room" and similar works as "completely ruthless studies in *discontinuity"* [italics mine] (*Swift: An Introduction* [Oxford, 1955], p. 185).

[9] *Gulliver's Travels,* ed. Herbert Davis (Oxford, 1941, rev. ed. 1959), p. 296.

discuss his demise while they pursue a game of cards. Through a series of five parallel stages, death and the business of playing cards are exactly equated, beginning with " 'The Dean is dead, *(and what is Trumps?)*' " and concluding with " 'He lov'd the Dean. (*I lead a Heart.*),' " each uttered in a single undiscriminating breath.[10] With alternatives each of which is equatable and interchangeable with the others, the seriate construction acts as a testing of the reader's powers of discrimination.

There is, then, a good deal to be said about craftsmanship in the poems. Criticism in its chilliest aspect, as methodological doctrine or systematic process, will find matters for analysis in many of the poems that have never yet been studied.

III

Commentators sympathetic to Swift's verse are likely to conclude their discussions with the observation that it is puzzlingly unique, or with an admission of critical inadequacy or bafflement. In the language and structure alone they do not find sufficient warrant for the peculiar emotional effect of some of the poems. Certain poems by Swift are characterized as "unlike anything else in our language" or "without quite their like in our literature"; and "we have not yet attained to an adequate appraisal" of Swift's poetic art; "for exact discussion of those very aspects of poetry in which Swift excels we still lack adequate tools." He is "a poet of a special kind." [11]

On reconsideration, I wonder whether the special quality in Swift's poems may not work through his own biographical presence.

All of Swift's poems—those with critical interest and those with none—may be said to evoke response beyond that implicit in the imaginative constructs they represent, simply because we know them to come from the author of *Gulliver's Travels* and *The Con-*

[10] "Verses on the Death of Dr. Swift," ll. 228–39.
[11] Dobrée, pp. 472, 473; Aden, p. 23; Peake, p. 88; Edmund Wilson, *The Shores of Light* (New York, 1952), p. 697.

duct of the Allies. To gain control over the "difficult" poems of
any author, we read them in relationship to his other works, which
are likely to interact among themselves and are all, taken together,
one manifestation of their author's life. We do this in spite of any
wish for critical "purity." For Swift as poet such a reading seems
especially desirable, as it does also for Herman Melville as poet:
Melville's "Billy in the Darbies" may have been originally intended to stand alone; but part of its impact for us comes from its
relationship now to *Billy Budd, Moby Dick,* and Melville's own
career.

The moving events of Swift's life cannot be dissociated from
his writings; as much as for any poet of his day, his own identity
and his poetry seem inseparable. In the drama of many of his
poems Swift deliberately creates a character for himself and plays
the leading role. He explores, defines, and identifies himself in his
poems, using that identity as a sort of intermediary to dramatize
the human predicaments his poems deal with.

One of Swift's most striking poems bears the open-faced title
"The Author upon Himself," but many of his other poems could
share that title, including "The Author's Manner of Living," "In
Sickness," "The Dean's Reasons," "The Dean to Himself on St.
Cecilia's Day," "Written by Dr. Swift on his Own Deafness," and
of course "The Life and Genuine Character of Doctor Swift" and
"Verses on the Death of Dr. Swift." He poses himself alongside
friends in "The Dean of St. Patrick's to Thomas Sheridan" and
"Dr. Swift to Mr. Pope While he was Writing the *Dunciad*." In
three of his liveliest poems he describes himself by means of an
altered perspective as though seen by Lady Acheson: "My Lady's
Lamentation and Complaint against the Dean," "Lady Acheson
Weary of the Dean," and "A Panegyrick on the Dean in the Person of a Lady in the North"; in another poem, "To Dean Swift,"
he assumes the guise of her husband Sir Arthur to address himself. Usually referring to himself in the third person in these and
other poems, as though recording what he sees in a mirror, he
appears—often humorously—as "the Chaplain," "Parson Swift,"

"Poor *S---t*," "Good Dr. *S---t*," "Cadenus," "Good Mr. Dean," "the DRAPIER," "thy Deanship," "the Dean," or "St. *P------*'s D--n." The important exception is in the eleven poems to Stella, all but one of which use the first person singular. Thus in his most affecting and personally tender group of poems the focus is properly on the woman to whom they are addressed. Use of the third-person seems more self-conscious in its effect than the use of "I"; and Lord Hervey, who egotistically refers to himself as "Hervey" in his *Memoirs,* is unconvincing when he explains his use of the third-person as a wish to avoid "the disagreeable egotisms with which almost all memoir writers so tiresomely abound." [12]

Openly egotistic like Montaigne in prose, Swift in poetry models his central figure upon himself, painting himself for others. Like Montaigne, Swift might have said he had written a body of work "consubstantial with its author, concerned with my own self, an integral part of my life"; and he might have noted with Montaigne that by training himself "to see my own life mirrored in that of others, I have acquired a studious bent in that subject, and when I am thinking about it, I let few things around me which are useful for that purpose escape my notice." [13] Montaigne was well known to Swift.[14] To symbolize Vanessa's superiority over most other females, Swift writes that in the shrill company of fashionable "glitt'ring Dames" of her acquaintance she quietly "held *Montaigne,* and read." [15] Montaigne could teach the art of self-scrutiny and self-depiction.

IV

Throughout his poetical career Swift showed himself in a series of remarkably varied lights and postures. His changing states

[12] *Lord Hervey's Memoirs,* ed. Romney Sedgwick (New York, 1963), p. 5n.

[13] Montaigne, "Of Giving the Lie," II:18, and "Of Experience," III:13, *Complete Works,* transl. Donald M. Frame (Stanford, 1957), pp. 504, 825.

[14] See Harold Williams, *Dean Swift's Library, with a Facsimile of the Original Sale Catalogue* (Cambridge, 1932), p. 66.

[15] "Cadenus and Vanessa," 1. 372.

of mind form a constant subject, but his visualized depictions of himself as he ages are numerous. A few examples will suggest his method. As a gowned young chaplain in Lord Berkeley's household in Ireland, he has Frances Harris, the lady-in-waiting who is attracted to him, describe how "he twisted his Girdle at me like a Rope." In London he makes Robert Harley, Lord Oxford, first see him as a priest who "shew'd some Humour in his Face" and "Look'd with an easie, careless Mien." Once installed by Oxford as an influential figure in the Tory government, Swift now "mov'd, and bow'd, and talk't with too much Grace;/ Nor shew'd the Parson in his Gait or Face"; when he enters the room at Windsor, "Waiters stand in Ranks; the Yeomen cry,/ *Make Room;* as if a Duke were passing by." He is out of favor and is returned to favor, so that *"Delaware* again familiar grows;/ And, in *Sw--t*'s Ear thrusts half his powder'd Nose." Elevated in the church, he becomes "a *Dean* compleat,/ Devoutly lolling in his Seat." After he assumes his duties as Dean in Ireland, however, he pretends to "College Aukwardness" with Lady Carteret and arrives sheepishly at her residence "by slow Approaches,/ Thro' Crowds of Coxcombs & of Coaches." He is renowned as patriot and author, both loved and feared, but when he is a guest of Lord and Lady Acheson in the north of Ireland, his pleasures are simple, rural ones: he helps to churn the butter and "He's all the day saunt'ring,/ With labourers bant'ring." [16] Finally, in his sixties, he versifies Lady Acheson's complaints about his incessant punning and railing at her, and provides an arresting face-to-face confrontation with him in his old age, with

> Tallow Face and Wainscot Paws,
> . . . Beetle-brows and Eyes of Wall.[17]

[16] "The Humble Petition of Frances Harris" (1701), l. 62; "Part of the Seventh Epistle of the First Book of Horace Imitated" (1713), ll. 8–9; "The Author upon Himself" (1714), ll. 13–14, 35–36, 67–68; "Part of the Seventh Epistle of the First Book of Horace Imitated," ll. 97–98; "An Apology to the Lady Carteret" (1725), ll. 148, 151–52; "My Lady's Lamentation and Complaint against the Dean" (1728), ll. 159–60.

[17] "Lady Acheson Weary of the Dean" (1728?), ll. 38–39.

The heavy, oppressive terms he chooses here, displaying himself with eyes staring out from under frowning brows in a pale face, his clumsy hands embrowned with age, are all humorously contemptuous and self-depreciating. "Wainscot" is the only unfamiliar term in the passage. In "Dick, A Maggot," written at about the same time, Swift uses "wainscot" again as a contemptuous adjective synonymous with "hazel," "tawney," and "Gypsey"; and his use is cited in the OED to illustrate an obsolete meaning for "wainscot." Although he causes Lady Acheson to describe him contemptuously in his poem, the description (except for the hands) is true to the portrait painted by Francis Bindon in Swift's old age and now in the Irish National Gallery. The Earl of Orrery wrote that "Dr. Swift had a natural severity of face, which even his smiles could scarce soften." [18]

Tested by his portraits, letters, and other people's accounts of him, the autobiographical glimpses of Swift in the preceding paragraph seem true to life. Yet some of them are taken from one of his imitations of Horace, so that the "Swift" who appears there—though perhaps absolutely true to life—is acting a role in a Latin poem brought up to date. Possibly, as other authors have been, Swift was assisted in formulating an idea of himself by taking clues from Horace and slightly altering the models Horace provides. Although he had reason to pride himself on his originality, Swift's "autobiographical" presentation of himself in his poems must have been associated in his consciousness with similar presentations elsewhere in literature. Perhaps he sometimes thought of himself in terms of Montaigne. Occasionally he seems to have imagined himself in verse as a Restoration wit manqué. His name is linked with that of Juvenal. He certainly associated the character "Swift" with characterizations in Horace's poetry, and Swift's contemporaries appreciated many of his poems by locating them in reference to the Latin Satires, Epistles, and Odes, as they were understood in eighteenth-century England.

[18] John Boyle, fifth Earl of Orrery, *Remarks on the Life and Writings of Dr. Jonathan Swift* (London, 5th ed. 1752), p. 78.

Had he lived in the same age with HORACE, he would have ap-
proached nearer to him, than any other poet. . . . Each poet was the
delight of the principal persons of the age. *Cum magnis vixisse* was
not more applicable to HORACE, than to SWIFT. They both were
temperate: both were frugal; and both were of the same Epicurean
taste. HORACE had his LYDIA, SWIFT had his VANESSA. HOR-
ACE had his MÆCENAS and his AGRIPPA. SWIFT had his OX-
FORD and his BOLINGBROKE. HORACE had his VIRGIL, SWIFT
had his POPE.[19]

    Two out of Swift's eight adaptations from Horace place him
in his relationship with Robert Harley, Earl of Oxford, who qualifies as nearly as any other contemporary to be called patron and
hero to Swift. In "Part of the Seventh Epistle of the First Book of
Horace Imitated and Addressed to the Earl of Oxford," the role of
the famous Roman lawyer, orator, and consul, L. Marcus Philippus, is taken over by Oxford; that of the freedman auctioneer Vulteius Mena—respectable, discreet, and lacking a fortune—is
taken by Swift. The ruinous gift to Vulteius of a farm he does not
want makes a nice parallel for Swift's preferment to his unwanted
deanery in Ireland. Vulteius, first seen by Philippus in a barber's
booth, is altered to Swift pricing books at a stall near the palace in
Westminster.

> Harley, the Nation's great Support,
> Returning home one Day from Court,
> (His Mind with Publick Cares possest,
> All *Europe*'s Bus'ness in his Breast)
> Observ'd a *Parson* near *Whitehall*,
> Cheapning old Authors on a Stall.   (1–6)

Although Swift has himself, like Vulteius, not responding to the
initial invitation from his future patron, the historical fact is that
it was Oxford who postponed their meeting.[20] Otherwise, the account seems close to the truth, and its effect is enhanced by what

[19] *Ibid.*, pp. 44–45.
[20] Letter IV, September 29 and 30, 1710, *Journal to Stella,* ed. Harold
Williams (Oxford, 1948), I, 33–35.

we bring to it from Swift's accounts of himself and Oxford in other poems, the *Journal to Stella,* pamphlets, and tracts. His *History of the Four Last Years of the Queen* incorporates a formal "character" of Oxford as a person who "hath been so highly Instrumental in changing the Face of Affairs in *Europe;* And hath Deserved so well of his own Prince and Country." [21] The poem cleverly versifies this prose matter, using Horace for a continuing line of reference.

In his *History* Swift goes out of his way to praise Oxford's "agreeable Conversation in a private Capacity." [22] Samples of that conversation, or "Tattle," shared with Parson Swift,

> As once a week we travel down
> To *Windsor,* and again to Town,

provide realistic entertainment in "Horace, *Lib.* 2 *Sat.* 6. Part of It Imitated." [23] Elsewhere Swift depicts himself as a suffering wit, a demanding friend, or a scourge of corruption; but in these two adaptations from Horace he is the naive parson, humorously put upon in the great world of Lords, Whitehall, Windsor, petitions, and Court secrets. Swift's Horatian poems, because they are based on models less familiar now than in the eighteenth century, and because they introduce public persons whose fame has faded, are in need of footnotes to explain their references.

The poems to Stella, however, need no explanation. They are as honestly affecting nowadays as when they were written. Perhaps it is not very surprising after all that Swift's most private and personal poems are his most universal. Biographically, their subject is the enduring power of affectionate friendship between a man and a woman as they grow old. Stella is pictured as she patiently attends him in his recurrent illnesses, while he lies "Lamenting in unmanly Strains," with "sinking Spirits," "Tormented with inces-

[21] *The History of the Four Last Years of the Queen,* ed. Herbert Davis (Oxford, 1951), p. 75.
[22] *Ibid.*   [23] ll. 77–78.

sant Pains." [24] Concern with personal ills in some modern "confessional" poetry is likely to encourage a mood apocalyptic and nearly hysterical. Swift's personal ills are introduced to explain a world in which mutual loyalty and assistance can make decay and dissolution endurable.

The last birthday poem to Stella before her death was written when she was ill and Swift was fifty-nine. The birthday itself is conventionally a day of "Joy," but it is also the annual reminder that "Time is running fast"; and Swift attempts in his poem to reconcile those two concepts. Acts of benevolent virtue, like those of Stella, he says, are neither chimeras nor merely their own reward. Such acts leave "lasting Pleasure in the Mind" to sustain us in "Grief, Sickness, Poverty, and Age."

> This Day then, let us not be told,
> That you are sick, and I grown old,
> Nor think on our approaching Ills,
> And talk of Spectacles and Pills;
> To morrow will be Time enough
> To hear such mortifying Stuff.[25]

When, at the age of seventy-five, Samuel Johnson had recovered from an illness, he recited the central couplet from this passage, "assuming a gay air," according to Boswell.[26] Johnson, grown old and sick, could enter into Swift's words precisely because they are so truly private, biographically personal, and universal in their application.

V

Swift's voice in his poems is like that which Montaigne praised, "succulent and sinewy, brief and compressed, not so much dainty and well-combed as vehement and brusque." [27] It is

---

[24] "To Stella, Visiting Me in My Sickness," ll. 99, 109; "To Stella, March 13, 1724," l. 1.

[25] "Stella's Birth-Day, March 13, 1727," ll. 17, 30, 32, 3–8.

[26] *Boswell's Life of Johnson,* ed. George Birkbeck Hill, rev. L. F. Powell (Oxford, 1934–50), IV, 285.

[27] Montaigne, "Of the Education of Children," I:26, p. 127.

speech that suggests an identifying presence and gesture. The brusque accents of Swift's voice can be heard even in the slightest of the trivia that one is often tempted to prune, lop off, and clear away from the overgrown canon of his verse. But it was Coleridge, the formulator of a new, "serious" concept of poetry after Swift's day, who suspected that he was "not perhaps the only one who has derived an innocent amusement from the riddles, conundrums, trisyllable lines, etc. etc., of Swift and his correspondents." [28]

Such an item is Swift's couplet of invitation to Lord Oxford to join members of the Scriblerus Club in Dr. Arbuthnot's rooms in St. James's Palace, where, Oxford is promised, he will encounter mirth and can assist in the ridicule of false learning. Arbuthnot addresses Oxford in a couplet, as does Thomas Parnell. John Gay's couplet, which he seems to have had trouble in versifying, alludes self-consciously to his own *Shepherd's Week*. Alexander Pope's couplet is even more complicated and allusive than Gay's. In Alexandrines and trisyllabic rhymes, Pope imposes a veneer of elegance by reminding Oxford of lines from the *Iliad* describing how Jove himself would willingly descend to consort with mortals and appear at "Feasts of *Æthiopia*'s blameless Race" (as Pope's own translation has it). Pope writes: "My Lord, forsake your Politick Utopians, / To sup, like Jove, with blameless Ethiopians."

Perhaps the friendly insolence of Swift's voice is as much an affectation as Pope's well-combed elegance, but one is not aware of it. The voice comes through with an authentic sound:

> In other Words, You with the Staff,
> Leave John of Bucks, come here and laugh.[29]

Intentionally, Swift restates in bare language, vehement and brusque, exactly what Pope has insinuated under a tissue of "po-

---

[28] *Biographia Literaria,* ed. George Watson (Everyman's Library, 1956, corrected 1965), p. 37.

[29] See *Poems,* ed. Williams, I, 187; *Memoirs of Martinus Scriblerus,* ed. Charles Kerby-Miller (New Haven, 1950), p. 353. The exact date of the invitation, in April, 1714, is uncertain.

etic" allusion. Exchange of Pope's formal "My Lord" for the blunt
"You" characterizes the difference between Pope's poetic voice
here and that in which Swift speaks. It is like the exchange of the
humorously vague "Politick Utopians" for the vulgarized and specific "John of Bucks." Pope's couplet is good-naturedly mocking,
for Oxford is neither a Lord engaged among ambiguous "Utopians" nor a God receiving an invitation from "blameless" out-
siders. In Swift's doggerel couplet a real Lord Treasurer, holding a
real staff of office, is brusquely commanded to excuse himself
from the real company of John Sheffield, Duke of Buckingham,
and other political planners, to join the real merriment of real
Scriblerians. Oxford is addressed as himself; Swift speaks as himself.

In hundreds of other lines that Swift revised with care—not
lines dashed off in a hurry among friends—there is still the immediate effect of a voice that singularly speaks concisely and out-
right, so that "In other Words" could serve as a kind of general
epithet for Swift's verse.

"In other Words" suggests a man impatient with conceits,
one who clarifies, exposes, and cuts through pretense. It represents
the biographical presence that one strongly feels but cannot quite
account for in much of Swift's poetry.

JOHN H. MIDDENDORF

Ideas vs. Words: Johnson, Locke, and the Edition of Shakespeare

Though the examining and judging of ideas by them-selves, their names being quite laid aside, be the best and surest way to clear and distinct knowledge: yet, through the prevailing custom of using sounds for ideas, I think it is very seldom practised. —LOCKE

THE PRAISE ACCORDED by Sir Walter Raleigh to Johnson's notes to Shakespeare in the edition of 1765 has been echoed to our time. In 1908 Raleigh pointed to Johnson's "strong grasp of the main thread of the discourse, his sound sense, and his wide knowledge of humanity," all of which enabled Johnson "in a hundred passages, to go straight to Shakespeare's meaning. . . . Whole pages of complicated dialectic and minute controversy are often rendered useless by the few brief sentences which recall the reader's attention to the main drift, or remind him of some per-fectly obvious circumstance." [1] In 1960 W. K. Wimsatt observed that Johnson "wrote a number of notes which were repeated by

[1] Sir Walter Raleigh, *Johnson on Shakespeare* (Oxford, 1908), p. xvi.

Shakespearian editors until at least as recently as the Furness *Variorum* volumes and which perhaps still deserve to be repeated more often than they are." [2] Too frequently, however, after acknowledging Johnson's achievement in the notes, critics have shifted their attention to the magnificent evaluations and statement of principles in the Preface, leaving the truth of their praise largely unsupported except for those who go to Johnson's pages to see for themselves.[3] Still to be presented are more precise answers to the question *why* Johnson was so often as successful as he was in illuminating the obscure corners of Shakespeare's world.

It is simply not enough to be reminded of Johnson's earlier work on the *Dictionary* or of his passionate responses to Shakespeare beginning perhaps even before his boyhood terror in the presence of the Ghost in *Hamlet.* Lexicographical training and deep personal involvement unquestionably provided him with valuable critical and aesthetic equipment to direct his course responsibly and sensitively, but we wish to know more particularly what habitual expectations and patterns of response—what method, if any—as an editor, he may have brought to his reading of the plays and to his writing of the illustrative notes.[4] It will be my purpose in this paper to point to a clue to Johnson's method, provided by himself; to suggest its origin in his earlier reading; to il-

[2] W. K. Wimsatt, Jr., *Samuel Johnson on Shakespeare* (New York, 1960), p. xvii.

[3] An exception, of course, is to be found in Arthur Sherbo, *Samuel Johnson, Editor of Shakespeare* . . . (Urbana, Ill., 1956), particularly in Chapter Five, where Sherbo rightly points to the neglect of the notes and offers an analysis of their usefulness in revealing Johnson's critical assumptions and predilections.

[4] In his Preface Johnson explains that his notes will be of three sorts: "illustrative, by which difficulties are explained; or judicial, by which faults and beauties are remarked; or emendatory, by which depravations are corrected" (p. 102 in *Johnson on Shakespeare,* ed. Arthur Sherbo with an Introduction by Bertrand H. Bronson [New Haven, 1968], vols. VII and VIII of the Yale Edition of the Works of Samuel Johnson. Subsequent quotations from Johnson's writings on Shakespeare will all be taken from these volumes). In this paper I shall be concerned only with the illustrative notes.

lustrate some of the results of its use in the notes; and, by implication, to account for their continuing value. I do not wish to
suggest that he was even conscious of a method himself; nor have
I evaluated the accuracy of his illustrative notes in the light of
subsequent interpretations of Shakespeare's text.

I

In his *Proposals for Printing . . . the Dramatic Works of William Shakespeare* (1756) and in his Preface to the completed edition, Johnson considered the problems faced by an editor of
Shakespeare. In brief he assumed his responsibility to be essentially
that of the classical scholar: "to correct what is corrupt, and to explain what is obscure." [5] He understood the particular theatrical
conditions and methods of publication that led to the corruption
of Shakespeare's text: the original texts were not printed, actors'
copies differed, actors' interpolations abounded, the printings were
carried out with no authorial supervision. Just as acutely he understood certain major causes of obscurity: the changes in idiom,
syntax, and casts of thought since Shakespeare's day; the changes
in fashions, traditions, superstitions, particularly troublesome in
dealing with a playwright like Shakespeare, who drew his scenes
and characters "from nature and from life." A further and even
more fundamental cause of obscurity, he insisted in the *Proposals,*
is Shakespeare's "fulness of idea, which might sometimes load his
words with more sentiment than they could conveniently convey,"
and his "rapidity of imagination which might hurry him to a second thought before he had fully explained the first." [6] In the Preface he presents a related notion:

Not . . . always where the language is intricate the thought is
subtle, or the image always great where the line is bulky; the equality
of words to things is very often neglected, and trivial sentiments and
vulgar ideas disappoint the attention, to which they are recommended
by sonorous epithets and swelling figures. (p. 73f.)

[5] Vol. VII, p. [51].   [6] *Ibid.,* p. 54.

Disproportion of ideas to words and truncation and compression of thought—to Johnson a failure to recognize these characteristics of Shakespeare's style is what allowed Hanmer, an editor for whom he had considerable respect,[7] to reduce to "grammar, what he could not be sure that his author intended to be grammatical. Shakespeare [Johnson continues] regarded more the series of ideas, than of words; and his language, not being designed for the reader's desk, was all that he desired it to be, if it conveyed his meaning to the audience."[8]

These beliefs—that Shakespeare was often unaware of the relationship of ideas and words, and regarded more the "series of ideas than of words" because he was writing for the stage—offer a clue as to how Johnson himself read Shakespeare and to how he composed many of his illustrative notes in order to share his understanding with his reader. It is a clue that involves Johnson's view of language and its relationship to the materials for which language is a set of signs.

II

Important aspects of Locke's psychology and epistemology underlay much of Johnson's thinking in, for example, the *Rambler*,[9] designated by Johnson himself as the "pure wine" of his writings;

[7] See Preface, pp. 97–98. Cf. Johnson's note on *Othello*, II. iii. 364 (p. 1029): ". . . there are few to whom that will be easy which was difficult to Hanmer."

[8] Johnson is here drawing upon established views of Shakespeare's language and its relationship to meaning. Dryden, in "The Grounds of Criticism in Tragedy" (*Essays*, ed. Ker [New York, 1961], I. 224) had complained that Shakespeare "often obscures his meaning by his words, and sometimes makes it unintelligible." The earlier editors of Shakespeare had noted the "ease and rapidity" with which Shakespeare wrote (Pope), and "his peculiar manner of *thinking,* and as peculiar a manner of *cloathing* those thoughts" (Theobald). Even Johnson's *bête noire* Warburton had observed that Shakespeare's "superiority of genius less needing the intervention of words in the act of thinking, when he came to draw out his contemplations into discourse, he took up (as he was hurried on by the torrent of his matter) with the first words that lay in his way. . . ."

[9] See, for example, *Rambler* 85, 89, 94, 137, 154, 160, 166 *passim*.

Locke has been aptly identified as "preeminently the philosopher of the *Dictionary,* one of its most important prose sources," [10] and as a significant contributor to the development of Johnson's moral and critical principles and his political thinking.[11] Certainly what bound Johnson to Locke at the deepest level was their shared scepticism of abstract speculation, their insistence upon experience as the foundation of all right reasoning. It should therefore come as no surprise that Johnson's views on language were essentially those of Locke, particularly when it is remembered that the works of one of Locke's most influential popularizers, Isaac Watts, were numbered by Johnson among those giving him most instruction and pleasure.[12]

Supporting most eighteenth-century speculation about language is some form of Locke's epistemology, the essential elements of which for my purpose are suggested by the key words *idea* and *word.* To Locke, *idea* meant many things—"whatsoever the mind perceives *in itself,* or is the immediate object of perception, thought, or understanding." [13] In its most fundamental sense, the term embraced particular external phenomena when presented by the senses or when consciously contemplated or remembered. To be sure, for Locke simple ideas are joined to form complex

[10] W. K. Wimsatt, Jr., *Philosophic Words* . . . (New Haven, 1948), p. 96.

[11] See Jean H. Hagstrum, *Samuel Johnson's Literary Criticism* (Minneapolis, 1952), Ch. 1 *passim;* Robert Voitle, *Samuel Johnson the Moralist* (Cambridge, Mass., 1961), Ch. 1 *passim;* Donald J. Greene, *The Politics of Samuel Johnson* (New Haven, 1960), p. 245.

[12] *Boswell's Life of Johnson,* ed. G. B. Hill, revised L. F. Powell (Oxford, 1934–1950), IV. 311; *Johnsonian Miscellanies,* ed. G. B. Hill (New York, 1897), II. 2; "Life of Watts," *passim.* My quotations from Watts will be taken from the 3d ed. corrected (London, 1742) of *Philosophical Essays* and from the 8th ed. corrected (London, 1745) of *Logick,* Johnson's copy of which, marked for his quotations in the *Dictionary,* is in the British Museum.

[13] John Locke, *An Essay Concerning Human Understanding,* ed. A. C. Fraser (New York, 1959), I. 169 (Bk. II, Ch. viii, par. 8). Subsequent quotations from the *Essay* will be taken from this edition. Locke's definition of *idea* is quoted in the *Dictionary.*

ideas (modes, substances, relations),[14] but the *fons et origo* of all ideas nevertheless remains sensation, reflection upon the experience of the senses, or a combination of both. This Lockean emphasis upon the origins of ideas as always to be found in experience is well known.

Just as frequently recognized is the tendency of Locke's explanations and terminology to encourage the root-metaphorical notion of *idea,* whether primarily sensory or conceptual, as a visual experience. Locke refers to ideas in the memory as "dormant pictures depending sometimes on the *will"* and to the unity of an idea as "one representation or picture, though made up of ever so many particulars." Echoing Locke, Watts tells us that an idea is "a picture of . . . things, as they are considered, or conceived in the mind," "a form under which . . . things appear to the mind." [15] Perhaps with an eye on Berkeley's distinction between *idea* (sensory image) and *notion* (unrepresentable concept), Watts stresses the importance of the visual by observing that "intellectual ideas by themselves cannot be traced, nor drawn, nor painted on the brain, and consequently can have no similar impressions made there," but "they may be closely connected or attached by custom to certain corporeal motions, figures, strokes, or traces which may be excited or delineated there." [16] To both Locke and Watts intellectual ideas—concepts—are both realized and anchored in the mind by association with the sensory and particularly the visual.

Again, to both Locke and Watts words are imperfect, sensible marks or signs of ideas established by custom. It follows, therefore, that many words are twice removed from the realities which supply the mind with the materials of thought. Emphasizing the inadequacy of words as the means by which ideas are signified and communicated was their belief that words, in their "primary or immediate signification, stand for nothing but *the ideas in the mind of him that uses them. . . ."* [17] Though the names of simple

[14] Locke, Bk. II, Ch. xii.
[15] Locke, I. 197 (II. x. 7), I. 424 (II. xxiv. 1); *Logick,* pp. 5, 9.
[16] *Philosophical Essays,* p. 93.   [17] Locke, II. 9 (III. ii. 2).

ideas are the least ambiguous, signifying, as they do, simple sensations (for example, hot, cold) common to all men, even these
names must necessarily refer to those sensations experienced and
understood by the user. The signs for modes, relations, and substances are much less reliable, particularly if they are used without
one's realizing their source in a multiplicity of simple sensations
or without one's making an attempt to limit their signification by
reference to those sensations or to the ideas attached to them by
usage. Two of the major purposes of Locke's *Essay on Human
Understanding* were to define the essences of things, ideas, and
words, and to point to their differences in order to free men from
slavery to the word and from the intellectual and emotional diso-
rientation which is its inevitable result.

III

Prior to the publication of his edition of Shakespeare in 1765,
the richest sources of information regarding Johnson's view of language and its indebtedness to Locke are the *Dictionary* and the
Rambler. The Preface to the *Dictionary* rests firmly upon Lockean
assumptions concerning the nature and relationship of things,
ideas, and words. The meanings of key words—particularly those
related to my purpose here—are supported and refined in the *Dictionary* by quotations from Locke's *Essay*. Illustrating the definition of *idea* ("mental imagination") is Locke's definition (see
above, p. 253). Quoted under the first definition of *word* ("a single
part of speech") is Locke's warning: "Amongst men who con-
found ideas with *words,* there must be endless disputes, wrangling,
and jargon." Locke or Watts—or both—are represented under related terms—*complex, image, sentiment, thought, train* (of ideas)
—with quotations pointing to Locke's epistemology and views on
language. More important, however, than establishing what is well
known, is to determine with greater precision the signification to
Johnson of these key terms.

In his mournfully realistic observation in the Preface to the
Dictionary—"I am not yet so lost in lexicography, as to forget
that *words are the daughters of earth, and that things are the sons*

of heaven"—Johnson was assuming a Lockean distinction that informed his remarks about language throughout his life.[18] His criticism of Pope's well-known definition of wit insists upon the irrevocable division between the content of thought and its vehicle: "How can the expression make it new? It may make it clear, or may make it elegant, but how new? You are confounding words with things."[19] Even as late as 1778, in one of those Boswell-inspired conversations about drinking, Johnson rebutted Sir Joshua by observing that "one of the disadvantages of wine" is that "it makes a man mistake words for thoughts."[20] Words are not things, words are not thoughts; rather, things are mirrored in the mind as ideas, and ideas, the material of thought stored in the memory, are realized in words.

There can be little doubt that when Johnson spoke of ideas he was often thinking of the form that sensory experience takes in the mind. Thus onomatopoetic words "contribute to enforce the impression of the idea. We hear the passing arrow in this line [IX. 632] of Virgil."[21] Such ideas, impressed by "sensible objects," are the least "fleeting, variable, and evanescent" of ideas and are to be distinguished from "conceits, or thoughts not immediately impressed by sensible objects."[22] Of the ideas so impressed by the sense, the most vivid and lasting are those of sight.[23] They are often enough indistinguishable from *image,* as defined by Johnson (definition 5): "An idea; a representation of any thing to the mind; a picture drawn in the fancy." It is in this

[18] Preface to the *Dictionary,* par. 17.
[19] C. B. Tinker, *Dr. Johnson and Fanny Burney* (New York, 1911), p. 151f.
[20] *Life,* III. 329.
[21] *Rambler* 94 (IV, 139 of *The Rambler,* eds. W. J. Bate, A. B. Strauss [New Haven, 1969], vols. III–V of the Yale Edition of the Works of Samuel Johnson; subsequent quotations from the *Rambler* will be taken from this edition).
[22] *Rambler* 110 (IV. 222) and 143 (IV. 400).
[23] See Donald J. Greene, " 'Pictures to the Mind': Johnson and Imagery," in *Johnson, Boswell and their Circle* (Oxford, 1965), particularly his discussion of *image* and *idea,* p. 153.

sense that Imlac uses *image* and *idea* interchangeably in his Dissertation upon Poetry:

I ranged mountains and deserts for *images* and *resemblances,* and *pictured* upon my mind every tree of the forest and flower of the valley. . . . The plants of the garden, the animals of the wood, the minerals of the earth, and meteors of the sky, must all concur to store his [the poet's] mind with inexhaustible variety: for every *idea* is useful for the inforcement or decoration of moral or religious truth. . . . All the *appearances* of nature I was therefore careful to study. . . . [italics mine]

But the *idea* (image, picture, resemblance, appearance) of a plant, an animal, a mineral, a meteor is relatively uncomplex. Johnson also uses the term more broadly and imprecisely to include the infinitely varied combinations which such ideas may assume in the mind. Although Locke, quoted in the *Dictionary* under *picture* (definition 4), assures that "it suffices to the unity of any idea, that it be considered as one representation or picture, though made up of ever so many particulars," such ideas must necessarily be less precisely impressed and are therefore more likely to shift and change kaleidoscopically in the mind:

The works and operations of nature are too great in their extent, or too much diffused in their relations, and the performances of art too inconstant and uncertain, to be reduced to any determinate idea. It is impossible to impress upon our minds an adequate and just representation of an object so great that we can never take it into our view, or so mutable that it is always changing under our eye, and has already lost its form while we are labouring to conceive it.

Rambler 125 (IV. 300)

Such ideas, of nature or of art, either because of their vastness or their complexity, or because they encompass operations and relationships unstable and contingent, can be realized only partially and fleetingly, and only by reference to the sensible objects which are at once their source and anchor. Johnson's tendency, when confronted by such an idea, is to analyze it, in the manner of Locke, into its components and to search for their parents in the world of "sensible objects." The alternative, to him, would be to surrender to the temptation to "feast the imagination with pure ideas," that is, to move into a world of order but a world unreal and therefore ultimately, perhaps, of madness.[24]

In sum, *idea* to Johnson is, first of all, a term defining the mental equivalent of simple experience in the world of sensible objects—the idea of cold, of bulk, and so on. It is also a term defining a unity of such simple experiences, as in Locke's definition of a swan, quoted in the *Dictionary:* "The idea, which an Englishman signifies by the name *swan,* is a white colour, long neck, black beak, black legs, and whole feet, and all these of a certain size, with a power of swimming in the water, and making a certain kind of noise." On a level approaching the abstract, *idea* signified to him the "works and operations of nature" or the "performances of art" which could be only partially and imperfectly realized in terms of components as related to each other and, as far as possible, to the "sensible objects" from whence they originally sprang. On a level almost totally abstract are those combinations of simple ideas with no immediately recognizable source in "sensible objects"—Locke's complex ideas, even the most abstruse of which, "how remote soever they may seem from sense, or from any operations of our own minds, are yet only such as the understanding frames to itself, by repeating and joining together ideas that it had either from objects of sense, or from its own operations about them. . . ." [25] Occasionally, going one step beyond, Johnson uses *idea* in the sense of vision—a prefiguration, for example, of which the work of art is an approximation. Of Dryden he said: "To write *con amore,* with fondness for the employment, with perpetual touches and retouches, with unwillingness to take leave of his own idea, and an unwearied pursuit of unattainable perfection,

---

[24] See *Rasselas,* Chap. xliv, on the "Dangerous Prevalence of the Imagination, and, as only one example from the *Rambler,* No. 89 (IV. 107): ". . . to regain liberty [from our musings we must] teach [our] desires to fix upon external things. . . ."

[25] Locke, I. 217 (II. xii. 8).

was, I think, no part of his character." [26] Such an idea has its roots in experience, but it represents an imagined order beyond experience.

To Johnson, words, the vehicles by which ideas are conveyed to the understanding,[27] at best do not add to the indeterminateness of ideas: "The uncertainty of terms, and commixture of ideas, is well known to those who have joined philosophy with grammar." [28] Indistinct to begin with, new words proliferate to keep pace with the increase of knowledge, existing words are increasingly "deflected from their original sense," and those words most in use— verbs like *get, do, put,* etc.—whose "sense [is] detorted . . . widely from the first idea . . . are hourly shifting their relations, and can no more be ascertained in a dictionary, than a grove, in the agitation of a storm, can be accurately delineated from its picture in the water." [29] Further contributing to the inadequacy of words are the associations and opinions arbitrarily and capriciously attached to them which, unless they are shared by writer and reader alike, weaken communication by setting up a "counteraction of . . . words to . . . ideas." [30] Indeed, though Johnson nowhere goes so far as to argue a doctrine of Coleridgean untranslatability, on at least one occasion he suggests a test of literary excellence close to it:

it . . . frequently happened, that in the works, which required [Criticism's] inspection, there was some imposture attempted; that false colours were laboriously laid; that some secret inequality was found between the words and sentiments, or some dissimilitude of the ideas and the original objects; that incongruities were linked together, or that some parts were of no use but to enlarge the appearance of the whole, without contributing to its beauty, solidity, or usefulness.

Rambler 3 (III.17)

---

[26] "Dryden," *Lives of the English Poets,* ed. G. B. Hill (Oxford, 1905), I. 413, par. 201.

[27] See, for example, *Rambler* 168 (V. 125).

[28] Preface to the *Dictionary,* par. 51.   [29] *Ibid.,* par. 45.

[30] *Rambler* 168 (V. 127).

Elsewhere, and usually, his stress is on the role of words as sign-posts to the world of sensible objects: "The pebble must be pol-ished with care, which hopes to be valued as a diamond; and words ought surely to be laboured when they are intended to stand for things." [31] In urging the use of words neither "too familiar" nor "too remote" he was expressing his conviction that "words to which we are nearly strangers, whenever they occur, draw that at-tention on themselves which they should transmit to things." [32]

IV

Understandably, Johnson's notes to his edition of Shake-speare offer much evidence not only of his Lockean assumptions about ideas, the nature of language, and the modes of its opera-tion, but also of his habitual resort to those assumptions as means of discovering and revealing the truth—of word, of line, of scene, of character—that Shakespeare struggled to realize and that provides the essential link of understanding between his audi-ence and the play. Johnson's notes may be categorized to provide evidence:

Sense as the source of ideas:
"[the five senses are the] five inlets of ideas"   *Much Ado,* I. i. 55
    (360) [33]

The distinction of ideas and words:
"[the   playwright]   attends   more   to   his   ideas   than   to   his
    words"   *Winter's Tale,* IV. i. 4 (299)
"[his] mind was more intent upon notions than words"   *Lear,* II. iv.
    255 (681)
        ("notion" is defined in the *Dictionary* [definition 1] as
        "thought, representation of anything formed by the mind;
        idea; image; conception")
"I would . . . direct the reader's attention rather to sense than
    words"   *Troilus,* IV. v. 79 (930)

---

[31] *Rambler* 152 (V. 47).   [32] "Dryden," *Lives,* I. 420, par. 220.
[33] Johnson's notes are quoted from the Yale Edition (see above, note 4). The number in parentheses refers to the page in that edition on which the note may be found. I shall use this system throughout.

Idea as picture:
"the idea of 'trimming' a lady to 'keep' her 'steady,' would be too risible for any common power of face" *John*, III. i. 208 (418)
"I am . . . inclined to believe . . . there is a confusion of ideas, and that the poet had at once before him a butcher carrying a calf bound, and a butcher driving a calf to the slaughter, and beating him when he did not keep the path. Part of the line was suggested by one image and part by another. . . ." *2 Henry VI*, III. i. 210 (586)
". . . finding no commodious allusion for the sands, he let that idea pass without any correspondent, and proceeds to the rocks" *2 Henry VI*, III. ii. 97 (588)

Idea of the works or operations of nature, external or human:
"a confinement of your mind to one painful idea; to ignominy" *Measure for Measure*, III. i. 69 (195)
"to be melancholy is to have the mind 'chained down' to one painful idea" *Lear*, IV. vi. 80 (696)
"all powers of action are oppressed and crushed by one over-whelming image in the mind" *Macbeth*, I. iii. 140 (760)
"having perhaps in the former plays completed his own idea, [the poet] seems not to have been able to give Falstaff all his former power of entertainment" *Merry Wives*, General Observation (341)
"This idea of dotage encroaching upon wisdom" *Hamlet*, II. ii. 86 (974)
"[The word 'wretch'] expresses the utmost degree of amiableness, joined with an idea . . . of feebleness, softness, and want of protection" *Othello*, III. iii. 91 (1030)
"the idea of times more civilized, and of life regulated by softer manners" *Lear*, General Observation (703)
"'Now o'er one half the world/Nature seems dead'. . . . This image, . . . perhaps the most striking that poetry can produce" *Macbeth*, II. i. 49 (769)
"I do not think, that in the word 'parted' is included any idea of 'division'; it means, 'however excellently endowed'" *Troilus*, III. iii. 96 (924)
"It is plain that 'perfume' is necessary to exemplify the idea of 'sweet, not lasting'" *Hamlet*, I. iii. 7 (964)
"the natural ideas of justice" *Lear*, General Observation (704)
"This is a true picture of a mind divided between heaven and earth" *2 Henry IV*, IV. v. 219 (517)

*The relationship between the natural or primitive meaning of a word
and its consequential or metaphorical meaning:*

" 'Leaven'd choice'. . . . [Shakespeare's] train of ideas seems to be
. . . choice *mature, concocted, fermented,* leavened" *Measure for
Measure,* I.i. 52 (177)

"I rather think that 'recollected' signifies, more nearly to its primitive
sense, 'recalled,' 'repeated' " *Twelfth Night,* II. iv. 5 (316)

"A 'rogue' is a wanderer or 'vagabond,' and, in its consequential signification, 'a cheat' " *Merry Wives,* II. i. 156 (332)

" 'Power' first signifies 'natural power' or 'force,' and then 'moral
power' or 'right' " *Coriolanus,* II. iii. 4 (805)

"That 'ignorant' at any time has, otherwise than consequentially, the
same meaning with 'impotent,' I do not know" *Coriolanus,* II. iii.
171 (806)

" 'Convictive' is only the consequential sense" *Hamlet,* II. ii. 599
(979)

" 'saucy' may very properly signify 'luxurious,' and by consequence
'lascivious' " *All's Well,* IV. iv. 23 (398)

"I can scarcely tell what signification to give to the word 'prone.' Its
primitive and translated senses are well known" *Measure for Measure,* I. ii. 175 (179)

                                V

Before considering more specifically how Johnson brought
his Lockean views of language to bear in his reading of Shake-
speare and in his editing of the plays, it is essential to remind ourselves of his larger idea of Shakespeare as a man and a writer.
Again the notes supplement the generalizations of the Preface. To
Johnson, Shakespeare's mind was, above all, rooted in the world
of things presented by the senses in the form of simple ideas.
Upon encountering a troublesome word in his text, therefore,
Johnson first tended to think of it in its primitive signification.
Thus, in *The Winter's Tale,* when Camillo says, "He thinks, nay,
with all confidence he swears,/As he had seen 't, or been an in-
strument/To vice you to 't," and Warburton defines "to vice" as
"to draw, persuade" and refers, for support, to "the character
called the Vice, in the old plays, [who] was the tempter to evil,"

Johnson simply notes that "the 'vice' is an instrument well known; its operation is to hold things together." [34]

But the greatness of Shakespeare lies in his enlarging the world of everyday things by releasing its metaphorical potential. Again and again the notes reveal Johnson's conception of Shakespeare's imagination leaping quickly, daringly, impatiently from one idea to another,[35] with the result that his thought was highly compressed,[36] his language often "ungrammatical, perplexed, and obscure." [37] Contributing to the metaphorical density and syntactical difficulty of his language was Shakespeare's conception of himself as a dramatist above all, and his subsequent understanding of the different expectations of readers and theatrical viewers, a conception and an understanding that resulted in dialogue in which, as in all talk, connections between ideas are taken for granted, and circumstance and tone supply meaning: "This poet is always more careful about the present than the future, about his audience than his readers." [38]

This view of Shakespeare as writer and dramatist vitally affected Johnson's view of himself as editor. Most important, since he perceived the plays as intricately and tightly woven nets of ideas,[39] he read them—as an editor—primarily as auditory and visual experiences. Hence his respect for the text. As he says in the Preface: "where any passage appeared inextricably perplexed, [I] have endeavoured to discover how it may be recalled to sense, with least violence. . . . My first labor is, always to turn the old

[34] I. ii. 414 (291f.)

[35] See, for example, *King John,* I. i. 27 (406), *Richard II,* IV. i. 21 (444f.)

[36] See, for example, *Comedy of Errors,* II. i. 40 (353), *All's Well,* IV. iii. 93 (396).

[37] Preface, p. 93.

[38] *Henry V,* III. vi. 96 (550). For Johnson's awareness of the particular nature of conversational style, see, for example, *Antony and Cleopatra,* I. ii. 36 (839), V. ii. 4 (868).

[39] See, for example, *Lear,* III. vi. 23 (687), IV. vi. 184 (697), *Hamlet,* III. iv. 102 (992).

text on every side, and try if there be any interstice, through which light can find its way. . . ." [40] Hence, too, his tolerance of Shakespeare's wrenching of diction and confusion of syntax, for they were the results, in part, of the playwright's impatience to reach the highest levels of psychological and dramatic truth. Hence, finally, his conception of his responsibility to deal with Shakespeare's words so as to "direct the reader's attention rather to sense than words" and untangle ideas by opening them up, loosening their texture. [41]

It remains now to consider how Johnson accomplished this task. We have seen how he often thinks first of the primitive meaning of Shakespeare's language. Behind this procedure is his tendency to explain a metaphorical word or phrase by pointing to its basis in the world of sensible objects and actions or by tracing its origin in other words or earlier meanings. Thus, "to trip the course of law" he explained as "to defeat the process of justice, a metaphor taken from the act of tripping a runner." [42] On the other hand, he was always alert to the danger of remaining in the world of sensible objects and actions as if it were the world of the play, as his literal-minded predecessor Warburton too often did. In *Henry VIII* the King speaks: "My life itself, and the best heart of it, / Thanks you for this great care." Warburton objected to the expression as "monstrous," because the heart is "the seat of life" and the King speaks "as if he had many lives, and to each of them, a heart. . . . A way of speaking that would have become a cat rather than a king." Johnson's note makes clear his understanding that Shakespeare here used "heart" in its metaphorical sense:

This expression is not more monstrous than many others. Heart is not here taken for the great organ of circulation and life, but, in a common and popular sense, for the most valuable or precious part. Our authour, in *Hamlet*, mentions the "heart of heart." Exhausted and effete ground is said by the farmer to be "out of heart." The hard and

[40] Preface, p. 106.   [41] *Troilus and Cressida*, IV. v. 79 (930).
[42] *2 Henry IV*, V. ii. 87 (518).

inner part of the oak is called "heart of oak." *Henry VIII,* I. ii. 1 (638)

Johnson often brings the play closer to his reader by associating Shakespeare's language with common, everyday phrases: "embrace heaviness" is explained by analogy with "hugs his sorrows"; "her eyes had lost her tongue" is explained by referring to a man who " 'loses' his company when they go one way and he goes another. So Olivia's tongue 'lost' her eyes; her tongue was talking of the Duke and her eyes gazing on his messenger"; "to take the head" is explained as "to act without restraint. . . . We now say, 'we give *the horse* his head,' when we relax the reins." [43]

In certain notes Johnson understands how ideas are related by association, as in *2 Henry IV,* when Henry V speaks—"My father is gone wild into his grave;/For in his tomb lie my affections,/And with his spirit sadly I survive . . ."—and Johnson explains "sadly" as "the same as 'soberly, seriously, gravely.' 'Sad' is opposed to 'wild'." [44] More frequently, acting upon his understanding of the often fragmentary, abrupt nature of talk, particularly at moments of emotional tension, he orders and fills out dialogue for his readers. The following are typical:

Orlando. As I remember, Adam, it was upon this fashion bequeath'd me. By will, but a poor thousand crowns.

[Warburton emended "fashion" to "my father."] There is, in my opinion, nothing but a point misplaced, and an omission of a word which every hearer can supply, and which therefore an abrupt and eager dialogue naturally excludes.

I read thus: "As I remember, Adam, it was on this fashion bequeathed me. By will but a poor thousand crowns; and, as thou sayst, charged my brother on his blessing to breed me well." What is there in this difficult or obscure? The nominative "my father" is certainly left out, but so left out that the auditor inserts it, in spite of himself. *As You Like It,* I. i. 1 (242)

[43] *Merchant of Venice,* II. viii. 51 (223); *Twelfth Night,* II. ii. 18 (314); *Richard II,* III. iii. 12 (442).
[44] V. ii. 125 (519).

Dromio of Ephesus. Marry, so it doth appear/By the wrongs I suffer,
and the blows I bear;/I should kick, being kickt

[Theobald emended to "don't appear"] I do not think this emendation necessary. He first says, that his "wrongs" and "blows" prove him
an "ass"; but immediately, with a correction of his former sentiment,
such as may be hourly observed in conversation, he observes that, if
he had been an "ass," he should, when he was "kicked," have
"kicked" again.   *Comedy of Errors,* III. i. 15 (355)

There are instances of Johnson's untangling syntax by attending to
the series of ideas in Shakespeare's mind, as he tells us in the
opening sentence of his long note on Hamlet's soliloquy:

Of this celebrated soliloquy, which bursting from a man distracted
with contrariety of desires, and overwhelmed with the magnitude of
his own purposes, is connected rather in the speaker's mind, than on
his tongue, I shall endeavour to discover the train, and to shew how
one sentiment produces another.   *Hamlet,* III. i. 56–88 (981)

And there are instances of his "opening up" the network of ideas
contained within Shakespeare's compressed figures:

Adriana. But if thou live to see like right bereft, / This fool-begg'd patience in thee will be left.

She seems to mean by "fool-begg'd patience," that "patience" which is
so near to "idiotical simplicity," that your next relation would take advantage from it to represent you as a "fool," and "beg" the guardianship
of your fortune.   *Comedy of Errors,* II. i. 40 (353)

VI

But it may be said of these notes that they represent, simply,
the workings of an acute, sensitive intelligence rather than the
workings of such an intelligence informed by the views we have
said Johnson shared with Locke. A common kind of glossarial
note may perhaps reveal the play of those views more fully.

Many of the glosses consist solely or essentially of a simple
list of three or more explanatory words. Frequently these words
fall into a pattern that reflects Johnson's lexicographical training

and suggests how he may have arrived at his own understanding of Shakespeare's words and how he may have hoped to bring his reader to the same understanding. The following are examples of this kind of simple gloss:

"spangled star-light sheen"
    "Sheen." Shining, bright, gay. *Midsummer Night's Dream,* II. i. 29 (142)
"Oh place! oh form!/How often dost thou with thy case, thy habit,/ Wrench awe from fools"
    "Case." For outside; garb; external shew. *Measure for Measure,* II. iv. 12 (187)
"Your salt tears' head"
    The source, the fountain of your tears, the cause of your grief. *All's Well,* I. iii. 163 (382)
"Unless some dull and favourable hand/Will whisper musick to my weary spirit"
    . . . "dull" signifies, "melancholy, gentle, soothing." *2 Henry IV,* IV. v. 2 (514)
"For all the soil of the atchievement"
    "Soil" is "spot, dirt, turpitude, reproach." *2 Henry IV,* IV. v. 190 (516)
"A ragged and forestall'd remission"
    . . . "ragged," in our authour's licentious diction, may easily signify "beggarly, mean, base, ignominious . . . ." *2 Henry IV,* V. ii. 38 (518)
"That I thy enemy due thee withal"
    To "due" is to "endue," to "deck," to "grace." *1 Henry VI,* IV. ii. 34 (574)
". . . thou shalt be met with thanks,/Allow'd with absolute power"
    "Allowed" is "licensed, privileged, uncontrolled." *Timon,* V. i. 159 (743)
"My dull brain was wrought/With things forgot"
    My head was "worked," "agitated," put into commotion. *Macbeth,* I.iii. 149 (761)
"The cognizance of her incontinency"
    The badge; the token; the visible proof. *Cymbeline,* II. iv. 127 (888)

In each of these lists we can see a rough progress from what Johnson would call the primitive meaning of the word in question to its consequential meaning. Johnson's reading seems first to have awakened within him a powerful sense of the dramatic situation —the setting and mood, the characters' temperaments, motivations, and interactions at the particular moment he found them— and then to have encouraged that sense, or *idea,* to point the way to the archetype of the situation, necessarily more readily grasped by the mass of readers. The movement of his mind, in other words, seems to have been from the particular experience of the play (the dramatic idea) to the common experience (the general idea) of which it is a facet. The list of words then serves to reverse the process for the reader, to carry his understanding from the familiar idea in his mind to its analogy, the less familiar idea of Shakespeare as expressed in the play. Put differently, the list establishes a bridge leading from the world of things and experiences, represented by the common store of words understood in their primitive meanings, to the world of the play represented by that same store of words with their full metaphorical meanings released. Admittedly, the progress is not always so clearly in one direction,[45] yet in a majority of Johnson's simple glosses the last word seems more often than not to be the one most appropriate for comprehension of the immediate dramatic situation.[46]

Less frequently Johnson's simple glosses take us directly into Shakespeare's mind to suggest *its* operation rather than to show us the operation of *Johnson's* mind as it moved outward from the play and then returned with his reader in tow. A note already quoted in part deserves to be given in full:

[45] Some additional simple glosses are as follows: *Tempest,* III. iii. 82 (130); *Two Gentlemen,* V. iv. 126 (173); *Merchant of Venice,* II. ii. 169 (221); *Love's Labour's,* IV. iii. 118 (277); *Twelfth Night,* I. v. 188 (313), II. iv. 44 (316), III. i. 73 (319); *Taming,* I. i. 191 (344); *2 Henry IV,* IV. v. 2 (514); *Henry V,* I. ii. 16 (531), IV. i. 239 (553); *Timon,* I. i. 75 (709), II. ii. 211 (720); *Coriolanus,* III. i. 158 (809); *Julius Caesar,* II. i. 113 (828); *Troilus,* II. ii. 176 (919); *Romeo,* III. v. 90 (951).

[46] Throughout the edition, although Johnson draws attention to readings which are "philosophical nonsense," he recognizes that his task is to explain "poetical sense." See, for example, *Henry V,* V. ii. 41 (564), *Romeo,* I. ii. 24 (941).

Duke. We have with a leaven'd and prepared choice / Proceeded to
     you

[Warburton emended to "level'd."] No emendation is necessary.
"Leaven'd choice" is one of Shakespeare's harsh metaphors. His train
of ideas seems to be this. "I have proceeded to you with choice *mature, concocted, fermented,* leaven'd." When bread is "leavened," it is
left to ferment: a "leavened" choice is therefore a choice not hasty,
but considerate, not declared as soon as it fell into the imagination,
but suffered to work long in the mind. Thus explained it suits better
with "prepared" than "levelled."   *Measure for Measure,* I. i. 52 (177)

Had Johnson written his more usual sort of gloss for this word his
note would probably have appeared thus: " 'Leaven'd' is 'fermented, concocted, mature'." Be that as it may, his reversal of the
transition from primitive to consequential meanings suggests how
his alertness to the full implications of a dramatic moment enabled
him to find the link between ideas essentially similar but different
in quality because held by different minds. Johnson's note would
appear to illustrate Locke's reminder, as echoed by Watts:

It is not the outward object, or thing which is perceived (*viz.*) the
horse, the man, &c. nor is it the very perception or sense, and feeling,
viz. of hunger, or cold, &c. which is called the idea; but it is the thing
as it exists in the mind by way of conception or representation that is
properly called the idea, whether the object be present or absent.[47]

The note also suggests Johnson's view of the creative process
as closely allied to the critical, and both processes as having a
common source in the everyday experiences that give rise to simple ideas. "So powerful is the current of the poet's imagination,"
says Johnson of *Lear,* "that the mind, which once ventures within
it, is hurried irresistibly along." [48] It was a current into which
Johnson was particularly willing to plunge, for, as his own vigorous image tells us, he found in Shakespeare a like spirit: "Shakespeare, whether life or nature be his subject, shews plainly, that
he has seen with his own eyes; he gives the image which he re-
ceives, not weakened or distorted by the intervention of any

[47] *Logick,* p. 8.   [48] General Observation, p. 703.

other mind; the ignorant feel his representations [*Dictionary,* definition 1: image, likeness] to be just, and the learned see that they
are compleat." [49]

Acting upon this sense of Shakespeare's *seeing* life in all its
concreteness, Johnson in his notes offers the results of his own seeing. He sees the completeness of Shakespeare's images because he
understands their origin in direct experience and their articulation
in terms reflective of a particular mind operating within the context
of a particular dramatic idea. In the following, from *2 Henry
IV,* Johnson visualizes the scene aware of the idea more than
the word, and of the fitness of the idea within its larger context:

Mowbray. Let us sway on, and face them in the field

I know not that I have ever seen "sway" in this sense, but I believe it
is the true word, and was intended to express the uniform and forcible
motion of a compact body. There is a sense of the noun in Milton
kindred to this, where speaking of a weighty sword, he says, "It de-
scends with huge two-handed *sway."*   IV. i. 24 (508)

Unlike Warburton, who had suggested an emendation—"way on"
—Johnson went to the idea signified, "saw" it, understood the link
between word and idea, and explained it by direct reference to the
thing itself. It is not enough to say that Johnson brought common
sense to his task as explicator; he brought a mind trained to think
of things, ideas, and words in certain relationships.

In *Measure for Measure* Johnson again disagrees with Warburton and illustrates his understanding of Shakespeare's idea by
referring to the primitive meaning of the word "base":

Duke. Thou art noble;/For all th' accommodations, that thou bear'st,
    /Are nurs'd by baseness.

Dr. Warburton is undoubtedly mistaken in supposing that by "baseness"
is meant "self-love" here assigned as the motive of all human actions.
Shakespeare meant only to observe, that a minute analysis of life at
once destroys that splendour which dazzles the imagination. Whatever
grandeur can display, or luxury enjoy, is procured by "baseness," by

[49] Preface, p. 89f.

offices of which the mind shrinks from the contemplation. All the delicacies of the table may be traced back to the shambles and the dunghill, all magnificence of building was hewn from the quarry, and all the pomp of ornaments, dug from among the damps and darkness of the mine.   III. i. 13 (192)

"Accommodations," defined in the *Dictionary* as "provision of conveniences" and "in the plural, convcniencies, things requisite to ease or refreshment," and "nurse," together with Johnson's instinctive attraction to the simple idea signified by "base," made his explanation inevitable. If we reduce to sequential form what must have been for Johnson a set of simultaneously occurring and interacting responses, we might speculate, first, that he conceived the simple idea of "base" and then, given the stimulus of the larger dramatic idea, that he moved to the complex idea of "base" as it resided in Shakespeare's mind at the time of composition. It is significant that, despite the relative elaborateness of the note, its fundamental movement is the same as that of his simple glosses, a kind of reverberation between primitive and consequential meanings, determined initially by the dramatic idea of which the speech is a part, and limited only by the boundaries of that idea. Though without the benefit of modern linguistic knowledge, it is clear that Johnson understood the extent to which words attain unique values because of the simultaneous presence of other words and, therefore, the extent to which a dramatic idea is more than the sum total of the individual significations of the words comprising it.

A final example of Johnson's power to visualize a scene—to see action and to understand the currents of thought it sets in motion—and to supply for his reader an expanded, more easily grasped version of a dramatic moment, occurs in *King John:*

[Stage direction] Enter Pandulpho.
Dauphin. And even there, methinks, an angel spake!

Sir T. Hanmer, and after him Dr. Warburton read here, "an angel *speeds.*" I think unnecessarily. The Dauphin does not yet hear the legate indeed, nor pretend to hear him, but seeing him advance and concluding that he comes to animate and authorise him with the power of the church, he cries out, "at the sight of this holy man, I am encouraged as *by the voice of an angel.*"   V. ii. 64 (427) [50]

Johnson, we know, loved to have "his wisdom actually operate upon real life." [51] And in Shakespeare he saw a man who "caught his ideas from the living world, and exhibited only what he saw before him." [52] Despite the undoubted vexations of living with the edition of Shakespeare from 1756 to 1765, there must have been for Johnson many moments of pleasure as he allowed himself to be hurried along in the current of the poet's imagination. Certainly at such moments he was not calmly and analytically relating a series of visual experiences to their verbal signs. Once ashore, however, as an editor with responsibilities to explain his plunge to less vigorous swimmers, he drew to the fullest upon his perceptual powers and his lexicographical knowledge, and it was then that Locke provided him with a vocabulary and a rationale. The view that he read the plays as ethical poems without the stage in mind, though surely not without some validity, must, I believe, be qualified. Between the crowded stage and the solitary editor was the intermediating world of idea explored by Locke.

[50] Some other examples of Johnson's power to visualize scenes: *Merchant of Venice,* II. ii. 144 (221); *Merry Wives,* IV. v. 25 (338); *Taming,* I. ii. 111 (345); *All's Well,* I. i. 16 (374).
[51] *Life,* II. 441.   [52] Preface, p. 63.

LOUIS T. MILIC

Observations on Conversational Style

THE TERM "conversational style" [1] is commonly
taken to be a useful description of a kind of writing which seems
somehow closer to speech than the norm. It is in fact more than
that. To say that a writer has a "conversational style" is to imply
a theory about the relation of speech to writing. The matter may
deserve discussion because it is improbable that what is called
conversational prose has any important or constant relation to
conversation or speech; because it seems likely that "conversational prose" is merely a mode of writing with its own conventions; and because the approval lavished on it seems to be the result of a fundamental misunderstanding about the relation of
speech to writing—a misunderstanding especially prevalent among
literary historians and critics unfamiliar with the nature of language and the history of English.

[1] The notion of "conversational style" developed well before the name.
There is no recorded use of the term in the eighteenth century, according
to the O. E. D.; nor does Johnson's *Dictionary* give an instance or a definition of it.

In the sixteenth century, when the use of the English language still required some defense, the poverty of everyday speech or conversation as a medium for the communication of serious or emphatic messages was taken for granted. Puttenham, for example, urges the use of figurative language in these terms:

> But as it hath been always reputed a great fault to use figurative speeches foolishly and indiscreetly, so it is esteemed no less an imperfection in man's utterance to have none use of figure at all, especially in our writings and speeches public, making them but as our ordinary talk, than which nothing can be more unsavory and far from all civility.[2]

Doubtless, Puttenham is laboring under a serious misapprehension, the ancient view that everyday speech differs from higher styles mainly in being undecorated. Nonetheless, it is curious that in the course of time the assumption developed that writing was better if it sounded like speech, or seemed to be like conversation or somehow conveyed to the reader the lack of planning and informality characteristic of conversation. Perhaps this tendency can be properly assessed as part of the general movement away from the forms of the old rhetoric—rhetoric is always old, unless it is the "new" rhetoric. Or it may be connected with the notion of the Plain Style, which has always waged a losing war with its elegant alternative, the style variously described as decorated, fancy, elaborate, formal, or ornate. The Asiatic oratory was challenged by the Attic, the Ciceronian by the Senecan, the Baroque by the Plain or Colloquial, later to be found inadequate by what Connolly has called the "Mandarin." [3] This constant shift may be attributed to two factors: the difficulties of expression, which have always been formidable, and the influence of fashion, which has extended even into the domain of language. Perhaps too the influence of mass education, remote from classical sources and formal discipline, has also played a part. Still, it cannot but seem eccentric to the undogmatic observer that the highest praise offered to a writer's

[2] *The Arte of English Poesy* (London, 1589), Bk. III, Ch. 2.
[3] Cyril Connolly, *Enemies of Promise* (Boston, 1939), Ch. 2.

style in this century is to say that his writing is like speech. Such eccentricity requires an accounting.

In trying to describe the change that overtook English prose during the Restoration, Sutherland rejects the usual influences (for example, the Royal Society's program as classically outlined by Bishop Sprat) in favor of speech:

Restoration prose is, in the main, a slightly formalized variation of the conversation of gentlemen. The gentleman converses with ease, and with an absence of emphasis that may at times become a conscious and studied under-emphasis, but is more often the natural expression of his poise and detachment.[4]

Edmund Wilson does not hesitate to attribute the effect of George Saintsbury's critical writings to the conversational element:

He has, in fact, invented a style of much charm and a certain significance: a modern, conversational prose that carries off asides, jokes and gossip as well as all the essential data by a very strong personal rhythm, that drops its voice to interpolate footnotes without seriously retarding the current, and that, however facetious or garrulous, never fails to cover the ground or make the points. . . . It is a fine and flexible English prose on the rhythms of informal speech rather than those of literary convention.[5]

Writers as disparate as Ruskin, Mark Twain, Henry James, and Hemingway, have been acclaimed in similar terms.[6] In view of the outrageous diversity of the writers described as conversational, it is reasonable to conclude that any written prose may be perceived as based on speech. In a sense, this is both true and self-evident. But in this sense the label is a tautology and useless as a critical term. If so, however, why do the critics labor so hard to pin this label on favored writers. Partly no doubt it is because the traditional vocabulary of stylistic description is poverty-stricken. A more important reason is that the label is always laudatory—and

[4] J. R. Sutherland, *On English Prose* (Toronto, 1957), p. 67.

[5] "George Saintsbury's Centenary," *Classics and Commercials* (New York, 1962), p. 307.

[6] See my "Metaphysical Criticism of Style," *New Rhetorics*, ed. Martin Steinmann, Jr. (New York, 1967), pp. 162–75.

laudatory in a peculiarly modern way. To a critic intent on rescu-
ing such museum pieces as Ruskin and Saintsbury, the most useful
card is the one that will demonstrate that these writers are after all
really modern. Since they are obviously not modern, it must be
shown that their apparent obsoleteness is a delusion. They are
really modern because their writing has the *je-ne-sais-quoi* of
modern speech-based prose. Those critics who feel that disorder
and complexity are at the root of speech-based prose are on solider
ground than those who use the term merely as a token of routine
approval.

Macaulay's style was once praised vastly beyond its considerable deserts. During this century Macaulay's dogmatic assurance
and his dishonesty have brought his style into disrepute. That the
historian Rowse should seek to reverse this trend may be a good
augury. That he should do it on the basis of "conversational style"
says nothing new about Macaulay. It merely adds to the vogue of
the term.

What then are the qualities which make the Essays such a prodigious
success?

They have the power of holding the attention in a most extraordinary way. And this arises from the fact that their style is essentially
conversational—but the conversation is dramatic, declamatory, excit-
ing. In fact, the Essays are debates. . . . You can hear the voice, the
torrent of that astonishing conversation, which made some people protest, though like Greville, they usually ended by submitting, fascinated, conquered by him. Again and again one has the sensation of
listening to a wonderful discussion among that brilliant circle of young
men at Cambridge, or to the famous talk at Holland House.[7]

If Macaulay was aware of this supposed attribute of his own
prose, perhaps that may account for the roasting he gave Dr.
Johnson for the lack of it in his work. The passage is familiar but
deserves quotation:

His conversation appears to have been quite equal to his writings in
matter, and far superior to them in manner. When he talked, he

[7] A. L. Rowse, *The English Spirit* (London, 1946), pp. 229–30.

clothed his wit and his sense in forcible and natural expressions. As soon as he took his pen in his hand to write for the public, his style became systematically vicious. All his books are written in a learned language—in a language in which nobody ever quarrels, or drives bargains, or makes love—in a language in which nobody ever thinks. It is clear, that Johnson himself did not think in the dialect in which he wrote. The expressions which came first to his tongue were simple, energetic, and picturesque. When he wrote for publication, he did his sentences out of English into Johnsonese.[8]

The implications of this censure are not generally noticed by the many who agree with its tenor, but they are of far-reaching importance in any consideration of the ideals of style in the eighteenth century and after.

To the reader of today, the primary assumption—that speech-based prose is a sufficient ideal—hardly needs justification.[9] It has achieved the status of an unexamined dogma, like the idea of progress in an earlier day. Moreover, it is consistent with a popular distortion of the linguists' view of the relation between speech and writing, that is, speech is the language, writing merely an inaccurate and incomplete record of it. Even so, Macaulay's assumption is a curious one, curious and naive. And if not naive, then dishonest, in accordance with his prejudices.

Macaulay censures Johnson's writing for not being like speech, but, more than that, he censures Johnson's writing for not being like Johnson's speech, which is very remarkable because Macaulay could not have known what Johnson's speech sounded like. Despite Macaulay's well-known tendency to assert his speculations as proven facts, it is probable that he thought he was on solid ground. Doubtless he thought there was some evidence he could rely on in making the comparison. Had not many of Johnson's contemporaries praised his conversation? And was there not the record of his speech in Boswell's volumes, the very work under review? To someone in need of evidence to press a tenden-

[8] *Critical and Historical Essays* (London, 1856), I, 188.
[9] Richard Bridgman, *The Colloquial Style in America* (New York, 1966), usefully surveys the influence and nature of this notion.

tious argument such evidence must have seemed more than sufficient. And in view of the tradition of considering speech as the
natural model for writing there must have seemed to Macaulay to
be no risk in arguing as he did.

He proves his case, he is confident, by adducing two passages
of Johnson's supposedly revealing how he "translated" his speech
into writing. The paragraph cited above concludes:

His letters from the Hebrides to Mrs. Thrale, are the original of that
work of which the Journey to the Hebrides is the translation; and it is
amusing to compare the two versions. "When we were taken up stairs,"
says he in one of his letters, "a dirty fellow bounced out of the bed on
which one of us was to lie." This incident is recorded in the Journey
as follows: "Out of one of the beds on which we were to repose,
started up, at our entrance, a man black as a Cyclops from the forge."
Sometimes Johnson translated aloud. "The Rehearsal," he said, very
unjustly, "has not wit enough to keep it sweet"; then, after a pause, "it
has not vitality enough to preserve it from putrefaction." [10]

The defect in Macaulay's argument as stated is that he is
blaming Johnson for the wrong fault, if it is a fault. He disapproves of Johnson's style for its inversions, its polysyllabic vocabulary, and his addiction to redundant "epithets," as he specifies a
little further on in the review. He disapproves, that is, of what has
been called the "Mandarin" style and prefers the Plain style. But
in choosing to justify his preference on the basis of the antagonism
between speech and writing he reveals his linguistic ignorance by
appealing to a tradition which he was sure his reader would respond to.

What, after all, do the differences between the original and
the translation consist of that he should make so much of them?
The Hebrides passage in the "written" version differs from the
"spoken" one in three main ways: (1) the inversion of the prepositional phrase with included clause ("out of one of the beds . . .")
from the post-verb complement position to sentence-initial position; (2) some lexical changes: *repose* for *lie, started up* for

[10] Macaulay, *Critical and Historical Essays* (London, 1856), I, 188.

bounced, man for *fellow;* (3) the substitution of a prepositional adverbial in middle position for the introductory adverbial clause; (4) a fancy simile in place of the adjective *dirty*. The second passage contains exclusively lexical substitutions. These alterations, though they may seem extensive when described, are merely stylistic variations of a conventional sort. They do not constitute a movement from speech to writing. They represent no more than a different set of stylistic choices, all within the framework of standard written English sentence patterns.

Macaulay could not judge the difference between speech and writing because, like most people, he had never really attended to the spoken word as it might look if it had been taken down and transcribed verbatim.[11] Speech is different from writing in many more ways than the size and difficulty of the words used. The following unedited transcription of a chunk of modern British conversation, spoken by someone with a University education and a good deal of experience at both speaking and writing, may be considered representative:

You see um the the um the chief lecturer there is is er um—he is the main lecturer though really he has one or two subordinates but he is the—he gives the lectures the main lectures—there are seminars as well and discussions following upon those but the main lectures are given by him—and he tries –to maintain—um a balance I mean he talks so far he's talked about I missed the last one um unfortunately but he's talked—er and given various sides he's given what he called

[11] It is interesting to compare Macaulay's later (1856) statement of his views on this subject with those of 1831: "As respected style, he spoke far better than he wrote. Every sentence that dropped from his lips was as correct in structure as the most nicely balanced period of the Rambler. But in his talk there were no *osity* and *ation*. All was simplicity, ease and vigor. He uttered his short, weighty, and pointed sentences with a power of voice, and a justness and energy of emphasis. . . . To discuss questions of taste, of learning, of casuistry, in language so exact and so forcible that it might have been printed without the alteration of a word, was to him no exertion, but a pleasure." (Macaulay, *Essay on Johnson,* ed. S. Thurber and L. Wetherbee, Boston, 1924, pp. 34–35). In the intervening quarter-century Macaulay had apparently acquired information on Johnson's stress and pitch phonemes.

the er the religious—um aspects of philosophy those who have—a religious point of view who believe in values you know er existing outside the human community—and then what he calls—the—the the secular point of view or the transsecular I think oh no secular point of view—opposed to the transsecular which embodies religious and er the other—er mystical er um approaches I suppose.[12]

Though it may be believed that conversation has degenerated in our time (as have so many things) and that this is the reason why educated people seem, when we read their transcribed remarks, to sound like mental defectives, it would be a serious misconception to suppose that Johnson did not sound somewhat like that when he talked. And if Johnson was the exception, he must have been the solitary one in the history of the language.

What characterizes the transcribed *sentence*—for it is punctuated like one—is the extremely weak sense of structure that it presents. It begins in one direction, is interrupted by appositives and modifications, proceeds in a different direction, and so on. It concludes not when the syntax requires that the sentence must end but when the speaker feels he has made his point, regardless where the syntax is going at that moment. It is a sort of logic that dominates the speaker's output, not a sense of form, as it does the writer's. If anything may be considered the essential feature of speech as distinct from writing, it is this very lack of interest in sentence-boundaries, at least for the speech which living speakers of modern English may claim to be acquainted with.

It may be objected to the foregoing comments on Macaulay that Boswell rendered Johnson's conversation accurately and even that the other renderings of Johnson's conversation, by Boswell's rivals, are very similar to what Boswell gives us. Certainly Macaulay, unaware of the details of Boswell's procedure and intent on showing Boswell as merely a superior stenographer, thought so. But what has been revealed about Boswell's practice by the discovery of his papers and notebooks declares that the Johnson who speaks in Boswell's pages has been edited for publication accord-

[12] Quoted in Randolph Quirk, *The Use of English* (London, 1962), p. 171.

ing to the conventions then current for rendering conversation in writing. Boswell's way of rendering conversation, however, was not the sole tradition of conversational writing in the eighteenth century. The "man Sterne" may claim a prior right.

Quite early in *Tristram Shandy,* Sterne takes the reader aside and tells him that "Writing when properly managed . . . is but a different name for conversation" (Bk. II, Ch. XI). Actually Sterne was only referring to the feature of his narrative method which consists of leaving things to the reader's imagination, that is, leaving them unsaid, a feature he believes to be especially characteristic of speech. Incompleteness of predication, however, is characteristic of all messages, whether spoken or written, which require an expanding circle of contexts to complete them. Nothing, evidently, can ever be wholly said and even apparently complete statements carry with them a dangling "I mean. . . ." Possibly because of Sterne's own emphasis on speech in the lines cited above or because readers were affected by other aspects of his style, the label "conversational" is firmly attached to Sterne's prose. Hazlitt's comment is probably representative: "His style . . . is at times the most rapid, the most happy, the most idiomatic of any that is to be found. It is the pure essence of English conversational style." [13] Many more have commented in this vein on Sterne's style, invariably in praise of it. Not too long ago, Virginia Woolf made the same observation but added to it a note of caution which is of the highest interest. She said: "The jerky, disconnected sentences [of *Tristram Shandy*] are as rapid and it would seem as little under control as the phrases that fall from the lips of a brilliant talker. The very punctuation is that of speech, not writing. . . ." But she added: "That Sterne achieved this illusion only by the use of extreme art and extraordinary pains is obvious without going to his manuscript to prove it." [14] The point is, of course, that a colloquial style is not achieved by reproducing conversation on paper

[13] William Hazlitt, *Lectures on the English Comic Writers* (London, 1819), Lecture VI.

[14] Virginia Woolf, *The Second Common Reader* (New York, 1932), pp. 81–82.

but by obtaining certain effects which the reader will perceive as similar to those he believes he responds to in speech. The fact seems to be that colloquial prose is more like other prose than it is like speech transcription, as has been suggested by the excerpt cited above.

When critics describe the colloquial quality of Sterne's prose, they do not mean that it resembles the "sentence" spoken by the anonymous university lecturer. They are thinking of his apostrophes to the reader, his asides and other aspects of interrupted syntax and his punctuation. Incidentally, they usually leave out of account his typographic playfulness (black and marbled pages, squiggles, odd placement of chapters . . .) which obviously require a paper surface to realize and which are in fact as essentially graphemic as his conversational style. The syntactic details of Sterne's prose have been closely described by Hnatko [15] but they have not otherwise been considered of much technical interest. It is, oddly enough, the punctuation which has enchanted the observer, above all the dash, the "Shandean dash." Fluchère, for example, citing Herbert Read's encomium with approval, raves in the following manner: "Neither the ordinary blank full-stop nor the commonplace comma is enough for him, because in themselves they give no indication of duration. The 'Shandean dash'. . . has the dual advantage of clearing a space round an incident without isolating it from its context as brackets do, and of indicating pauses of varying length, as rests do in music." [16]

The frequent occurrence of dashes in *Tristram Shandy* can hardly be argued. A glance at any page reveals how frequently Sterne used this device. Nor can it be doubted that the dash provides Sterne with an unusual (and additional) mark of punctuation, though it may be questioned how long in his progress through the book the reader responds freshly to this device.[17]

[15] Eugene Hnatko, "Sterne's Conversational Style," in *The Winged Skull,* eds. Arthur H. Cash, John M. Stedmond (Kent, O., 1971), pp. 229–36.

[16] Henri Fluchère, *Laurence Sterne: From Tristram to Yorick,* tr. and abr. by Barbara Bray (London, 1965), p. 422.

[17] I have argued elsewhere ("Information Theory and the Style of *Tristram Shandy,*" in *The Winged Skull,* pp. 237–46) that the profusion of devices,

What is seriously open to question is the relation of Sterne's dash in print to the pauses that occur in speech. Pauses in actual speech, as reference to the previously cited specimen will reveal, generally come in the middle of syntactic constructions. For instance, they are found between the article and the nominal: "the the um and chief lecturer"; within verb clusters: "and he tries—to maintain"; between verb element and object: "to maintain—um a balance." Cursory listening to speech will reveal that such junctures are found whenever a substantive part of speech (for example, noun or adjective) must be selected to fit into a ready-made structure of function words.

Sterne, however, uses the dash in places where a punctuation mark in writing, not a pause in speech, would normally be found. In fact, his dashes are frequently found next to standard punctuation marks and they come at the legitimate boundaries between constructions. The following passage is typical:

—My mother, who was sitting by, look'd up,—but she knew no more than her backside what my father meant,—but my uncle, Mr. *Toby Shandy*, who had been often informed of the affair,—understood him very well. [*Tristram Shandy*, Bk. I, Ch. 3]

Although there is some evidence that Sterne's practice in using the dash changed in the later books, this specimen supports the belief that Sterne's dash is Sternian, not colloquial. That it may be perceived by a willing reader as further evidence of Sterne's colloquial quality is not evidence that Sterne's prose is like speech, only that it was intended to appear so.

It has been adequately shown in the foregoing, I believe, that the term "conversational style" provides no very accurate description of a writer's linguistic procedure. The most diverse writers are lumped together as conversational and conversation itself is visualized under such varying aspects that nothing emerges but a sense of generalized approval. The confusion inherent in this criti-

---

both typographical and stylistic, used by Sterne in *Tristram Shandy* is an effort to counter the tendency of any deviation from the norm to become part of the norm and thereby to lose the power of emphasis.

cal tactic can perhaps be seen in its purest form in the following comment on Sterne, whose colloquial style is here contrasted with Macaulay's, which by this writer is considered of a different sort:

But if we can hardly describe Sterne's style as being in the literary sense a style at all, it has a very distinct colloquial character of its own, and as such it is nearly as much deserving of praise as from the literary point of view it is open to exception. Chaotic as it is in the syntactical sense, it is a perfectly clear vehicle for the conveyance of thought. We are as rarely at a loss for the meaning of one of Sterne's sentences, as we are, for very different reasons, for the meaning of one of Macaulay's. And his language is so full of life and colour, his tone so animated and vivacious, that we forget we are reading and not listening, and we are as little disposed to be exacting in respect to form as though we were listeners in actual fact. Sterne's manner, in fact, may be that of a bad and careless writer, but it is the manner of a first-rate talker; and this of course enhances rather than detracts from the unwearying charm of his wit and humour.[18]

Traill, here, like Hazlitt and Macaulay in excerpts cited earlier, makes the automatic assumption that speech-based prose must be good, or rather that the assertion that a prose is based on speech or is colloquial, vernacular, or conversational necessarily qualifies it for praise. One may be sympathetic with the distrust of classical rhetoric and its procrustean forms implied by this view without feeling satisfied with this reasoning. What is striking is not only the weakness and circularity of the reasoning but also the remarkable carelessness with evidence manifested by the writers who have been cited.

The author of the standard work on the history of English speech, the British philologist Wyld, takes the trouble on the first page of his book to point out the danger of relying on written records as sources of material about the spoken language:

It is an unfortunate circumstance for students of the history of a language, but one from which there is no escape, that they are dependent on written documents for a knowledge of all but the most recent de-

[18] H. D. Traill, "Laurence Sterne," *English Prose,* ed. Henry Craik (New York, 1895), IV, 208–209.

velopments, since, in the nature of things, they can gain no direct and personal access to the spoken language earlier than the speech of the oldest living person they may know.[19]

Perforce Wyld relies on letters, dialogue in plays, popular literature and various other records but always with the consciousness that they are distortions of the actual speech because they have undergone certain conventional changes, the original being forever out of reach.

In the context of such scholarly caution it is startling to find Sutherland's, Rowse's, and Wilson's divergent views of what a conversation is: that is, an exchange, a speech or debate, and a monologue. Despite these divergences of definition, the identical term is applied to all three cited examples. Further, the question how we may verify whether any definition of conversation is consistent with the practice of a given time is never even considered. Rowse speaks of Macaulay's brilliant discussion as if he had heard it. Macaulay speaks of Johnson's style and delivery as if he had a tape-recording. Sutherland might have been present at the gentlemanly exchanges of the Restoration courtiers. Obviously no one is expected to take such fiction seriously. Behind these statements is a conviction that conversation (or speech) must have been as these writers believe it was; that is to say, there is in all this an implicit theory of the relation of speech to writing. Since this is nowhere formulated, it must be reconstituted speculatively from internal evidence. Probably an outline sketch of this implicit hypothesis would take somewhat the following form.

Speech, it has always been supposed, is prior to writing. Since people speak naturally and effortlessly but learn to write only after long and painful exposure to lessons in logic, grammar, and rhetoric (the medieval trivium), a gradual sense of the disharmony between these two means of communication developed. The rules of grammar, the forms of rhetoric, could be waived in informal discourse but were essential in writing, which for a long time

[19] H. C. Wyld, *A History of Modern Colloquial English,* 3d. ed. (London, 1936), p. 1.

occupied only a small part of the population and only a small part of the time. With the rise of educational opportunities for women and for the public at large, the disjunction between the stilted formality of certain kinds of writing and the lack of attention to form in speech and other more occasional compositions became obtrusive and led to calls for reform. Actually the realization of the disjunction between what are really only two ways of writing—the simple and the ornate—is not located at any point in time but occurs over and over in the history of English prose. The proponents of the plain style (like Bishop Sprat), reject what they consider to be vicious abundance and superfluity of phrase in favor of "a close, naked, natural way of speaking." [20] The earlier complaint against inkhorn terms was similarly based on a contrast with the mother tongue, the ordinary spoken language.[21] Whenever the call for reform of the formal style occurred—it should be noted that the move toward ornate prose was never preceded by a manifesto but merely happened—it was grounded on the supposed simplicity and soundness of the native idiom. The qualities of speech were supposed in the main to be shorter sentences and a less Latinate vocabulary. That the conscious practitioners of a conversational style, like Sterne, did not in any sense follow this pattern was ignored. Practice is never taken into consideration by proponents of ideals of style. Speech, the native idiom, the natural rhythms of English—whatever these phrases mean, they are the slogans which dictate approval of anything that can possibly be classified under the rubric "conversational."

The difficulty, then, in understanding the details of this complicated dispute is that the struggle between speech and writing is really concerned with two contrapuntal ideals of English prose, the formal and the plain. The reference to speech is a systematic error, since the modes of emphasis characteristic of speech cannot be reproduced in ordinary writing but must be replaced by a com-

[20] Thomas Sprat, *The History of the Royal Society of London* (London, 1667), p. 113.

[21] Thomas Wilson, *The Arte of Rhetorique* (London, 1553), folio 86.

plex system of conventions commonly known as the rules and devices of rhetoric.

In suggesting that the term "conversational style" be abandoned as a critical term in the discussion of style, I would call attention to the primary fact that no coherent definition of it can be found which covers with any adequacy the variety of phenomena which have been so labeled. If it is anything, "conversational style" is a way of writing which selects any of a variety of features popularly and erroneously thought to be connected with speech. It is merely, like the adjectives "lucid," "simple," and "terse," a term signifying approval with the barest minimum of descriptive power. Somebody's conversational style may be described, but it is unlikely that the description will fit anyone else's. Like many terms in the traditional vocabulary of stylistic description it is a mythical entity and ought to yield to newer views of what style is and how it ought to be described.

T. S. Eliot's comment on this subject, despite its age and his lack of affiliation with the linguistic tradition, is worth restating for its unusual good sense:

People sometimes talk vaguely about the *conversational style* in writing. Still more often, they deplore the divorce between the language as spoken and the language as written. It is true that the spoken and the written language can drift too far apart—with the eventual consequence of forming a new written language. But what is overlooked is that an *identical* spoken and written language would be practically intolerable. If we spoke as we write we should find no one to listen; and if we wrote as we speak we should find no one to read.[22]

[22] "Charles Whibley," *Selected Essays, 1917–1932* (New York, 1932), p. 407.

INDEX